Broken Dreams

BOOKS BY THOMAS HAUSER

BOXING NON-FICTION

The Black Lights: Inside the World
of Professional Boxing
Muhammad Ali: His Life and Times
Muhammad Ali: Memories
Muhammad Ali: In Perspective
Muhammad Ali & Company
A Beautiful Sickness
A Year at the Fights
Brutal Artistry
The View from Ringside
Chaos, Corruption, Courage, and Glory
I Don't Believe It, but It's True
Knockout (with Vikki LaMotta)
The Greatest Sport of All
The Boxing Scene
An Unforgiving Sport
Boxing Is . . .
Box: The Face of Boxing
The Legend of Muhammad Ali
(with Bart Barry)
Winks and Daggers
And the New . . .
Straight Writes and Jabs
Thomas Hauser on Boxing
A Hurting Sport
A Hard World
Muhammad Ali: A Tribute to the Greatest
There Will Always Be Boxing
Protect Yourself at All Times
A Dangerous Journey
Staredown
Broken Dreams

GENERAL NON-FICTION

Missing
The Trial of Patrolman Thomas Shea
For Our Children
(with Frank Macchiarola)
The Family Legal Companion
Final Warning: The Legacy of Chernobyl
(with Dr. Robert Gale)
Arnold Palmer: A Personal Journey
Confronting America's Moral Crisis
(with Frank Macchiarola)
Healing: A Journal of Tolerance
and Understanding
With This Ring (with Frank Macchiarola)
Thomas Hauser on Sports
Reflections

FICTION

Ashworth & Palmer
Agatha's Friends
The Beethoven Conspiracy
Hanneman's War
The Fantasy
Dear Hannah
The Hawthorne Group
Mark Twain Remembers
Finding the Princess
Waiting for Carver Boyd
The Final Recollections of Charles Dickens
The Baker's Tale

FOR CHILDREN

Martin Bear & Friends

Broken Dreams

Another Year Inside Boxing

Thomas Hauser

The University of Arkansas Press
Fayetteville
2021

ISBN: 978-1-68226-179-8
eISBN: 978-1-61075-753-9

25 24 23 22 21   5 4 3 2 1

♾ The paper used in this publication meets the minimum requirements
of the American National Standard for Permanence of Paper for Printed
Library Materials Z39.48-1984.

Library of Congress Cataloging-in-Publication Data

Names: Hauser, Thomas, author.
Title: Broken dreams: another year inside boxing / Thomas Hauser.
Description: Fayetteville, Arkansas: The University of Arkansas Press,
    2021. | Summary: "Thomas Hauser's latest collection of articles about
    the contemporary boxing scene"—Provided by publisher.
Identifiers: LCCN 2021003485 (print) | LCCN 2021003486 (ebook) |
    ISBN 9781682261798 (paperback) | ISBN 9781610757539 (ebook)
Subjects: LCSH: Boxing—Anecdotes.
Classification: LCC GV1135 .H379 2021 (print) | LCC GV1135 (ebook) |
    DDC 796.83—dc23
LC record available at https://lccn.loc.gov/2021003485
LC ebook record available at https://lccn.loc.gov/2021003486

For Jessica, Bayo, Simon, Oye, and Judy

Contents

Author's Note

Broken Dreams contains the articles about professional boxing that I authored in 2020.

The articles I wrote about the sweet science prior to 2020 have been published in *Muhammad Ali & Company*; *A Beautiful Sickness*; *A Year at the Fights*; *The View from Ringside*; *Chaos, Corruption, Courage, and Glory*; *I Don't Believe It, but It's True*; *The Greatest Sport of All*; *The Boxing Scene*; *An Unforgiving Sport*; *Boxing Is . . .* ; *Winks and Daggers*; *And the New . . .* ; *Straight Writes and Jabs*; *Thomas Hauser on Boxing*; *A Hurting Sport*; *A Hard World*; *Muhammad Ali: A Tribute to the Greatest*; *There Will Always Be Boxing*; *Protect Yourself at All Times*; *A Dangerous Journey*; and *Staredown*.

Fighters and Fights

There were far fewer fights than usual in 2020 because of COVID-19. The rematch between Deontay Wilder and Tyson Fury was contested before the coronavirus shutdown and was a particularly intriguing matchup.

Wilder–Fury II in Perspective

On February 22, 2020, at the MGM Grand in Las Vegas, Tyson Fury knocked out Deontay Wilder in round seven of a rematch of their December 1, 2018, draw. With Anthony Joshua having faltered as a fighter since his victory over Wladimir Klitschko three years ago, the consensus is that Fury is now the #1 heavyweight in the world.

Wilder–Fury II shaped up from the start as an intriguing drama. Fury has a fighter's name (first and last). "Deontay" sounds like a fashion designer's moniker. But Wilder has an aura of menace about him. In the ring, he evokes images of a deadly raptor ripping its prey to shreds with a single strike.

Fury has an erratic persona. By his own admission, he has struggled with severe depression for most of his life. On November 28, 2015, he decisioned Wladimir Klitschko to claim the WBA, IBF, and WBO belts. Then he began spouting homophobic, misogynist, anti-Semitic dogma before abandoning boxing to deal with his emotional problems.

"Part of the attraction with Fury," British journalist Ron Lewis writes, "has always been, you genuinely don't know what he is going to say. Sometimes he will just make stuff up. In the modern boxing media where video journalists generally outnumber writers, the soundbite is king. Soundbites are rolled out and the outlandish remarks are gobbled up as good material. And Fury gives good soundbites. Whether they are true or not doesn't really matter. What counts is that people click."

Fury returned to the ring in 2018 after a thirty-month absence and notched lackluster victories over Sefer Seferi and Francesco Pianeta. On December 1, 2018, he survived ninth- and twelfth-round knockdowns en route to a draw against Wilder. Less-than-impressive triumphs over Tom Schwarz and Otto Wallin followed.

In his most recent ring appearance, Fury journeyed to Saudi Arabia for an October 31, 2019, staged wrestling spectacle that pitted him against WWE strongman Braun Strowman.

Fury has good boxing skills for a man his size. He stands six feet, nine inches tall and fights in the neighborhood of a non-svelte 260 pounds. There's a lot of jiggling when he moves around the ring. At age thirty-one, he entered Wilder–Fury II as an undefeated professional boxer with 29 wins, 20 knockouts, and a draw in 30 fights.

Wilder captured a bronze medal at the 2008 Olympics as a raw twenty-three-year-old. Seven years later, he annexed the WBC heavyweight title by decision over Bermane Stiverne. Since then, he has successfully defended his belt ten times against mostly pedestrian opposition. His most credible opponents were Luis Ortiz (twice) and Fury.

Deontay has made some good life choices and also some bad ones. There have been incidents of violence outside the ring and public utterances that made him look and sound like a bully. That said, Wilder can punch. Bigtime. Entering the ring on February 22, he had 40 knockout victories in 42 fights, with only Fury and Stiverne having gone the distance against him. And Stiverne was obliterated on a first-round knockout when they met in the ring for the second time.

As writer Carlos Acevedo noted, "There is no softening-up process necessary for Wilder to demolish an opponent. Cumulative damage is not a prerequisite. He picks his high-spots (moments when he fully commits to his bludgeonous right hand) with care, and few can withstand its direct impact."

Fighters are associated with certain phrases . . . Joe Louis: "He can run but he can't hide" . . . Mike Tyson: "They all have a plan until they get hit" . . . Wilder sums up nicely when he says of each opponent, "He has to be perfect for twelve rounds. I have to be perfect for two seconds."

Let's say it again. Wilder can punch. His right hand is devastating. And not only isn't he afraid to throw it; his entire fight plan (at the risk of losing round after round on the judges' scorecards) is about trying to land it. His conventional boxing skills are limited. His chin is suspect, but he has learned to use his height and reach to protect it. Give him time to set up and proceed at his leisure, and he will destroy you.

Moreover, Wilder carries his power late. As Fury found out in round twelve of their first encounter, Deontay is dangerous until the final bell.

"This is a gladiator sport," Wilder says. "It ain't no room for weakness in this sport, especially when you're a champion because you'll always be a target. You're always gonna have a bull's-eye on your back. So you've gotta have a mentality like that. It's good to be nice and kind and shit like that. But when it comes to boxing, you can't show no weakness. You've gotta show that you're a savage, that you ain't nothing to be messed with, and that's what I show. Put fear in these guys' hearts and really mean it. When you fight Deontay Wilder, I take something from you. I take years from your life."

As for Fury's psychiatric issues, Wilder acknowledged, "We all have mental problems. Ain't nobody one hundred percent. I'm crazy at times. I go do things at times. I been had a gun in my hand before thinking about committing suicide. I mean, shit. It ain't no different. I can be a role model, but you have to accept me and embrace me for who I am. I may say some crazy stuff. I may make up my own words at times. I'm human. I don't walk a straight path and a lot of things may go wrong in my life and it's going to be up to me to correct them. I just tell people to accept me for who I am. I am who I am. I'm not perfect."

For a while, Wilder was skeptical that the rematch would take place.

"Fury doesn't want to fight me again," Deontay said. "He's satisfied with the draw and he wants to run with a moral victory." That was followed by reference to Fury rising from the canvas after what initially seemed to be a fight-ending knockout: "I knocked some marbles out his head. When a man doesn't know how he got knocked onto the ground or how he got up, that ain't no good sign. His family don't even want him to fight me again. He don't want to either, but he's got to."

In due course, the rematch was signed with the two sides agreeing to a fifty-fifty revenue split.

It would be Wilder (backed by Premier Boxing Champions and FOX) versus Fury (in league with Top Rank and ESPN). Thereafter, Top Rank CEO Bob Arum predicted that Wilder–Fury II would engender two million pay-per-view buys. That left a lot of observers willing to bet the "under," since Wilder–Fury I was generously estimated to have generated 325,000.

In truth, neither Fury or Wilder had sold well to the public in the past.

Wilder had headlined two previous fight cards in Las Vegas. According to numbers released by the Nevada State Athletic Commission, 4,074 tickets resulting in a live gate of $755,200 were sold for his 2015 outing against

Bermane Stiverne. Deontay's 2019 rematch against Luis Ortiz generated a live gate of $4,063,141 on 7,403 tickets sold. Depending on whom one believes, Wilder–Ortiz II (which was distributed on pay-per-view by FOX) engendered between 225,000 and 275,000 buys. Since FOX is reported to have guaranteed 500,000 buys for Wilder-Ortiz II, that translated into a lot of red ink.

Meanwhile, the live gate for Fury–Schwarz at the MGM Grand was $882,145 with 5,489 tickets sold. The live gate for Fury–Wallin at T-Mobile Arena was $999,723 with 3,577 tickets purchased. There were more comps (3,898) for Fury–Wallin than tickets sold.

To state the obvious, these are not good numbers. But ESPN and FOX (which jointly handled the pay-per-view for Wilder–Fury II) went all in on promotion of the rematch.

FOX is available in 120 million American homes. ESPN has 83 million domestic subscribers. ESPN put the promotion into high gear on December 28 when Fury appeared on its *College Gameday* program prior to the College Football Playoff semifinal game between LSU and Oklahoma. Then, on February 2, FOX broadcast two Wilder–Fury II commercials during Super Bowl LIV. According to Nielsen Media Research, the first Super Bowl promo (which ran at 8:02 p.m. Eastern time) was seen by 103.5 million viewers. The second (which aired thirty-five minutes later) drew 101.1 million. There were also seven pre-game promotional spots that averaged 18 million viewers each.

Given the fact that in-game Super Bowl commercials normally cost advertisers as much as $10 million a minute, this marked a significant investment by FOX in the promotion.

The lead-up to Wilder–Fury II was marked (and sometimes marred) by back-and-forth utterances between the fighters.

Fury did his part to debase the public dialogue during a media scrum immediately after the January 13 kickoff press conference in Los Angeles. Discussing his preparation for the rematch, he declared, "I'm masturbating seven times a day to keep my testosterone pumping. Pump it, pump it, pump it, pump it up! Don'tcha know! I gotta to keep active and the testosterone flowing for the fight."

Later, Tyson declared, "I look at Wilder and I don't see a tough fight. I see a long-legged pussy that I'm going to break in. A big six-foot, seven-inch virgin that ain't been rodded before. I'm going to bend him over and scuttle him backwards nice and slowly."

Fury further pledged, "After this fight, I'm going to binge on cocaine and hookers. Is there anything better than cocaine and hookers? I go to the cheap thirty-dollar ones. Always give yourself a shot of penicillin before shagging 'em. If you haven't got the penicillin, always double-bag up."

Wilder responded more simply, saying, "This is unfinished business that I will finish. Come February 22, I'm going to rip his head off his body. The first fight was a very controversial fight. We left people confused about who won. This is where we come and settle everything. This is judgment day."

When fight week arrived, the hype machine went into in overdrive, proclaiming that Wilder–Fury II was one of the most anticipated heavy-weight championship matches of all time. There was a massive amount of network shoulder programming including extensive onsite coverage from February 18 until fight night.

ESPN and FOX, which talk breathlessly about "unified titles" when matchups like Vasyl Lomachenko vs. Jose Pedraza occur, suddenly forgot that the WBA, WBO, and IBF (each of which recognizes Anthony Joshua as its heavyweight champion) exist. Also forgotten was the fact that, in Wilder–Fury I, the fighters had landed a total of only 155 punches between them. That's six punches per fighter per round.

No matter. The twelfth-round knockdown and Fury getting up from it had elevated Wilder–Fury II as a commercial attraction. The fight sparked high interest in the boxing community. Whether or not this interest was spilling over to general sports fans and beyond was a separate issue. Tickets were available at list price until three days before the fight.

Fury predicted that he'd knock Wilder out in the second round. That earned a scornful rejoinder from Deontay, who proclaimed, "Fury has got pillows as fists. We all know he don't have no power. He's just a tall big man that can move around a ring and that's about it. As far as him knocking me out, he don't believe that himself. He can't even see that in his dreams."

There was the usual idiotic (and dangerous) shoving and shouting at the final pre-fight press conference on Wednesday, all of which was gleefully distributed as a marketing tool by the promotion (except for the part where Wilder and Fury trashed each other as being unmarketable).

Among other things, Wilder berated Fury, saying, "When I found you,

you was strung out on coke. When I found you, you was big as a house, contemplating about killing yourself. So don't you ever forget who brought you to bigtime boxing. I brought you back. I put food on your table for your family to eat. Don't you ever forget that."

On Thursday, to its credit, the Nevada State Athletic Commission ruled that, for security reasons, the fighters would not be allowed to engage in the ritual staredown at the close of Friday's weigh-in. Arum complained about the ruling, but all was not lost. After the weigh-in, as Fury and Wilder stood on opposite sides of the stage with six commission inspectors between them, Fury gave Wilder the finger and Deontay responded by grabbing his crotch.

For their first encounter, Wilder had weighed in at 212½ pounds. This time, he tipped the scales at 231 (his heaviest ever). Fury had weighed 256½ pounds the first time around. Now it was 273 (three pounds less than his all-time high). The general feeling was that the extra weight would help Wilder and hurt Fury.

It was a pick 'em fight with a slight edge in the odds, if any, toward Wilder. Looking at the two bouts that each man had engaged in subsequent to their first encounter, Deontay seemed to be improving (against Dominic Breazeale and Luis Ortiz). Fury, on the other hand, appeared to be stagnating (against Tom Schwarz and Otto Wallin).

"Deontay does not get the credit that he deserves for the improvement," Jay Deas (Wilder's co-trainer and adviser) said in a February 12 media conference call. "I don't think people totally get what they're seeing, and sometimes they don't understand the nuances of the sport. We do what we call a six-month test. Every six months, we ask ourselves, 'Would you right now beat you from six months ago?' And I can answer one hundred percent honestly that, since the beginning of the first day that he came in the gym, that answer has been yes. He keeps getting better and better and better and smarter and refined with the technique. The things that people don't really get is the timing, the distance, the spacing, the positioning, all those things that allow you to land those big punches. That's skill. And he wants to learn. He's the kind of guy that is still hungry to get better and better."

ESPN commentator Teddy Atlas was in accord, saying, "I feel like Wilder has added something. He's added a delivery system where he mesmerizes you with the jab and then BOP, the right hand is right behind it,

George Foreman did it, Teófilo Stevenson did it. They lie to you. They make you think you're safe because they're only throwing the jab three-quarters, so you think that's the end of the line for danger. But it's not. It's about three inches further because they didn't extend the jab. And Wilder has learned how to do that by making you think you're safe. You cooperate a little, and then BOOM!"

In December, Fury announced that he was replacing trainer Ben Davison with Sugar Hill and that Stitch Duran (not Jorge Capetillo) would be his cutman for the February 22 rematch. Fury and Hill soon began talking about tapping into a new reserve of power. But as Don Turner (who trained Evander Holyfield and Larry Holmes late in their respective ring careers) observed, "You don't take a fighter in his thirties, change his style, and teach him to punch with more power in an eight-week training camp."

Those who picked Wilder to win the rematch noted that, as Wilder–Fury I progressed, Deontay seemed to figure Tyson out. He'd knocked Fury down in both the ninth and twelfth rounds and was likely to set up his punches more effectively the second time around.

Also, there was the matter of "the cut." Fury had suffered a gruesome gash along his right eyebrow courtesy of a left hook from Wallin in round three of their September 14 bout. The cut bled profusely throughout the fight and required forty-seven stitches to close.

The scar tissue from that cut would be an attractive target for Wilder. "No matter what he does," Deontay said, "when he fights me, it's going to open right back up. I'm going to pop it right back open. He can get plastic surgery, duct tape or staples, superglue or hot glue, cement glue. Shit, he can go get some of that flex glue. It ain't gonna to matter. I definitely look forward to re-cutting open that eye."

And finally, there was the biggest factor of all—Wilder's power.

"I've never seen anything like it," Bob Arum (who co-promotes Fury with Frank Warren) said. "It's actually accentuated by the fact he doesn't know how to box. He's a horrible boxer. He puts on a clinic of how not to box, but he has that right hand."

"For one punch," Teddy Atlas added, "just one punch, I think Wilder is the hardest puncher in the history of the sport."

Yes, Wilder was a one-trick pony. But it was quite a trick.

Meanwhile, the case for a Fury victory began with Wilder's limited repertoire. Bart Barry spoke for many when he wrote, "Wilder only took what he did best and committed to doing it better. If the holes in his style aren't any larger now than when he started, they are, surprisingly, no smaller."

Fury's partisans also reasoned that their man would be in better shape for the rematch than for the first fight and wouldn't tire down the stretch as he had before. Also, they were confident that, this time, in addition to making Wilder miss, he'd make Deontay pay when he missed.

Asked what he'd learned from Wilder–Fury I, Tyson responded, "He's got a big right hand and that's it. He's a one-dimensional fighter. I didn't know what I had in the tank last time. This time, I know I can go the distance. I'll throw everything but the kitchen sink at him, and he won't know what hit him."

As for the knockdown in round twelve of their first encounter, Fury explained, "I backed up in a straight line and got clipped with a right hand and it was good night, Vienna. That was all she wrote. But then I rose from the canvas like a phoenix from the ashes to get back into it, take him up, and finish the fight the stronger man."

There were a host of battles between ESPN and FOX behind the scenes with regard to a range of issues. Where on-air talent was concerned, it was agreed that Joe Tessitore (ESPN) would call the blow by blow with expert commentary from Lennox Lewis (FOX) and Andre Ward (ESPN). Host Brian Kenny (FOX) would be joined at the fight-night desk by Max Kellerman (ESPN), Shawn Porter (FOX), and Timothy Bradley (ESPN). In addition, Mark Kriegel (ESPN), Kate Abdo (FOX), and Bernard Osuna (ESPN) would serve as ringside reporters while Larry Hazzard (FOX) would be the unofficial scorer and rules expert.

There was a lot of chatter during the televised portion of the pay-per-view undercard about how this would be Wilder's eleventh consecutive heavyweight title defense, breaking a tie that he'd held with Muhammad Ali. This ignored the fact that Ali was the undisputed heavyweight champion of the world during his reign while Deontay was one of many. Max Kellerman then analogized Fury's boxing skills and elusiveness in the ring to that of Wilfred Benítez and Willie Pep.

Viewers were also told that the live gate for Wilder–Fury II had surpassed $17 million, which made it the largest live gate in the history of heavyweight boxing in Nevada. Lewis–Holyfield II in 1999 had grossed $16.86 million. Of course, accounting for inflation, $16.86 million in 1999 would be worth $26.28 million today.

Fury, wearing a red velour robe and sitting on a throne, was wheeled to the ring by four buxom women while a recording of "Crazy" sung by Patsy Cline played over the public address system. Wilder opted for glitzy black body armor accessorized by a black mask during his ring walk, with rapper D Smoke providing the soundtrack.

Then came the moment of reckoning.

Fury dominated the action from beginning to end. He came out aggressively in the first two rounds, stalking and outjabbing Wilder, who hardly jabbed at all. As is usually the case, Deontay did little to set up his punches and looked simply to land the big one. His deficiencies as a boxer showed.

Boxing Fury is a bit like boxing a mountain. Wilder was having trouble coping with a bigger man who chose this time to come right at him, throwing punches.

With 38 seconds left in round three, Fury dropped Wilder with a clubbing overhand right that landed on Deontay's left ear. If Wilder had looked bad before, from that point on, he looked awful. His legs were weak. His balance was unsteady. He bled profusely from his left ear and seemed confused if not dazed. He wasn't just losing rounds. For the first time in his career, he was getting beaten up.

Referee Kenny Bayless helped Wilder a bit by breaking the fighters at times when Fury was working effectively inside. Then, not long after Tyson dropped Deontay with a hook to the body in round five, Bayless (without previous warning) took a point away from Fury for hitting on the break.

By round six, Wilder was fighting like he was out on his feet. And more significantly, his power had deserted him. It no longer looked as though he had the ability to change the course of the fight with one punch. It was then that Fury had the poor taste to lick Deontay's neck during a clinch to taste the blood that was flowing from his ear.

The mauling continued. One minute, 37 seconds into round seven, with Wilder trapped in a neutral corner and Fury pounding away, Mark Breland (Deontay's chief second) threw in the towel.

In the end, Fury had learned more from Wilder–Fury I than Wilder had. Deontay thought that, this time around, he'd be able to set up the big punch more effectively than before and still fight at his chosen pace. Fury, on the other hand, learned in the desperate minutes after being knocked down in round twelve of their first encounter that, if he moved forward aggressively throwing punches, Wilder couldn't deal with his size and strength.

"Things like this happen," Wilder said in a post-fight interview with Bernard Osuna. "The best man won tonight. I just wish my corner would have let me go out on my shield."

He's fortunate that they didn't.

Meanwhile, in the weeks ahead, there will be a lot of talk about "greatness." Thus, it's worth considering the thoughts of writer Carlos Acevedo who wrote, "Of all the concepts, phrases, and words that have devolved in boxing over the years, none has slipped so drastically as the notion of greatness. Writers and reporters take many of their cues directly from press releases, publicists, promoters, and network puffers. This is like taking advice from a three-card monte dealer on where the queen of hearts may be."

In his most recent fight preceding Wilder–Fury II, Fury struggled against Otto Wallin. Against Wilder on Saturday night, at times he looked sloppy. Two victories—against Wladimir Klitschko and now Wilder—don't qualify a fighter for greatness.

Fury himself seems to understand that notion. During a media conference call to promote Wilder–Fury II, he declared, "The only thing that means anything to me is winning these fights. That's it, period. I'm a purebred fighting man through and through. And when it's over, it's over. I'm not really concerned about the legacy. I'm not overly concerned about what happens when I'm done. We can only take one chapter of our lives at a time, and I'm just enjoying living in the moment right now. I'm living my dream, my childhood dream, my young adult dream, and my midlife dream. I really don't care about legacy because what somebody thinks of me when I'm finished is unimportant. It's all sticks and stones. Whether it's good or bad, everyone is entitled to their opinion. And there will be somebody else to replace me just like every other champion."

Boxing returned from a three-month layoff on June 9, 2020.

Top Rank on ESPN
and What Comes Next

Two boxing cards promoted by Top Rank were televised on ESPN this past week. But the primary storyline wasn't the fights, which were largely fungible. It was the return of boxing in the Coronavirus Era.

Promoting a boxing match in a jurisdiction with responsible oversight is hard under the best of circumstances. It's more difficult during a pandemic. The Nevada State Athletic Commission and Top Rank put responsible coronavirus protocols in place. Responsible—not foolproof. "That's the best I can do," Top Rank CEO Bob Arum acknowledged. "I can't just wave a wand and make everything perfect."

Top Rank also took a step in the right direction when Arum pledged, "If we do it right, then any promoter that wants to look at our protocols and look at what we did, we're happy to provide them with our protocols. There's no copyright on it. If they want to see how it should be done, assuming everything goes well, we're happy to show them. There are about thirty pages. They're all designed for safety. And we're happy to share it with our colleagues in the sport."

That position was in marked contrast to UFC's attempt to keep its coronavirus protocols "confidential," claiming that they were "proprietary information." Coronavirus protocols should be made public for two reasons: (1) if they have flaws, the flaws should be spotted and corrected; and (2) if they're well constructed, state athletic commissions and other promoters can learn from them.

Top Rank's fight cards took place on June 9 and June 11, 2020, in the Grand Ballroom at the MGM Grand in Las Vegas. There were no spectators other than those in the room on official business. Here, it might be noted that empty rooms are not uncommon at fights. When Oscar De La Hoya fought Floyd Mayweather at the MGM Grand Garden Arena in 2007, there were fourteen paying customers in the stands when the first bout began.

Ring announcer Mark Shonuck performed his duties on June 9 and 11 from outside the ropes. It was nice to see fighters in the ring without sanctioning-body officials jostling with commission personnel to be on camera while entourage members surround their fighter shouting "You da man!" Stitch Duran and Mike Bazzel worked in opposing corners as cutmen for each of the fights except in instances where a fighter's trainer or assistant trainer doubled as his cutman.

ESPN's announcing team was situated with safety in mind. Blow-by-blow commentator Joe Tessitore called the action from a studio at ESPN headquarters in Connecticut. Tim Bradley, Andre Ward, and Mark Kriegel offered analysis from their respective homes. Roving reporter Bernardo Osuna was the only on-camera member of the announcing team positioned on site.

A supporting bout for the June 9 card was scratched when Mikaela Mayer (who was scheduled to fight Helen Joseph) tested positive for COVID-19. That left five fights.

Cuban Olympic gold medalist Robeisy Ramirez knocked out a grossly overmatched Yeuri Andujar at 54 seconds of round one.

Quatavious Cash won a unanimous decision over Calvin Metcalf in a bout that went to the scorecards after being stopped as the result of a cut caused by an accidental head butt.

Italian heavyweight Guido Vianello took on 294-pound Don Haynesworth, who looked as though he wasn't in shape to shadowbox—let alone, fight—for the scheduled six rounds. Conditioning became a moot point when the first solid right hand that Vianello landed ended matters at 2:16 of round one.

After that, heavyweight Jared Anderson mercilessly pounded Johnnie Langston before stopping him at the 1:55 mark of the third round.

That set the stage for the main event: WBO 126-pound champion Shakur Stevenson vs. Felix Caraballo in an over-the-weight non-title bout.

Stevenson is a good, well-schooled fighter who has made his mark in the professional ranks against light-punching slow opponents. Caraballo, who works in a supermarket and took the fight on less than four weeks' notice, fit that mold. Asked during a pre-fight media conference call whether he'd watched video of Caraballo, Shakur answered, "I watched like one round. I seen everything I needed to see in that one round. He's nowhere near on my level."

As expected, Stevenson dominated from start to finish, ending the beatdown with a well-placed body shot at 1:31 of round six.

Top Rank's June 11 fight card was more competitive. Adam Lopez opened the show with a majority decision over Luis Coria in a spirited fight. Then, after Gabriel Muratalla blew out 40-to-1 underdog Fernando Robles in the first round, Eric Mondragon and Mike Sanchez fought to a four-round draw. In the main event, Yenifel Vicente was knocked down twice by Jessie Magdaleno and penalized four points for low blows before being disqualified in the tenth round.

What should boxing fans make of the June 9 and 11 fight cards on ESPN?

First, let's repeat what was said earlier in this article. Promoting a boxing match is hard under the best of circumstances. It's more difficult during a pandemic.

Within that framework, the fight cards and telecasts were implemented in a professional manner. It might have seemed strange to viewers for the announcing team to call the fights from offsite TV monitors. But HBO and Showtime commentators have done the same thing in the past. And Epix's announcing team called fights from a studio in New York throughout the network's two-year boxing run.

The absence of an onsite crowd took away from the drama. Crowd response adds to the excitement of a good fight. It's one of the reasons that telecasts sometimes originate from the home town of a main event fighter.

The bigger problem—particularly with regard to ESPN's June 9 show—was the quality of the fights. The introduction at the top of the telecast declared that "bigtime boxing" was back. But June 9 wasn't bigtime. The fights were gross mismatches with odds like 40–1 (Stevenson–Caraballo), 35–1 (Anderson-Langston), and 30–1 (Vianello–Haynesworth). In five fights, the underdog won zero rounds.

Shows like this leave boxing's fan base with a sour taste in its collective mouth. According to Nielsen Media Research, the June 9 telecast was watched by an average of only 397,000 viewers with a peak viewership of 609,000. These are poor numbers given ESPN's reach. The totals for June 11 were worse—an average viewership of 311,000 with a peak of 392,000.

By way of comparison, more than 1.14 million viewers watched the July 4, 2019, Nathan's Hot Dog Eating Contest on ESPN.

Also, at times, the ESPN telecasts toyed with boxing fans in a particularly aggravating manner. For the first half of the June 11 telecast, viewers were told to stay tuned for a major announcement from Tyson Fury regarding his upcoming fights. But the major announcement turned out to be nothing more than a statement from Fury that he intended to fight Deontay Wilder next and that the Fury and Anthony Joshua camps had loosely agreed upon the parameters for two fights to be contested in 2021. All of that had been previously reported. And as Fury conceded, "Nothing is really set."

The ESPN announcing team also went overboard in hyping Shakur Stevenson as "the next Floyd Mayweather" and "the best young fighter on the planet" with the promise that "he's gonna be the number one pound-for-pound fighter in the world for certain."

Stevenson is a talented young fighter. He'd be well matched against Gary Russell Jr. But there are other young fighters who show just as much, if not more, potential. And before anyone gets too upset by that declaration, consider the following.

ESPN's panel of twelve "experts" (which includes TV commentators Joe Tessitore, Tim Bradley, and Andre Ward) doesn't list Stevenson among its top ten pound-for-pound fighters, nor was Shakur among the other eight fighters who received points in the ESPN.com poll.

Stevenson is not listed among the twenty fighters who received votes in the Boxing Writers Association of America pound-for-pound rankings.

Boxing Scene doesn't list Stevenson in its top-ten pound-for-pound rankings or among "five more who could easily be here" or "five for the future."

And going six rounds against Felix Caraballo isn't a credential that should lift anyone into the pound-for-pound conversation.

Also, the ESPN commentating team repeatedly made the point that Stevenson wants to become boxing's premier attraction "without having to play the villain role." In that regard, it might be instructive to go to YouTube and type in "Shakur Stevenson garage."

Perhaps Stevenson's thinking has evolved in a positive way since this incident in a Miami Beach garage occurred two years ago and he has become a model citizen. But I haven't heard him address what happened that evening in a meaningful way.

As for the immediate future, there will be at least two Top Rank cards each week on ESPN in the months ahead. And they will be held without spectators in attendance for the foreseeable future.

"We're probably going to be doing this for three months," Bob Arum told Boxing Scene with regard to the present formula. "It's one step at a time. People have got to understand that we don't have experience in what we're doing here. Nobody does. Better to go slow and be on solid ground than to just rush ahead and fuck everything up." Translation: It will be a long time before boxing fans see the fights that we want to see.

There's an oft repeated tale about Joe Namath, the charismatic quarterback who led the New York Jets to an upset of the mighty Baltimore Colts in the 1969 Super Bowl, a game that established parity between the NFL's warring factions. Namath had an eye for women and a sexual appetite to match. One night, he and running back Ed Marinaro were in a hotel lounge at closing time. A woman, not particularly attractive, was alone at the bar. Namath went over to her. They exchanged a few words. Then he returned to Marino and said, "I'm going upstairs with her. I'll see you in the morning."

Marinaro was astonished.

"Joe? Why her?'

"It's three o'clock in the morning," pro football's #1 matinee idol answered. "Miss America ain't coming in."

Boxing fans, get used to it. Miss America ain't coming in. Not anytime soon, anyway.

Jack Dempsey is one of boxing's most iconic figures and an enduring part of boxing lore.

Jack Dempsey and the Newsboy: Debunking a Myth

It's one of boxing's most endearing legends. Jack Dempsey went to bed on the night of July 4, 1919, after knocking out Jess Willard to claim the heavyweight championship of the world and dreamed about the fight. Except in Dempsey's dream, Willard knocked him out. It wasn't until a newsboy selling papers on the street assured him he'd won that the Dempsey felt like the champion again. It's a heartwarming story. Except it probably isn't true.

Once upon a time, the Fourth of July was an important day on the boxing calendar. In the course of twelve years, four heavyweight championship bouts were fought on Independence Day.

Tommy Burns vs. Billy Squires on July 4, 1907, was the first. Their fight in Colma, California, on the San Francisco peninsula was scheduled for forty-five rounds, but Burns knocked out Squires in the first. The event had a slightly un-American flavor since Burns was from Canada and Squires was from Australia. The referee was former heavyweight champion James J. Jeffries.

Three years later, Jeffries was in the ring again on the Fourth of July, this time in Reno as a combatant against Jack Johnson. It was one of the most celebrated sports events of all time. Johnson was in control from the opening bell and stopped Jeffries in the fifteenth round.

Two years passed before Johnson returned to the ring. When he did, it was against Fireman Jim Flynn in East Las Vegas, New Mexico, on July 4, 1912. A totally outclassed Flynn was disqualified for repeated fouls in the ninth round.

Ultimately, Flynn laid claim to a more favorable entry in boxing's record book. On February 13, 1917, he knocked out a twenty-two-year-old prospect named Jack Dempsey in 25 seconds. Seven months later, Dempsey avenged the defeat by knocking out Flynn in the first round.

That brings us to Dempsey vs. Jess Willard on July 4, 1919. BoxRec.

com reports that there were fight cards at sixty-four venues in the United States that day. Sam Langford lost a decision to Harry Wills in St. Louis. Jack Britton decisioned Johnny Griffiths in Canton. Harry Greb decisioned Bill Brennan in Tulsa.

As for Dempsey–Willard, Randy Roberts is a professor of history at Purdue University and the author of several trailblazing books about boxing. One of these books, published in 1979, is the most reliable of the Dempsey biographies. Roberts didn't include Dempsey's newsboy anecdote in his book. Why not?

"Because I don't think it's true," Roberts says. "It has the feel of the type of manufactured apocryphal story that sportswriters made up in those days when they were more interested in building legends than accurately recounting what happened. If I'd read about the incident in a contemporaneous newspaper account of the fight, it would have given the story credibility and I would have included it in my book. But as best I can tell, it wasn't told until Dempsey's first autobiography which was written twenty-one years later. I can't say with absolute certainty that it's not true because I wasn't there. But it's highly improbable, like the story of Cassius Clay throwing his Olympic gold medal into the Ohio River, which wasn't told until Ali's [1975] autobiography and almost certainly never happened."

In Dempsey's first autobiography, co-authored in 1940 with Myron Stearns, the former champion wrote, "I didn't get to bed until two o'clock. That night, I dreamed I had been knocked out. It was a strange sort of nightmare. When I woke up, I couldn't get to sleep again. I dressed and went out onto the street. Newsboys were still hollering their extras 'all about the new champ.' I called to one of them and said, 'Say, Buddy, who won the fight?' He said, 'Dempsey. Say, aren't you Dempsey? You ought to know.' I was so tickled, I gave him a dollar and went back up to my room and read the accounts all through three or four times, convincing myself that at last I was really the champion."

Here, it should be noted that newsboys were popular in feel-good stories of the day such as the hugely successful film *Mr. Smith Goes to Washington* that was released in 1939 (one year before Dempsey's first autobiography was published).

In Dempsey's second autobiography, published in 1960 and authored with Bob Considine and Bill Slocum, the newsboy story was recounted as follows: "That night, I went to bed at ten o'clock. About midnight, I had a nightmare. I dreamed that Willard had knocked me out. It was so realistic I fell out of bed. I got up and turned on the lights and looked at myself in a mirror. I had dreamed I was all cut up around the eyes. There wasn't a mark on me. I dressed in a hurry and went down to the street in front of the hotel. A kid was selling extra papers. 'Who won the fight?' I asked him. He looked at me. 'Aren't you Jack Dempsey?' he squeaked. 'Yeah.' 'You damn fool, you did!' the kid said. I gave him a buck, went back upstairs and to bed."

Finally, in a 1977 autobiography written with his stepdaughter Barbara Piattelli, Dempsey maintained, "I woke up in a cold sweat, confused. I climbed out of bed and stumbled into the bathroom, turning on the over-head light. I peered at my face and saw some small dried patches of blood on it. I felt paralyzed. Pulling on my pants and shirt, I rushed out into the hall. Not realizing I had forgotten to put my shoes on, I ran outside, my heartbeat sounding in my ears. A newsboy was hollering 'Extra, Extra! Read all about it!' 'Ain't you Jack Dempsey?' the newsboy asked. 'Yeah. Why?' I grabbed a paper. There it was, my name in big, bold headlines. I was the Heavyweight Champion of the World. All of a sudden, standing barefoot on the street with a newsboy at my side, I felt the full impact of my victory. I reached into my pockets to give the kid a buck but found my pockets empty. I told him to pick it up in the morning from the room clerk. 'You don't owe me nothin, Champ!'"

Now let's look at the contradictions in Dempsey's three versions of the story.

> Autobiography #1: I didn't get to bed until two o'clock.
> Autobiography #2: I went to bed at ten o'clock.

> Autobiography #2: It was so realistic I fell out of bed.
> Autobiography #3: I climbed out of bed.

> Autobiography #2: I looked at myself in a mirror. There
>   wasn't a mark on me.
> Autobiography #3: I peered at my face and saw some small
>   dried patches of blood on it.

Autobiography #1: "Say, Buddy, who won the fight?" He said, "Dempsey. Say, aren't you Dempsey? You ought to know."

Autobiography #2: "Who won the fight?" I asked him. He looked at me. "Aren't you Jack Dempsey? he squeaked. "Yeah." "You damn fool, you did!"

Autobiography #3: "Ain't you Jack Dempsey?" the newsboy asked. "Yeah. Why?" I grabbed a paper. There it was, my name in big, bold headlines. I was the Heavyweight Champion of the World.

Autobiography #2: I gave him a buck, went back upstairs and to bed.

Autobiography #3: I reached into my pockets to give the kid a buck but found my pockets empty. I told him to pick it up in the morning from the room clerk. "You don't owe me nothin, Champ!"

Dempsey might have had a nightmare that he lost to Jess Willard. The rest of the story seems to be—shall we say—embellished.

Despite a strong push from Premier Boxing Champions and Showtime, Jermall and Jermell Charlo have yet to develop a profitable fan base.

How High Can the Charlos Climb?

Jermell and Jermall Charlo, identical twins, turned pro respectively in 2007 and 2008. Now thirty years old, they've compiled a 65–1 (40 KOs) ring record between them. But they haven't gone in as tough as boxing fans would have liked and they haven't become stars. A September 26, 2020, doubleheader on Showtime-PPV was designed to chip away at these issues and launch them into a higher orbit.

A fighter doesn't need cruelty to be great. Cruelty implies deriving joy from another person's pain. Many fighters disassociate themselves from the pain they cause. That's typical of sports. When a baseball player hits a home run, he doesn't empathize with the pitcher's pain. So cruelty isn't necessary. But it helps for a fighter to have a wellspring of anger to motivate him. And the Charlos have that.

Jermall came into the September 26 fight card with an unblemished 30–0 (22 KOs) ring record and a World Boxing Council 160-pound belt around his waist. But he lacked a signature win on his résumé, and Canelo Álvarez is widely regarded as both the real WBC middleweight champion and the best middleweight in the world.

Jermell Charlo (33–1, 17 KOs) had previously held the WBC 154-pound title, lost it by decision to Tony Harrison in 2018, and regained it by knocking out Harrison last year.

"Twin power is better," Jermall has said. "If you don't like the Charlos, stay out of our lane and keep the hate down."

The fights on September 26 were contested at Mohegan Sun in Uncasville, Connecticut, without spectators on site. Showtime styled the promotion as a two-part, six-fight pay-per-view doubleheader and charged $74.95 for the show. The fact that the event was on pay-per-view didn't speak to the Charlos' marketability. Rather, it signaled that no sponsor would put up enough money for the fight to be televised on FOX, nor would Showtime pay a license fee large enough to cover the fighters' purses.

The first half of the doubleheader was headlined by Jermall Charlo vs. Sergiy Derevyanchenko with Brandon Figueroa vs. Damien Vazquez and John Riel Casimero vs. Duke Micah on the undercard. Part two featured Jermell Charlo vs. Jeison Rosario for the WBC, WBA, IBF, and *Ring Magazine* 154-pound titles, preceded by Luis Nery vs. Aaron Alameda and Danny Roman vs. Juan Carlos Payano.

The two Charlo fights were the bouts that mattered most.

"I see people grumbling they aren't pay-per-view fighters," Showtime Sports president Stephen Espinoza said. "But no one is a pay-per-view fighter until they get put in a pay-per-view fight."

Still, there were questions as to how the numbers would add up. Derevyanchenko was guaranteed a purse in the neighborhood of $2.2 million. And Rosario was well compensated by Showtime and Premier Boxing Champions (which represents the Charlos) for bringing his belts to the table. That meant the Charlos would be fighting for modest guarantees and hoping for a profitable upside on pay-per-view buys.

"This one is more a roll of the dice than usual," Espinoza acknowledged.

Derevyanchenko (13–2, 10 KOs) was a step up in the quality of opposition for Jermall. Sergiy grew up in Ukraine and has lived in Brooklyn since 2014. He's a tough out and had come up short in losses by decision to Danny Jacobs and Gennady Golovkin in fights that could have gone either way on the judges' scorecards.

"The green color of the WBC belt suits me," Derevyanchenko said at the final pre-fight press conference for the Charlo doubleheader. "I want that green belt. I've fought twice for the title and I'm more ready than ever for the third time."

That said, Sergiy was thirty-four years old with the wear and tear of four hundred amateur bouts and fifteen pro fights on his body. Jermall was a 2-to-1 favorite.

Rosario (20–1–1) had scored a surprise knockout of Julian Williams as a 30-to-1 underdog in January to claim the IBF and WBA belts. Speaking through a translator at the final pre-fight press conference for the Charlo fight, Jeison declared, "People are going to see on Saturday that it was no fluke that I beat Julian Williams the way that I did. There's no room in my mind for the possibility of not winning."

In response, Jermell, a 4-to-1 favorite, proclaimed, "During the fight, you're going to find out who really is the hunter. I'm a warrior and we're going to see that night who really is the hunter and who is the one that's going to be hunted."

The clear consensus going in was that it wouldn't be easy for either Charlo but that Jermall and Jermell would both win.

Charlo–Derevyanchenko was a spirited action fight with Charlo in control for most of the bout. Sergiy kept trying to pressure Jermall but was rarely able to land effectively. Charlo fought a disciplined fight, relied heavily on a good jab, and landed the more telling blows. He was more skilled and also more athletically gifted than Derevyanchenko. A succession of jabs opened a cut on Sergiy's right eyelid in round five. A more dangerous cut on Sergiy's left eyelid that was partially obscured by swelling followed. The decision of the judges was 118–110, 117–111, 116–112 in Jermall's favor.

"Sort of, it was easy," Jermall said afterward. "I don't wanna call him like an easy fight. No fight is easy. It's always a hard fight. At any given time, anything can change. But we stuck to the game plan and we made it happen. I let my jab dictate and do what it do, and we got the victory. I wanted to knock him out, if that's what you wanna know. I wanted to knock him out, but you can't knock out every fighter. I landed the shots that I needed to land to win."

Meanwhile, the defeat was a bitter disappointment for Derevyanchenko who cried in his dressing room after the bout. "I'm sick of fighting a good fight and losing," Sergiy told those who were gathered around him. "I want to win a title."

Later that night, seven stitches were etched into Derevyanchenko's skin to close the cut on his left eyelid. On Sunday, the cut was reopened by a plastic surgeon who restitched it.

Jermell Charlo vs. Jeison Rosario was the second featured fight of the night. Rosario won four of the first seven rounds on two of the judges' scorecards and three on the third. But from beginning to end, it had the feel of being Jermell's fight. He knocked Rosario down in the first and sixth rounds before ending matters on a strange note in round eight with a jab to the beltline that, because of its landing angle, might have jammed Rosario's protective cup into his private parts. As it was, Rosario lay on his back in pain and seemed to be having difficulty breathing.

"Something must've been seriously done to him prior to that in the earlier rounds," Jermell said afterward. "I don't know; I never seen it. I mean, have you ever seen somebody with a jab to the body put him out? That's different. I hit him right in the right spot, took the air out of him. I don't know what happened, man."

Three years ago, I wrote, "The Charlo brothers are good fighters. It would be nice if they were matched tougher so we can find out how good."

That sentiment still holds true.

This was Jermall's most impressive performance to date, a solid victory against a world-class opponent. It would be interesting to see him next against Canelo Álvarez, Gennady Golovkin, Demetrius Andrade, or Danny Jacobs. It would be less interesting to see him against Chris Eubank Jr. or Jarrett Hurd.

Jermell, like his brother, has a good chin, good boxing skills, and world-class athletic gifts. He also has three of the four belts at 154 pounds and a legitimate claim to being the #1 junior-middleweight in the world. But like Jermall, he needs better opposition—not belts—to take him to the next level. That could come from above if he moves up to 160 pounds. Or it could come from below; for example if Errol Spence were to beat Danny Garcia and then move up to challenge Jermell.

At the post-fight press conference following his victory over Rosario, Jermell declared, "I hope that we proved all of these haters wrong tonight. I seen a whole lotta yak on that Instagram and on them Twitters and all of them pages and all of that media. They don't understand the skills and the levels of boxing, and that's what we present. We here for it. We here to stay. Everybody in boxing—the Charlo twins are taking the fuck over!"

But while the Charlos will be formidable opponents for anyone they fight, neither has moved the needle in a significant way in terms of marketability. Most sports fans have no idea who they are. Many casual boxing fans don't know which Charlo is which. Tickets for their past fights have not sold well.

The September 26 doubleheader was a test-drive for making the Charlos an ongoing dual pay-per-view attraction. Showtime has not released PPV numbers as of this writing and might never do so. But indications are that the doubleheader drew poorly. The network has been plagued by poor ratings since its return to boxing following its shutdown for the pandemic. One week prior to the Charlo card, a *Showtime Championship Boxing* telecast headed by Erickson Lubin vs. Terrell Gausha averaged a meager 122,000 viewers. Had the Charlo doubleheader been on "regular" Showtime, it likely would have generated a substantial rating. But economic considerations forced it to pay-per-view.

Thus the centuries-old philosophical question: "If a tree falls in a forest and no one is around to hear it, does it make a sound?"

Fight cards were few and far between in 2020 because of the pandemic.

Fight Notes

Boxing made its debut at Barclays Center on October 20, 2012, with a fight card headlined by four world title bouts. Danny Garcia, Erik Morales, Paulie Malignaggi, Peter Quillin, Devon Alexander, Danny Jacobs, and Luis Collazo were in the ring that night. The franchise grew nicely. Fans who went to Barclays saw good featured fights with solid undercard bouts. But as of late, the arena's fistic offerings have faded.

Barclays cast its lot with Premier Boxing Champions. And PBC has moved its prime content to greener pastures (green being the color of money). There were five fight cards at Barclays Center in 2019. Each one struggled to sell tickets.

January 25, 2020, marked the thirty-ninth fight card at Barclays. The arena was half empty. The announced attendance was 8,217 but that included a lot of freebies. There were six fights on the card. As expected, fighters coming out of the blue corner won all of them. That's what happens when 6–0 squares off against 2–10–1.

Three of the fights were televised by *Showtime Championship Boxing*, which has also been diminished as a consequence of a multiyear output deal with PBC.

In the first of these bouts, Stephen Fulton (17–0, 8 KOs) and Ukrainian-born Arnold Khegai (16–0, 10 KOs) met in a junior-featherweight bout. Each man had fought the usual suspects en route to their confrontation. There was a lot of holding and rabbit-punching, which referee Steve Willis ignored. Eventually, Fulton pulled away for a unanimous-decision triumph.

Next up, Jarrett Hurd (23–1, 16 KOs) took on Francisco Santana (25 7, 12 KOs).

Hurd is a big junior-middleweight who held the WBA and IBF 154-pound titles until losing to Julian Williams last year. Santana is a career welterweight who had lost three of his most recent four fights and had won only three times in the last five years.

Hurd was expected to walk through Santana. But he was strangely passive for much of the fight, which led to the strange spectacle of Santana (the noticeably smaller, lighter-punching man) walking Jarrett down for long stretches of time. Francisco is a one-dimensional fighter and was there to be hit. When Jarrett let his hands go, he hit him. But he fought like a man who didn't want to fight and didn't let his hands go often enough.

By round seven, the boos and jeers were raining down. Hurd won a unanimous decision but looked mediocre. That's the most honest way to put it. One wonders what tricks losing to Julian Williams last year played with his mind.

Also, it should be noted that, when the winning fighter thanks God in a post-fight interview and the crowd (which supported Jarrett at the start of the bout) boos at the mention of the Almighty, there's a problem.

"The crowd didn't love it," Hurd acknowledged afterward. "But you gotta understand; I got the unanimous decision and I did what I wanted to do."

The main event matched Danny Garcia (35–2, 21 KOs) against Ivan Redkach (23–4–1, 18 KOs).

Garcia had a nice run early in his career, winning belts at 140 and 147 pounds. But later, he came out on the losing end of decisions against Keith Thurman and Shawn Porter. Other than that, he has gone in soft for the past five years.

Redkach is a junior-welterweight who had won 5 of 10 fights during the same five-year period.

There was the usual pre-fight nonsense with Garcia telling reporters, "We picked Redkach because he's dangerous and we knew he'd be tough." But in truth, Redkach had been whitewashed by Tevin Farmer at 135 pounds and was knocked out at the same weight by John Molina Jr. (who never won again).

Garcia, like Hurd, was a 30-to-1 betting favorite.

Redkach fought a safety-first fight. Also safety second and third. There wasn't one second when it looked as though he had a realistic chance of winning the fight or fought like he did.

One of the few proactive things that Ivan did do was stick out his tongue from time to time when Garcia hit him. Then, at the end of round eight, he bit Danny on the shoulder while they were in a clinch. At that point, one might have expected referee Benjy Esteves to disqualify Redkach. But Esteves seemed to not notice.

Rather than go for the kill after the bite, Garcia eased up and cruised to a unanimous decision. Meanwhile, by round eleven, the crowd was streaming for the exits. Most of the fans were gone by the time the decision was announced.

Garcia and Hurd had set-up showcase fights put on their plate. And neither man delivered the way he should have.

★ ★ ★

On March 7, 2020, FOX offered viewers a heavyweight tripleheader from Barclays Center in Brooklyn.

Frank Sánchez (14–0, 11 KOs), who came out of the Cuban amateur system, was a 10-to-1 favorite over Joey Dawejko (20–7–4, 11 KOs). Efe Ajagba (12–0, 10 KOs), a Nigerian Olympian now living in Texas, was a 30-to-1 favorite over Razvan Cojanu (17–6, 9 KOs). And Adam Kownacki (20–0, 15 KOs) was listed at 20-to-1 over thirty-six-year-old Robert Helenius (29–3, 18 KOs).

Things went according to plan. Until they didn't.

Sánchez, age twenty-seven, has been matched professionally against a series of limited opponents. Dawejko, who comes from the Andy Ruiz school of physical conditioning, fit that mold. He's generously listed as five feet, ten inches tall and weighed in for the bout at 247 pounds. He'd also lost three of four fights since 2017.

Don Elbaum promoted Dawejko early in Joey's ring career. At one point, Elbaum thought he might have a prospect. Then Dawejko struggled through a stretch when he won once in five fights against ordinary opposition, and Elbaum realized that he'd never get beyond being a club fighter.

Still, Elbaum respects Dawejko. "Let me tell you something," he says. "Joey's not afraid of anybody. Maybe he should be, but he isn't. Joey always gives you everything he has trying to win."

Against Sánchez, everything that Dawejko had wasn't enough. The fight resembled a sparring session. Sánchez settled into a safety-first, jab-and-move mode. Dawejko plodded forward but rarely landed cleanly and didn't have the power to hurt Sánchez on the all-too-few occasions when he did hit him.

CompuBox credited Sánchez with outlanding Dawejko by a 116-to-46 margin. Mystifyingly, judge Kevin Morgan gave rounds one and ten to

Joey. Those were the only rounds that Dawejko won on any of the judges' scorecards.

Put Dawejko in the ring with a guy like Dawejko and it will be a good fight. Put him in the ring with a guy like Sánchez and it will be a stinker.

Ajagba vs. Cojanu was next up.

Ajagba, age twenty-five, has fought the usual suspects. Cojanu, a thirty-three-year-old Romanian now living in California, has beaten one fighter with a winning record in the past five years and has now lost five of his last six outings while being knocked out in four of them.

In the early rounds, Ajagba kept jabbing and trying to set up his right hand. He has a somewhat wooden style that suggests a fighter who's boxing by the numbers. Cojanu fights in slow motion, throws wide punches, and leans forward, chin out, when he throws them. By round five, there were scattered boos from the crowd. In the press section, more people than usual were checking their smartphones for messages.

Then, in round six, Cojanu tired and Ajagba started landing consistently. By round eight, Razvan was exhausted and dropped to the canvas from an accumulation of blows. That would have been a good time to stop the fight, but referee Ron Lipton chose not to. So Cojanu took an ugly beating until dropping to one knee at the 2:46 mark of round nine when Lipton waved off the carnage. Ajagba had a 244-to-83 advantage in punches landed.

That set the stage for Kownacki–Helenius.

Kownacki who will turn thirty-one on March 27, is a likeable man with a crowd-pleasing "hit me, and then I'll hit you back, and then we'll hit each other some more" style. In recent years, he has fought a series of overmatched opponents while (some would say) being readied as a sacrificial lamb with the intention of serving him to Deontay Wilder.

Helenius, who was born in Sweden and fights out of Finland, was regarded as a "safe" opponent for Kownacki. Ten years ago, "The Nordic Nightmare" was being groomed as a prospect himself. He beat Lamon Brewster, Samuel Peter, and Sergiy Liakhovich at a time when they'd been reduced to non-threatening opponents. He also won a controversial split decision over Dereck Chisora in Finland while Chisora was in the midst of a stretch that saw him lose four of five fights. More recently, Helenius had lasted twelve rounds against Dillian Whyte but lost eleven of them. He'd been knocked out by Johann Duhaupas and (eight months ago) Gerald Washington.

Kownacki matches up poorly against slick boxers. Helenius was once described as having the footwork of a stalagmite.

"Beating him doesn't really do a lot for me," Kownacki acknowledged at the final pre-fight press conference, "because I'm a big favorite in this fight."

The crowd at Barclays Center was wholeheartedly behind Kownacki. This was his fifth fight in a row at the venue.

Adam had weighed in for the bout at 265 pounds (one under his career high); Helenius, a trimmer 238.

Earlier in the week, Cliff Rold had made a good point. Writing about Kownacki (a volume puncher without much defense), he'd noted, "Watching boxing is supposed to be fun. That's really the bottom line, isn't it? A fun fighter is still something to look forward to. Everyone isn't necessarily going to be the future of their division, a future great, a legacy carver, or any of the other things that can distract from the root of why fans devote time and attention to the sweet science. Saturday night against Helenius, no matter how long it lasts, we're going to see some leather fly. Isn't that really all we're asking for?"

Kownacki won round one against Helenius by coming forward and throwing punches while Robert jabbed ineffectively and held. Round two was closer with Helenius inclined to trade and throwing the straighter punches. The third stanza belonged to Kownacki. He was throwing more and getting off first, outlanding Helenius by a 28-to-8 margin. Then . . .

Twenty seconds into round four, Kownacki got whacked with a straight right hand followed by a stiff jab that sent him to the canvas. He rose immediately, and referee David Fields incorrectly ruled it a slip. That call was soon academic.

Kownacki had been shaken. Five seconds after the action resumed, Helenius dropped him with a straight right hand followed by a left hook up top. Adam was on his feet at the count of three. This time, though, his legs were wobbly. Helenius battered him around the ring, and Fields halted the battle 68 seconds into the round.

Helenius had more left as a fighter than Kownacki and his team had realized. They disrespected him as an opponent and paid the price.

Kownacki had been in line for a huge title-bout payday. Now he was reduced to saying, "It wasn't my night. It's boxing. Things just didn't go my way tonight. He hit me with a good shot. I knew what was going on. I'm just upset with myself. It is what it is."

There are two morals to the story: (1) Things can change very quickly in boxing. (2) A fighter should never go into the ring thinking he has an easy fight ahead of him. In boxing, despite the odds, anything can happen.

★ ★ ★

Matchroom Boxing's monthlong "Fight Camp" ended with a BANG. On August 22, after a month of less than scintillating action, DAZN viewers in the United States saw two fights that were well worth watching.

First, Katie Taylor (15–0, 6 KOs) stepped up to scratch and accepted the challenge of a rematch against Delfine Persoon (44–2, 18 KOs). The two women met previously last year with Taylor unifying the four major 135-pound titles by decision in a fight that most onlookers thought Persoon won. To Katie's credit, she said immediately that she'd fight Delfine again and then made good on her promise.

As in their first encounter, Persoon was the physically stronger fighter. She moved forward for the entire ten rounds, mauling and brawling as best she could. This time, Taylor boxed more and stood her ground less, rendering Persoon's pressure tactics less effective.

Katie tired a bit as the fight wore on. Her punches lost some of their sting and she got hit with some good shots. She was never able to discourage Persoon but she did outbox her.

This time, there was no controversy as to the winner. Taylor emerged triumphant by a 96–94, 96–94, 98–93 margin.

"She deserves this time to win," Persoon acknowledged.

No one should be fooled by Taylor's physical grace and gentle outside-the-ring demeanor. In the ring, she's a tough, skilled professional fighter.

Taylor–Persoon set the stage for Fight Camp's grand finale: Dillian Whyte (27–1, 18 KOs) vs. Alexander Povetkin (35–2–1, 25 KOs).

Whyte was putting his status as the mandatory challenger to WBC heavyweight champion Tyson Fury on the line and was a 4-to-1 betting favorite. The feeling was that Povetkin, who's closing in on his forty-first birthday, had faded to the point where he no longer had the tools to compete successfully against Whyte, who was bigger (252 to 224 pounds) and stronger.

Povetkin was busier in the early going, but Whyte put some good hooks to the body in the bank. Then, in round four, Dillian went upstairs and dropped Alexander twice; first with a left hook up top and next with a left uppercut.

At that point, Whyte was in control and Povetkin's chances looked as good as Peter McNeeley's against Mike Tyson. Dillian's ring walk had been preceded by an impressive display of fireworks and he was enjoying the party.

Except Povetkin was the wrong guy to invite to the party.

Thirty seconds into round five, Whyte got sloppy. Povetkin moved inside.

BOOM!!!

A left uppercut landed flush on Whyte's jaw, laying Dillian out flat on his back, unconscious. It was a spectacular, highlight-reel, knockout blow and the last thing anyone expected.

Whyte made a brief post-fight appearance with promoter Eddie Hearn and said simply, "I'm good. It's one of them things where it just landed."

★ ★ ★

WBC-IBF 147-pound champion Errol Spence raised his record to 27–0 (21 KOs) with a dominant twelve-round performance against Danny Garcia on Saturday night (December 5, 2020). There were questions before the fight as to whether Spence had fully recovered from injuries sustained in an October 10, 2019, automobile accident. But one had to assume that a less formidable comeback opponent would have been chosen had there been doubts in Errol's camp about his health or what a punch from Garcia might do to the bone and tissue structure beneath his face.

Garcia (now 36–3, 21 KOs) is a tough out. But at the highest levels of competition, he's an out. Spence gave Danny next to nothing to work with and had enough hurt on his punches to keep Garcia from challenging his narrative for the flow of the fight. Errol's jab was effective as an offensive weapon and defensive shield. Danny's left hook—normally the most potent punch in his arsenal—seemed to have been packed in mothballs for the night.

The judges favored Spence by a 117–111, 116–112, 116–112 margin (which was kind to Garcia). Danny is now 0–3 in fights against Spence, Keith Thurman, and Shawn Porter. If there's a criticism of Spence's performance on Saturday night, it's that (as was the case when he fought Mikey Garcia twenty months ago) he never put the pedal to the metal in an effort to finish with a knockout.

Hector Camacho wasn't malevolent as much as he was sick, hurting, and out of control.

Macho Time

Hamilcar Publications is becoming a leader in the publication of books about boxing. *Macho Time: The Meteoric Rise and Tragic Fall of Hector Camacho* by Christian Giudice is its most recent offering.

As Carlos Acevedo writes in his foreword to the book, "In the 1980s, Camacho was one of the most talented fighters in the world and personified the hedonistic philosophy of the decade with boorish aplomb. He was garish, crude, outlandish, lewd, reckless, and loud. Everybody paid attention to him. He made sure of that."

Giudice has written biographies of Alexis Arguello, Roberto Duran, and Wilfredo Gomez. Camacho is his latest subject.

Camacho was born in Bayamón, Puerto Rico, on May 24, 1962. His father was seventeen and his mother fourteen when they married. When Hector was four, his mother moved with her children to Spanish Harlem in New York to escape her violent, alcoholic husband. Growing up, Hector fell in with street gangs, habitually used drugs, and was kicked out of seven schools. He also took up boxing and compiled a 96–4 amateur record while winning three New York Golden Gloves titles.

Camacho turned pro in 1980 with a four-round decision over David Brown in the Felt Forum at Madison Square Garden. He was a hot prospect from the start with blinding handspeed and deft footwork that separated him from opponents. The fact that he was a southpaw made things even more complicated for the men he fought.

"No one could outbox him, overpower him, out-quick him, or out-smart him in the ring," Giudice writes. "His grace and speed made up for his flaws. But speed was only part of the package that included incomparable defensive instincts, precision punching, a menacing jab, and sharp angles that rarely put him in harm's way. Casual fans loved what they saw because of his energy, flair, and talent. Hardcore fans saw glimpses of greatness."

"He would always create angles," Camacho's son, Hector Jr., later noted. "It was like art. The way he blocked punches—jab, jab, hold. And he always knew where he was in the ring."

Camacho was also a dirty fighter who took advantage of what compliant referees allowed him to do. One of his signature moves was to illegally pull down on an opponent's neck with his right glove to move the opponent into an uppercut.

"He had a maturity in the ring that belied his age," boxing analyst Steve Farhood later recalled. "But I don't remember the maturity as much as I remember the pure speed and skill level. He had the tricks and the moves. But his pure speed combined with the southpaw style and the command of being center stage made him the total package."

Camacho quickly established himself as a gate attraction. He was good looking and had CHARISMA marked by a smile that enabled him to project as a charming fun-loving boy while proclaiming himself to be "The Macho Man." Among other things, he designed his own ring wardrobe at a time when most fighters wore traditional trunks and robes. His sartorial choices for entering the ring, as catalogued in *Macho Time*, included "tassels, epaulets, masks, fringe, diapers, capes, panchos, codpieces, loincloths, sequins, glitter, Cazals, and a variety of bizarre headdresses."

"He had presence," Sugar Ray Leonard (who Camacho hoped to supplant as the face of boxing) told Giudice. "The way he carried himself. He walked into the ring with authority and I saw something. Not just physically but mentally, spiritually. He walked into that ring like 'I'm going to win.' I just knew this kid was going to be a star."

Camacho won his first title in 1983 with a fifth-round knockout of Rafael "Bazooka" Limón to claim the World Boxing Council 130-pound belt. Two years later, after moving up in weight, he annexed the WBC lightweight crown with an almost flawless twelve-round performance against José Luis Ramírez.

Then Camacho hit a speed bump. On June 13, 1986, he brought a 28-and-0 record into Madison Square Garden to defend his title against Edwin Rosario.

Camacho had hoped from the start of his career to follow in the footsteps of Carlos Ortiz, Wilfred Benítez, and Wilfredo Gómez to become a Puerto Rican icon. But boxing fans from the island had been slow to embrace him, thinking of him as a New Yorker.

"The perception that he wasn't a true Puerto Rican hurt Camacho deeply," Giudice writes. "In his mind, he was just as Puerto Rican as anyone else."

Meanwhile, Rosario, who had lived his entire life in Puerto Rico, was the crowd favorite that night at Madison Square Garden. And after feeling Edwin's power, Camacho ran for much of the fight, clinching whenever Rosario got in close. Hector retained his title on a narrow 115–113, 115–113, 113–114 split verdict. But a clear majority of fans and media on site thought that Rosario deserved the decision.

The Rosario fight raised questions about Camacho's self-proclaimed machismo, toughness, and heart. He'd won the fight on the judges' scorecards. And for the most part, he would keep winning in the years ahead. But he was never the same confident fighter again.

"Hector no longer performed like the star he was," Giudice notes. "Some fighters thrive when opponents force them out of their comfort zones. Marvelous Marvin Hagler, Thomas Hearns, and Roberto Duran all delivered in the clutch. Sugar Ray Leonard set the standard for finding the opportune times to shine. When one fighter provides a blueprint of greatness as Hector had, it is discouraging when that fighter doesn't fulfill those expectations."

Thereafter, clinching and survival tactics became Camacho's stock in trade. The public perception of him as a fighter changed. The primary entertainment value in his fights came to derive from his personality rather than his ring skills.

"He was a flamboyant showman," Larry Merchant recalled. "And that was a talent in itself. Not many people could pull it off. But that's what he was largely known for after the first phase of his career."

Three months after fighting Rosario, Camacho won a decision over Cornelius Boza-Edwards in what Giudice calls "the dawn of a new era in which escaping replaced attacking and preservation replaced calculated risk."

On March 6, 1989, Hector fought Ray Mancini, who (although only twenty-seven years old) had been retired for four years. At the kickoff press conference for the fight, Mancini declared, "Camacho runs like a dog and holds like a woman."

"I'd rather run than get beat up," Hector countered.

Camacho prevailed over Mancini on a 115–113, 115–113, 112–116 split verdict. Mancini would fight only once more, ending his career with four consecutive losses. Two years after beating Mancini, Camacho lost for the first time in 39 fights when he was decisioned by Greg Haugen. He decisioned Haugen in an immediate rematch and proceeded, in the words of Hector Jr., to "resurrect his career off old men."

Camacho fought Roberto Duran when Duran was forty-five and again when Duran was fifty. Ray Leonard was forty when he returned to boxing after a six-year layoff to fight Camacho (who drove Leonard into permanent retirement).

Over time, Camacho was defeated by Julio César Chávez Sr., Félix Trinidad, and Oscar De La Hoya. As his career wound down, he fought draws against Sal Lopez, Jorge Vaca, and Yori Boy Campas and lost by decision to Chris Walsh and Saul Duran. The last of these fights—the final bout in Camacho's long ring journey—came when he was ten days shy of his forty-eighth birthday. He fought professionally for three decades (from September 12, 1980, though May 14, 2010), and compiled a 79–6–3 (38 KOs) ring record. He was never knocked out.

But Camacho's ring exploits are only part of his story. He walked on the wild side and was embroiled in street life and street conflicts throughout his life. He consorted with known drug dealers and used cocaine and other recreational drugs before, during, and after his ring career.

"Hector did not think twice about putting his loved ones and closest friends in peril to get a fix," Giudice writes. "He grew up with drugs. They were not just part of a hellish phase but a way of life ingrained in the environment in which he was raised."

In city after city, Camacho traveled into dangerous territory in search of drug dealers and a fix. At one point, he moved to Clewiston, Florida, to distance himself from the streets. But he brought his street ways with him. For every person who tried to steer him in the right direction, there were multiple enablers who reinforced his self-destructive tendencies.

Camacho was a father at sixteen and a poor one. Before Hector Jr. was in his teens, his father pressured him into an assignation with a prostitute to introduce him to sex. Soon after, he introduced him to drugs.

"Pop was explosive," Hector Jr. told Giudice. "You had to be careful around him. He was a street thug. Rob. Steal. He was mean. You had to fuck with him to see that side."

Hector Jr. also recalled, "When I was growing up in Spanish Harlem, I had a lot of resentment. I was always wondering, 'What the fuck am I doing in the projects?' He let me down."

Camacho's erratic behavior carried over into boxing. He had a long string of trainers that included Negro Gonzalez, Mickey Rosario, Patrick Flannery, Robert Lee, Billy Giles, Jimmy Montoya, Chuck Talhami, Rudy Mata, Pepe Correa, and Jesse Reid. More and more as time went by, his drug use and drinking adversely affected his ring performance. There were erratic post-fight interviews on national television that ranged from Camacho sobbing and asking Tim Ryan of CBS, "Will you be my friend? I need friends," to his uttering a racial epithet on HBO. The night before Hector fought John Montes in Alaska, he got high and had to be talked out of jumping from a hotel window by CBS matchmaker and boxing analyst Gil Clancy.

There was no social media or TMZ to report on Camacho's every misstep outside the ring when he was in his prime as a fighter. If there had been, he would have been skewered.

In his late teens, while on probation for an earlier car theft, Camacho was sentenced to six months in prison for stealing another car and leading police on a thirty-block chase. In 1988, he was arrested in Florida for pulling a gun on a student in a local high school and was caught on camera trying to hide a bag of cocaine when he was arrested. That led to charges of assault and illegal drug possession. Later that year, he was arrested for driving down a highway while having sex with a woman who was seated on his lap. An arrest for shoplifting followed. Most often, because of his status as a boxer, the cases were adjudicated with fines and probation.

Multiple complaints alleging domestic violence were lodged against Camacho by his wife and various girlfriends. In 1998, his wife was granted a restraining order against him. He owned Uzis and shotguns and was involved in multiple car accidents. In 2004 and again in 2007, he was arrested on charges of burglary and felony possession of drugs.

On November 20, 2012, a drug deal in Bayamón went bad. Camacho was shot four times and removed from life support four days later. He was fifty years old when he died.

"There was no way to spin Hector's death," Giudice acknowledges. "Drugs and violence had reduced him to a pale version of himself."

Macho Time is the first full biography of Camacho. Hamilcar deserves credit for infusing the project with superb production values and an eye-catching design for the book. Overall, Giudice does a solid job of reporting. At times, the fight reports seem repetitious and some of them are too long. But on the other side of the ledger, there's a good recounting of Camacho–Rosario—a fight that warrants in-depth coverage.

One concern a reader might have is that there are places where it seems as though someone told something to Giudice and he accepted it as fact without further checking it out. For example, Jimmy Glenn was a fixture on the New York boxing scene for more than fifty years. But he was not—as written in *Macho Man*—a "former Golden Gloves champion and Muhammad Ali sparring partner." Factual errors like this are worrisome, not for what they say about Glenn but for questions they raise regarding the presentation of more important issues.

That said, *Macho Man* is often entertaining and as thorough a biography as we're likely to see of this man-child who could have been a great fighter but became a cautionary tale instead.

Carlos Monzon: *A Fistful of Murder*

Carlos Monzon was born into extreme poverty in Argentina on August 7, 1942. He was mean, violent, surly, brutal, arrogant, occasionally charming, handsome with a smoldering sensuality, and remorseless. His life was marked by street fighting, drunken behavior, domestic violence, and more than forty arrests. In the midst of it all, he found boxing.

Monzon's story is told by Don Stradley in *A Fistful of Murder: The Fights and Crimes of Carlos Monzon*. It's the latest in a series of short books from Hamilcar Publications published under the imprint Hamilcar Noir that deal with boxers whose lives were marked and often terminated by violent crime. Told in 128 pages, the story moves at a brisk pace.

Monzon had one hundred professional fights in a career that began in 1962. He reigned as middleweight champion from 1970 until his retirement in 1977 and was honored as the 1972 "Fighter of the Year" by the Boxing Writers Association of America. All told, he compiled an 87–3–9 (59 KOs) record with one no contest. The three losses came during the first two years of his career when he was a novice.

Monzon was a big, strong, tough fighter with a good chin and a basic skill set: stand tall, throw a sharp jab, and follow with a hard right hand behind it. Mark Kram described him as "a perfectly shaped middleweight, tall with long arms and with style running through every sinew up to his dramatic Belmondo face."

By contrast, British boxing commentator Reg Gutteridge described Monzon as having "little ring grace" and added that "he clubs as if wearing a Roman cestus on his fist."

Those who question Monzon's greatness point to the fact that the best of the fighters he beat were past their prime (e.g., Nino Benvenuti) or both past their prime and naturally smaller men (e.g., Emile Griffith and José Nápoles). Monzon was also held to a draw by Benny Briscoe before besting

Briscoe on a close decision in a rematch. And he only narrowly defeated Rodrigo Valdéz in the last two fights of his ring career.

But as Stradley writes, "A strange thing happened to Monzon in retirement. He became a better fighter. The boxer who had often been dismissed as a classless thug was now revered as an all-time great. During the next decade when lists were made of the top middleweights or of great championship reigns, Monzon's name would always be near the top."

How good was Monzon?

Hall of Fame matchmaker Bruce Trampler says that he would have been competitive with any middleweight in any era. More significantly, in 2007, I had a conversation with Bernard Hopkins in which I asked Bernard to speculate as to how he would have fared in the ring against Sugar Ray Robinson, Marvin Hagler, and Monzon. Hopkins's answer is instructive:

"Sugar Ray Robinson at 147 pounds was close to perfect," Bernard said. "But at middleweight, he was beatable. I would have fought Ray Robinson in close and not given him room to do his thing. He'd make me pay a physical price. But at middleweight, I think I'd wear him down and win. Me and Marvin Hagler would have been a war. We'd both be in the hospital afterward with straws in our mouth. We'd destroy each other. My game-plan would be, rough him up, box, rough him up, box. You wouldn't use judges for that fight. You'd go by the doctors' reports. Carlos Monzon? I could lose that fight. Monzon was tall, rangy, did everything right. I see myself losing that fight more than winning it."

Stradley's recounting of Monzon's ring career is largely pro forma. The more compelling portions of the book lie in the portrait he paints of Monzon's personal life.

Monzon had virtually no formal education and was close to illiterate. At age nineteen, he married fifteen-year-old Mercedes Beatriz García. The newly wed couple lived with her family in a two-room shack where they slept on a mattress on the floor.

"In many ways," Stradley writes, "Monzon was the typical wife abuser. He was obsessed with control; he had an evil temper; he drank too much." In 1973, Mercedes shot her husband in the arm and shoulder after a quarrel between them.

Monzon's pattern of physically abusing women, assaulting people in public, reckless driving, and other antisocial acts was a constant in his life before, during, and after his championship reign. But as his fame grew, so did his following.

"Monzon," Stradley notes, "didn't look like other fighters of the day. He was photographed to look like a stylish Latin pop star, usually in a long leather coat, with plenty of gold jewelry. Argentina's *El Gráfico* [a popular magazine] treated Monzon like a model, featuring him in regular photo spreads."

In 1974, while married to Mercedes, Monzon met Susana Gimenez (a popular actress and talk show host). Soon, they were involved in a torrid affair that lasted for four years. At one point, Mercedes complained to Monzon about Susana and he punched her in the face, breaking the superciliary arch above her eye. Monzon was arrested and avoided a prison term by pleading temporary insanity. A divorce followed.

Susana's film credits included adult-oriented comedies. In Stradley's words, "Monzon had abandoned the mother of his children for a slutty clown. It didn't help that her sartorial sense ran towards pink denim."

Even so, Stradley recounts, "Monzon and Susana were now the most photographed twosome in Argentina. Journalist Alfredo Serra estimated they appeared on more than three hundred magazine covers, describing the pair as combining 'the strength, beauty, fame and glamour of the world in a single couple.'"

During his championship reign, Monzon parlayed his fame as a fighter into several film roles. Then he retired, his relationship with Susana ended, and he met Alicia Muñiz Calatayud.

Alicia had worked as a model and belly dancer in addition to once managing a hair salon. She and Monzon married in Miami because his divorce from Mercedes wasn't recognized under Argentine law. They lived together from May 1979 through August 1986 and again during a brief reconciliation in 1987. On several occasions, Alicia filed complaints with the police alleging that Monzon had beaten her.

By 1988, Stradley writes, "Monzon was still famous but no longer important. Most of the time he was drunk."

On February 14, 1988, during a weekend they were spending together, Monzon murdered his estranged wife.

"Here's what probably happened," Stradley posits. "When Alicia came for the weekend, she reminded him that he was late with his monthly payments [for child support]. They returned from their night out, a night where they'd been unfriendly to each other and a witness had seen Monzon hitting Alicia. At some point before 6:00 a.m., she said something that made the dynamite in his head go off."

Monzon told conflicting stories after Alicia's death, all of which centered on the claim that she'd accidentally fallen over a balcony railing during an argument between them. Then an autopsy report revealed that Alicia had been strangled to death.

"Medical examiners," Stradley recounts, "estimated thirty-five pounds of pressure or more had been applied to Alicia's throat. Strangling only requires eleven pounds. They estimated it had been done with a two-fingered grip, probably thumb and forefinger in a kind of one-handed death clamp. It takes only twenty seconds or so to strangle someone into unconsciousness. The damage to Alicia's throat would take much longer. It wasn't done by accident or in the heat of the moment. It took a few minutes of full-on rage. Alicia had been strangled long after she had passed out. It's also rare that a strangling victim has visible marks on the neck or throat. The imprints on Alicia were clear and deep, as if someone had tried to squeeze her head off at the neck. He dumped her body over the balcony to make it look like she'd fallen."

Monzon was charged with murder. The trial was broadcast live on radio throughout Argentina. Monzon testified that he and Alicia had argued about money and admitted that he had slapped her. "I have hit women on other occasions and nothing happened to any of them," he told the court. "I hit all of my women except one. My mother."

A three-judge panel found Monzon guilty of murder. He was sentenced to eleven years in prison with the possibility of time off for good behavior.

By 1993, Monzon was allowed to spend daytime hours and weekends outside of prison. On Sunday, January 8, 1995, after attending a barbecue, he was behind the wheel of a car, probably drunk and definitely speeding.

"By the rules of his furlough agreement," Stradley writes, "he had to be back at the Las Flores prison by 8:00 p.m. He didn't want to risk being late. He only had a short time left to serve on his sentence and didn't want any infractions on his record. So he drove fast. He'd always been a terrible driver. Being in prison hadn't made him any better at it."

While speeding back to the prison, Monzon lost control of the vehicle, which turned over multiple times, killing him instantly. Two other passengers also died in the accident. He was fifty-two years old.

After Monzon's death, his body lay in state at City Hall in his hometown of Santa Fe. An estimated ten thousand people filed past it. Twenty thousand more lined the route to the Municipal Cemetery while six thousand mourners waited at the cemetery entrance.

Argentine president Carlos Menem told the nation. "Remember Carlos Monzon as a champion, not as a man jailed for murder." But Argentinian journalist and political commentator Bernardo Neustadt took a contrary view, declaring, "We are a macho society that idolizes a man who beats or violates a woman; a macho society that taught Monzon to dress up, to speak a bit better, but didn't teach him to think; a macho society that wasn't horrified when Monzon said he beat all his women."

More than a decade after his death, Arturo Gatti still stirs passions.

Killed in Brazil

Killed in Brazil: The Mysterious Death of Arturo "Thunder" Gatti by Jimmy Tobin is the latest in a series of short books published by Hamilcar that focus on the untimely deaths of well-known fighters.

Gatti was regarded by many as the ultimate blood-and-guts warrior. His ring record was 40 wins against 9 losses with 31 knockouts and 5 KOs by. But as Tobin notes, "He was judged less by the outcomes of his fights than by their violence." Gary Shaw, once COO of Main Events (Gatti's promoter) declared, "Nobody ever said he was the greatest fighter in the world. But they did say he was the most exciting."

When sober, Gatti was a likeable man who inspired fondness and loyalty among those who knew him. His fans idolized him. But his life outside the ring was marred by heavy drinking, drug use, and other wildly irresponsible conduct. Pat Lynch (Gatti's manager) said that, whenever the phone rang in the wee small hours of the morning (which it did on more than one occasion), he always hoped it was Arturo asking for help rather than someone calling to tell him that Arturo had wrapped his car around a tree and was dead.

Gatti died in Brazil in 2009, two years after he retired from boxing. He was thirty-seven years old. Depending on which version of events one believes, either he committed suicide by using the strap from his wife's purse to hang himself from a staircase after a night of hard drinking and quarreling, or he was murdered by his wife, possibly with the assistance of one or more accomplices. Initially, his wife—a former exotic dancer named Amanda Rodrigues—was arrested and charged with murder. Three weeks later, the charges were dismissed.

Lengthy court proceedings in Quebec (where Gatti lived) resulted in a court judgment upholding a Last Will and Testament that bequeathed Arturo's entire estate to his widow.

Killed in Brazil is divided into three parts. Part Two summarizes Gatti's ring career. Parts One and Three explore the issues surrounding his death.

"Gatti," Tobin writes, "had become a myth incarnate, a fighter for whom giving up was impossible. It isn't difficult to understand why so many people refuse to believe he killed himself. Surely, Gatti, who never gave up in the ring, would never give up in life."

In keeping with that view, Gatti's family and friends hired their own investigators who interviewed witnesses, gathered forensic evidence, and disputed the findings of the Brazilian authorities.

But Tobin, who never takes a position as to whether he believes Gatti was murdered or committed suicide, also lays out the case that Arturo died by his own hand.

Gatti's marriage was in crisis at the time of his death. Court documents filed in 2006 include testimony from a former girlfriend that Arturo had previously attempted suicide by overdosing on cocaine, alcohol, and prescription drugs.

"In the minds of the people who knew him best," Tobin writes, "he was a warrior. He earned this reputation in the ring, where his capacity for enduring punishment had become mythological. He was a man who could endure absurd suffering. How easy then is it to assume this toughness extended beyond his body, that Gatti was psychologically rugged too?"

But, Tobin continues, "We should ask whether it is reasonable to limit a person's capabilities to actions in keeping with our understanding of them. Gatti's own career is instructive here. Before he turned the impossible into a routine, he first had to surprise us."

Thus, Tobin cautions, "Gatti might not have been as resolute in the face of life's challenges as he had been in the face of men's fists. Pain in the ring has an end, and very often that end saw Gatti's hand raised. It has a ceiling too. Pain in the ring? You know your opponent is susceptible to it and that, however much you both may hurt, you can put the pain behind you after the bell. Pain dissipates, heals, and is replaced by the flush of health and power that allows you to take it on anew. But not all pain is like that. And there were signs that Gatti's resolve trembled a bit in response to the hurt you don't stitch up or hide behind Ray-Bans."

Most of the people who believe that Gatti was murdered focus on his love for life. I lean toward the conclusion that Arturo was murdered but for a different reason, one that I've previously stated.

The case that Gatti committed suicide rests, in Tobin's words, on the following scenario: "Grimly fashioning a noose, adjusting it for size, positioning a stool, calculating the stability of his makeshift gallows—alone in this despairing ritual. He had to climb the stool too. His body betraying him from the seven cans of beer along with the two bottles of wine he'd consumed at dinner, betraying him from the head injury he'd suffered when that mob attacked him for throwing Amanda to the ground."

And I might add, tying the makeshift noose to the staircase.

I don't think Arturo was capable of doing all of that on the night he died.

Why not?

In 2003, I was at the annual Boxing Writers Association of America dinner at a hotel in midtown Manhattan when Gatti and Micky Ward were co-honored for participating in the 2002 "Fight of the Year." Midway through the dinner, I left my seat to go to the men's room. When I got there, an intimidating young man was blocking the entrance.

"You can't go in there," he said.

"Why can't I go in there?"

"It's in use. You'll have to go to another floor."

"What do you mean, it's in use? There are a dozen urinals and toilets in there."

At that point, Arturo staggered out of the men's room, dead drunk, accompanied by a woman who looked very much like a dancer at a not-very-exclusive adult club.

"Blow job," Arturo announced when he saw me.

And he pointed to his fly. Which was still unzipped.

In that condition, Arturo couldn't have walked a straight line, let alone figured out the mechanics of detaching his wife's purse strap, hooking it over a staircase railing, and hanging himself.

In the end, most people will believe what they want to believe.

Teofimo Lopez Stakes His Claim to Stardom

Seven months after the coronavirus shut down sports in the United States, boxing fans finally got what they were waiting for on October 17, 2020, when Vasyl Lomachenko and Teofimo Lopez met in the "bubble" at the MGM Grand in Las Vegas. It was a high-profile fight to unify the four major 135-pound titles. And it would be televised on ESPN—the most anticipated fight on "free" television in the United States since Keith Thurman fought Danny Garcia on CBS on March 4, 2017.

Lomachenko turned pro in 2013 after a stellar amateur career that saw him win two Olympic gold medals on behalf of Ukraine and compile an otherworldly amateur record of more than 300 wins against a single loss. Now thirty-two years old, he had been at or near the top of most pound-for-pound lists for much of his pro career while building a 14–1 (10 KOs) record and annexing belts at 126, 130, and 135 pounds. He entered the ring to face Lopez holding the WBC, WBA, and WBO lightweight titles.

Lomachenko carries himself like a champion and has always been willing to go in tough. But in recent years, due to the economics and politics of boxing, his opposition has been frustratingly limited. The twenty-three-year-old Lopez (15–0, 12 KOs) represented a refreshingly stern challenge. Fast-tracked for stardom by Top Rank, Teofimo was the 2018 ESPN and *Ring Magazine* "prospect of the year." On December 14, 2019, he knocked out Richard Commey in the second round to claim the IBF 135-pound title.

It wasn't easy for Top Rank (which promotes both fighters) to put the promotional pieces for Lomachenko–Lopez together. The pandemic precluded a live gate. A pay-per-view promotion was possible. But major PPV cards in the United States carry a price tag in the neighborhood of seventy-five dollars. And the only major pay-per-view card in America since the pandemic began—the September 26 doubleheader featuring Jermall and Jermell Charlo—drew poorly.

Eventually, ESPN offered a license fee large enough to pay Lomachenko a purse of roughly $3.25 million while Lopez received $1.5 million. Arum spoke without hyperbole when he said, "It's clearly the best fight since the pandemic started. It would have been a major fight even without the pandemic, and now it's being shown to the public without an extra charge. Nobody [in the United States] has to pay five cents to watch it. If they're a cable subscriber or a satellite subscriber, they get it for nothing."

ESPN promoted the Lomachenko–Lopez telecast heavily on multiple platforms. Lomachenko, by winning three belts at 135 pounds and standing at or near the top of most the pound-for-pound lists, had done the heavy lifting to give the fight its elite status. There was talk of the bout being a "grudge" match because the fighters were trained by their respective fathers and Lopez and his father were shooting off their mouths a lot. But no one had kicked anyone's dog, insulted anyone's wife, or stolen anything that belonged to the other fighter.

Soundbites that Lopez offered included, "I don't like the guy and I'm going to have fun as Lomachenko's face is beaten and marked up by my hands. . . . The takeover is here and the reign of Lomachenko, the little diva, is coming to an end. . . . I don't like the way he carries himself. After this fight, I don't want to hear about him or talk about him again. . . . I don't think any fighter has ever given Loma this much disrespect. I don't give a shit about him. . . . I'm not looking at Lomachenko. I'm looking through him. . . . Loma is on his way out. I'm on my way in."

Lomachenko (unlike Lopez) is not one to run his mouth. But as time passed, he responded: "I've heard this a lot of times from a lot of boxers. Then you come in the ring and you forgot about your words and your promise. For me, it's just trash talk, it's just words. We'll see what happens in the ring. . . . Teofimo Lopez can talk all he wants. He's very good at talking. He has done nothing but say my name for the past two years. When we fight in Las Vegas, he will eat my punches and his words. . . . I don't like them [Teofimo and his father] because they've been talking bad things about me. I want to beat him very badly, very, very badly. . . . In my country, if you insult somebody, you'd better be prepared for them to hurt you. If I get a chance to cause him pain, I'm going to do it."

The odds were 7-to-2 in Lomachenko's favor. But most insiders thought the fight shaped up as being much closer than that.

Lomachenko's partisans noted that, while each man had fifteen previous professional fights, Vasyl had won two Olympic Gold medals, fought far tougher competition in the pros than Lopez had, and established himself as an elite boxer. Also, Lomachenko had gone twelve rounds on five occasions while Lopez had fought past six rounds only twice.

"I started to watch his fights," Lomachenko said during an interview on ESPN. "And I started to learn him. He is an excellent puncher. He has a high boxing IQ. He is younger. But I have vast experience during my fights in twelve rounds. So we will see how he can hold his own during the fight."

However, on the other side of the coin, Lopez would be the most dangerous opponent that Lomachenko had faced. He had the freshness and audacity of youth on his side and the power to turn the fight around with one punch.

Teofimo's size was perhaps his biggest advantage. As Lomachenko has moved up in weight, the size and strength of opponents has blunted the superiority afforded him by his ring craftsmanship. "One-thirty-five is not my weight class," Vasyl conceded. "For me, my weight class that is more comfortable is 130. But I need four belts. I need to be the undisputed world champion. That is why I moved to 135."

Lopez punched harder than anyone Lomachenko had fought and would enter the ring as the much bigger man. He'd turned pro at 133 pounds and could easily move to 140. "I'm a big lightweight," Teofimo proclaimed. "Come October 17, I'm going to bring him back down to 130. This is not his weight class."

Few people expected Lopez to outbox Lomachenko. But Teofimo is at a point in his career where he's getting more skilled and stronger with the passage of time. Vasyl, by contrast, seems to have plateaued and might be on the verge of decline. It wouldn't be shocking, insiders agreed, if Lopez were to turn the tide with one big shot or break Lomachenko down with a sustained body attack.

"He's very talented," Teofimo said. "And so am I."

It was all talk. On Saturday night, the action began.

There were two introductory fights on the ESPN telecast. In the first, Edgar Berlanga (14–0, 14 KOs) sought to extend his consecutive first-round knockout streak to fifteen against Lanell Bellows (20–5, 13 KOs). No one thought Bellows would win. The question was whether Lanell (who had never been knocked out but hadn't faced much in the way of competition) would survive the first round. He didn't. Then Arnold Barbosa (24–0, 10 KOs) won a ten-round decision over Alex Saucedo (30–1, 19 KOs).

Meanwhile, the ESPN telecast was marked by over-the-top claims that sounded like dubious advertising in a presidential campaign. Blow-by-blow commentator Joe Tessitore proclaimed that Lomachenko–Lopez was "the biggest fight that boxing can make" (which came as a surprise to fans who are hoping for Tyson Fury vs. Anthony Joshua). He also called televising the fight on ESPN "a paradigm shift for the sport."

In a different time, Lomachenko–Lopez would have been contested in a packed house at Madison Square Garden with partisans on both sides cheering for their standard-bearer. In this instance, the Nevada State Athletic Commission had ruled that 250 fans and members of the media could be present. Tickets were distributed primarily to the fighters' camps and to first responders who had worked to combat the COVID-19 pandemic. No tickets were available for sale to the general public.

One day earlier, Lomachenko had ignored social distancing guidelines after the Friday weigh-in (each fighter weighed 135 pounds) and moved aggressively into Lopez's space. But when the bell rang for round one of their actual fight, that aggression was lacking.

The notes I took during the fight read as follows:

> Round 1—A feeling-out round. Lopez trying to engage
> behind a marginally effective jab. Lomachenko fighting
> cautiously. Very cautiously.
>
> Round 2—Lomachenko throwing next to nothing, which
> is allowing Lopez to gain confidence and believe that he
> belongs in the ring with him. One gets the feeling that
> Lopez can hurt Lomachenko more than Lomachenko can
> hurt Lopez.
>
> Round 3—Lopez the aggressor. Lomachenko isn't looking to
> land as much as he's looking to avoid confrontations. He
> hardly looks like a generational talent.
>
> Round 4—Lopez fighting a smart, disciplined fight. His
> power—or Lomachenko's fear of it—is the key factor
> so far. Lomachenko is doing virtually nothing to score
> points.

Round 5—More of the same. Lomachenko letting Lopez dictate the pace of the fight, not showing much in the way of angles and not letting his hands go. Vasyl usually does more than just frustrate opponents; he hurts them. Right now, he's doing neither.

Round 6—Lopez stalking. Virtually no offense from Lomachenko. He's conceding round after round, doing little damage to Lopez and not doing much to tire Lopez out. If this was at Madison Square Garden, the crowd would be booing.

Round 7—Lopez in command. Not only is he bigger, he seems to be almost as fast as Lomachenko.

Round 8—Finally, Lomachenko becoming more aggressive, opening up. Lopez willingly trading with him.

Round 9—Lopez coasting a bit.

Round 10—Lomachenko throwing more and landing more. Lopez standing his ground.

Round 11—Lomachenko throwing, scoring.

Round 12—Lomachenko going all out. Lopez standing his ground and finishing stronger. Teofimo cut badly on his right eyelid from a head butt near the end of the round. This was Teofimo's coming-out party.

This writer scored the bout 116–112 for Lopez, giving Lomachenko rounds eight through eleven. That was identical to Tim Cheatham's scorecard. Steve Weisfeld scored it 117–111. It's hard to know what Julie Lederman was thinking to get to 119–109 in Lopez's favor.

As for the future, it's good for boxing to have another talented young fighter in the mix and Lopez meets that criteria. Also, the number of viewers who tuned in for Lomachenko–Lopez will be a significant factor in determining the extent to which television networks in the United States are willing to underwrite quality fights on free television in the year ahead. Early reports are that Lomachenko–Lopez averaged 2,729,000 viewers exclusive of ESPN Deportes and ESPN+. That makes it the most watched boxing match on television since the 2017 bout between Manny Pacquiao and Jeff Horn.

Meanwhile, Lomachenko–Lopez could lead to a reevaluation of Lomachenko's greatness. Vasyl's fights have long been portrayed as being about his extraordinary technical prowess and physical conditioning rather than the ability to dig deep and gut a fight out. Indeed, in the two fights when Lomachenko was called upon to gut it out—first against Orlando Salido and now against Lopez—he came up short.

One might say that, when Lomachenko was tested, greatness was lacking. Or one might say that, against a skilled opponent with a big punch, 135 pounds was simply a bridge too far.

The Tyson–Jones Exhibition

There was a time when people who understood boxing talked about Mike Tyson vs. Roy Jones as a real fight.

In 1996, I had a long sit-down with Jones. Tyson had been released from prison a year earlier and had reclaimed the WBC and WBA titles by knocking out Frank Bruno and Bruce Seldon. Roy was undefeated and gaining recognition as boxing's pound-for-pound king.

"Would you fight Mike Tyson?" I asked.

"If the money was right," Jones answered. "But you have to understand, if I did it, I'd go in there to win. I'm not the kind of guy who says, 'If they pay me enough, it's all right if I lose.' When I fight, I fight to win."

My next question was, "What would you key on if a Jones–Tyson fight came about?"

"First, I'd key on his power," Roy said. "Because if Tyson catches me with a big punch, I'm losing out. I'd have to avoid his big punches and make sure I landed all my punches so he couldn't counter. That wouldn't be easy because Tyson bobs and weaves and he's quick. One area where I'd have an advantage is, I'd work on his footwork, make him chase me, because his footwork is ordinary. If I get past three rounds, Tyson is in trouble. I doubt if I'd knock him out. But if it goes past three rounds, I'd win a decision."

On Saturday night (November 28, 2020), twenty-four years later, Mike Tyson and Roy Jones squared off in a boxing ring. The occasion was an exhibition marketed as a fight—a pop culture event that exemplified the valuation of fame, hype, and glitz over substance and reality.

In their prime, Tyson and Jones were awesomely gifted fighters. Tyson at his best was a more subtle boxer than most people gave him credit for. Jones was more brutal than acknowledged. There was a time when Mike was considered the best fighter in the world. Then Roy earned that designation. They were historic talents.

But their greatness is in the past.

Tyson was a .500 fighter with five wins, five losses, and two no contests during the last nine years of his ring career. He hasn't fought a "real" fight in fifteen years and is no longer "the baddest man on the planet." Jones hasn't won a big fight since he decisioned Félix Trinidad in 2008. When they stepped into the ring together on Saturday night, Mike was fifty-five years old and Roy was fifty-one.

The Tyson–Jones event was put together by a music/video-sharing platform called Triller. Event organizers floated the rumor that they would invest "north of fifty million dollars" in the venture. That seemed unlikely. But whatever the number, Triller hoped to turn a profit on pay-per-view buys and, more important, use the proceeds as an infomercial for Triller.

Initially, Tyson–Jones was slated to take place at Dignity Health Sports Park in Carson, California, on September 12. Then it was rescheduled for November 28 at Staples Center in Los Angeles. Each fighter wore 12-ounce gloves, not the 10 ounces worn by heavyweights in standard competition. Originally, the exhibition was scheduled for eight three-minute rounds. But on October 14, the rounds were shortened to two minutes each.

Jones was guaranteed a one-million-dollar payday with an upside dependent upon the number of pay-per-view buys. Tyson's guarantee was a matter of conjecture. He told TMZ that he was "not getting anything" for the fight and added, "It's going to be for various charities. Nobody has to ever worry about me getting rich or getting jealous or saying I'm doing this for money. I'm not getting anything. I just feel good doing this because I can."

That said, the assumption was that the lion's share of the purse money would go to Tyson or one or more entities controlled by him.

The question hovering over it all was whether Tyson–Jones would be an "exhibition" or a "fight."

Boxing has a long history of exhibitions by elite fighters dating back to the days of John L. Sullivan. Most often, they have been marketed as such whether the fighter exhibiting his skills was Jack Johnson, Joe Louis, Sugar Ray Robinson, or Muhammad Ali.

Either a fighter is trying to hurt his opponent or he isn't. If he's trying to hurt his opponent, it's a fight. If not, it's an exhibition. A boxing exhibition is essentially a sparring session.

Andy Foster (executive director of the California State Athletic

Commission, which had jurisdiction over the event) was adamant that Tyson–Jones would be an exhibition. He stated that again and again:

* "I understand the interest that people have in Tyson. I grew up being knocked out by Mike Tyson on *Punch Out*. But this isn't a situation where they're going out there to try to take each other's heads off. They're just going to be in there, moving around the ring and letting fans see these legends."

* "I don't care if they spar. I don't care if they work. They can move around and make some money. They can get into it a little bit, but I don't want people to get hurt. They know the deal. It's an exhibition. They can exhibit their boxing skills, but I don't want them using their best efforts to hurt each other. They're going to spar hard, but they shouldn't be going for a knockout. This isn't a record-book type of fight. People shouldn't be getting knocked out."

* "Ray Corona will referee it. I'm sure there are going to be times where it heats up. Ray's job is going to be to put the ice back on without having to kill the whole thing. He's that kind of referee. I feel that he's going to be good at that. He's the right guy for this kind of a fight. Ray won't let people get hurt. He understands what an exhibition is. It's not a fight-fight."

Foster was sincere in his desire to regulate Tyson–Jones as an exhibition and that this be made clear to prospective pay-per-view buyers. "We can't mislead the public as to this is some kind of real fight," he said. Toward that end, he announced that the exhibition would not be scored by any judge representing the California State Athletic Commission and that no winner would be announced.

Even then, there were medical concerns. Jones sought to discount them, telling ESPN.com, "Wait a minute! You've boxed for how many, thirty-nine years? And now, you're all of a sudden worried about your health. Be for real. C'mon!"

But the brain is more susceptible to injury as it ages. Men in their fifties shouldn't be punching each other in the head. And as Jones's career wound down, he'd suffered severe concussive knockouts at the hands of Antonio Tarver, Glen Johnson, Danny Green, Denis Lebedev, and Enzo Macarinelli.

As Tyson–Jones drew near, Foster was between a rock and a hard place. Regardless of his dictates, the event was being marketed to the public with a wink that said, "We don't care what the rules are. This will be a fight."

There were casino betting lines on who would "win" (leaving open the question of how a winner would be determined). The World Boxing Council inserted itself into the proceedings, announcing that Tyson–Jones would be remotely scored by three former WBC champions (Christy Martin, Vinny Pazienza, and Chad Dawson) with the winner being awarded the WBC "frontline battle belt." An undercard composed of commission-approved bouts reinforced the storyline that Tyson–Jones as the main event would also be a "fight." The Voluntary Anti-Doping Association was hired to test Tyson and Jones for performance-enhancing drugs (but not recreational drugs).

So yes; Foster had articulated the rules. But would they be enforced?

Three days before the event, Ryan Kavanaugh (the driving force behind Triller) issued a statement that read, "Know there have been some false rumors swirling, so to be crystal clear. The WBC is scoring the fight. There could be a knockout and there will be one winner. Anyone who says there is no judging or no winner either does not understand the rules or has their own agenda. Unquestionably, 100 percent. DraftKings is the betting partner and is taking bets on the fight in New Jersey, New Hampshire, and Illinois."

"It's being marketed to the public as a fight," a frustrated Andy Foster told this writer. "It's not supposed to be a fight. And I'm doing what I can to see that the public is not misled. This is not being presented to the public the way it was presented to me. They talk to me one way, and then they have an interview and say something else. I've reminded both fighters that, in California if you get disqualified, you don't get paid. And we will disqualify someone if it's appropriate to do so."

And what was the expressed intent (genuine or otherwise) of the two fighters?

* Tyson: "I'm looking to be one hundred percent of Mike Tyson in the ring. I'm a neophyte in taking it easy. I don't know how to do it that way. I am one speed, forward. Roy is just going to have to deal with that."

* Jones: "Who goes in the ring with the great legendary Mike Tyson

and thinks this is an exhibition? Twelve-ounce gloves, no headgear. Really, this is an exhibition? Come on."

★ Tyson: "We're throwing punches at each other. This is going to be my definition of fun. Broken eye sockets, broken jaw, broken rib. That's fun to me."

★ Jones: "When it comes time to fight, we're going to fight. If it comes down to bite, we're going to bite. Whatever has to happen is going to happen. That's just what it is."

★ Tyson: "I'm coming to fight and I hope he's coming to fight and that's all you need to know."

★ Jones: "Mike comes to that ring and Mike's coming to kill. When I go in there, I'm going in there to kill or die. So you know how it's gonna go. People are gonna get what they paid for, trust me."

More than a century ago, outlaw fights were contested on barges and in remote locations to circumvent legal proscriptions against prizefighting. The marketing of Tyson–Jones was based on fans believing that an outlaw fight would take place right in front of the eyes of the law.

Tyson was the draw. Tyson–Jones was largely about Mike. From a marketing point of view, the promotion could have substituted Shannon Briggs for Roy and not missed a beat.

Once upon a time, the entire world stopped to watch when Mike Tyson fought. Even today, there are people who will buy into anything Tyson. Mike Tyson on Broadway, Mike Tyson versus a shark. Triller wasn't selling boxing. It was selling Tyson.

Computers and cameras are facile tools. The much-circulated short video clip of Tyson vigorously hitting workout pads didn't prove anything from a competitive point of view. But news outlets that rarely cover boxing fixated on it and devoted time and space to Tyson–Jones. There was extensive coverage of the event in the general sports media and on boxing websites.

"It's almost like a reality show," Tyson told writer Joe Santoliquito. "All of these cameras and these strange motherfuckers descending upon me. It's crazy that people think that this is that important."

Fourteen years ago, Tyson fought a pay-per-view exhibition against Corey Sanders (the club fighter from Maryland, not the Corrie Sanders from South Africa). It was an artistic and financial disaster. People who bought the pay-per-view felt cheated when it was over.

Tyson–Jones was better organized than that earlier venture and promised to be a more entertaining promotion. The event also got a commercial lift when Donald Trump Jr. (who has 6.4 million Twitter followers) sent out five tweets during fight week (including two on fight day) accompanied by links to promotional videos and pay-per-view ordering information. It would be interesting to know how much, if anything, Trump was paid for the tweets.

Meanwhile, people who bought the pay-per-view were hoping for a fight. In that regard, Tyson's mental state was an unknown and potentially explosive variable. Some thought that this was the wrong psychological environment for Mike; that he might snap and go in any one of a multitude of wrong directions.

"You never know with Tyson," Teddy Atlas (who assisted Cus D'Amato in training the young Mike Tyson) said. "I think he'll try to establish some kind of dominance at the start. If he gets it, he'll make it whatever he wants—a fight, an exhibition. And if he gets resistance, either he'll treat it as an exhibition or give in."

That led to another intriguing question: If it was a fight, who would win?

According to DraftKings, Tyson was a 2-to-1 betting favorite. A more credible betting line circulated by Jimmy Shapiro acknowledged, "The fight will have no winner. But a KO can take place and, if either boxer suffers a bad cut, the exhibition is over." Within that framework, the odds were roughly 3-to-1 that the fight would go the distance.

One day before the event, Tyson weighed in at 220 pounds (his lightest for a ring appearance in 23 years). Jones (who at five feet, eleven inches stands an inch taller than Tyson) weighed in at 210 pounds—six more than for any of his previous fights and seventeen more than the 193 pounds he weighed when he defeated John Ruiz for the WBA heavyweight title in 2003.

If it turned into a fight, Jones would try to make Tyson look silly. Mike would try to knock Roy out. Jones has two bad knees, which would make it difficult for him to move out of the line of fire. In recent years, he has also seemed to have balance problems. And there was the matter of Roy's chin.

On the other hand, Jones has more of an ego than Tyson. And Roy has some mean in him, perhaps more mean than there now is in Mike.

As the voice of boxing for HBO Sports, Jim Lampley helped shape the historical record for Tyson and Jones when they were great fighters and sat next to Roy behind a microphone for years. How did he feel about the event?

"It appears to me to be a frivolous sideshow," Lampley told this writer. "I hope that, when it's over, people look back on it with the understanding that, whatever the outcome, it does nothing to alter either man's legacy as a fighter."

Staples Center was closed to the public on fight night because of coronavirus protocols. The financial success of the venture was almost completely dependent on pay-per-view buys.

It's relatively easy to stream an event. YouTube is proof of that. But it's complicated to stream an event on a transactional basis. The Tiger Woods vs. Phil Mickelson streaming fiasco on Thanksgiving weekend 2019 speaks to that. The online pay-per-view ordering system for Woods–Mickelson crashed under the weight of last-minute orders, after which the promotion opened up a free internet stream and cable companies were pressured into refunding the cable purchase price to buyers who had paid for the promotion.

Tyson–Jones was streamed live on TysonOnTriller.com at a cost of $49.99. In addition, Triller turned to FITE to help distribute the stream on various FITE platforms in the United States and Canada. FITE (which has close to four million registered users and has streamed more than four thousand events during the past five years) also distributed the event digitally in thirty-six other territories ranging from Germany and the Netherlands to Bangladesh and the Faroe Islands. BT Sport Box Office distributed the pay-per-view in the United Kingdom.

The fight-night video stream was built around familiar on-camera faces. The commentating team consisted of Mauro Ranallo, Ray Leonard, and UFC middleweight champion Israel Adesanya. Mario Lopez was the event host. Jim Gray conducted fighter interviews. Michael Buffer was the ring announcer for the main event.

Lopez characterized Tyson–Jones as a real competition, calling it "this epic fight." Ranallo brought his usual over-the-top style to the telecast. The pre-packaged videos were heavily skewed toward the idea that this was Mike Tyson in a real fight. Once the undercard bouts began, there was artificial "crowd noise" every time a punch landed or a big one missed.

Perhaps this was what led Ranallo to tell viewers that there was "an amazing atmosphere" in the arena.

DraftKings and Weedmaps (a company involved with the legal use of cannabis) were event sponsors. Much of the streaming package was aimed at an urban audience. This was particularly true of the music, which included profanity-laced performances by Wiz Khalifa, French Montana, YG, and Snoop Dogg. Ne-Yo performed the National Anthem.

The featured undercard fight of the evening was a celebrity toughman-style confrontation matching Jake Paul (1–0, 1 KO) against Nate Robinson (making his ring debut).

Paul, the brother of loud-mouthed "YouTube sensation" Logan Paul, is a less well-known version of his brother. Jake knocked out Ali Eson Gib (a third loud-mouthed YouTube sensation) in a trash-sport fight on DAZN on January 30, 2020. Robinson (a five-foot, nine-inch former point guard) logged eleven years with eight different teams in the National Basketball Association, was a three-time NBA Slam Dunk Champion, and is now thirty-six years old. The fight was scheduled for six rounds in the cruiser-weight division.

Robinson was once an elite athlete. That was his biggest edge. But his fight plan was limited to throwing an inartful jab followed by a clumsy right hand and holding when the fighters got close.

Meanwhile, Paul can whack a bit. He dropped Robinson—and hurt him—with a right hand behind the ear in round one. He decked him again with a right hand that landed high on the forehead early in the second stanza. At that point, incomprehensibly, referee Thomas Taylor let the fight continue, whereupon Paul knocked Robinson face first to the canvas, out cold, with another right.

Then it was time for Tyson–Jones.

After all the talk, it wasn't a fight but a hard sparring session. Tyson was the aggressor. He looked like the main man, while Jones looked like a hired sparring partner. Roy had nothing to challenge Mike with. He tried to stay out of range. But Mike has always been good at cutting off the ring, particularly when he isn't getting hit. He was dominant in every round, although he never dug his shots to Jones's body as hard as he could have.

Both men were breathing heavily after two rounds. Snoop Dogg (who by this time had joined the commentating team) described the scene as looking "like two of my uncles fighting at a barbecue."

As noted, the WBC had designated three unofficial scorers for the contest. Possibly by prearrangement, they ruled it a draw: Christy Martin 79–73 for Tyson, Vinny Pazienza 80–76 for Jones, and Chad Dawson 76–76 even. The fact that there was no outrage over the WBC "decision" showed clearly that neither the commentating team nor Tyson took the event seriously as an actual fight.

Overall, the promotion was a success. Advance pay-per-view sales were strong. Remarkably, the event appears to have engendered well over one million PPV buys. It's conceivable that someone will bring a class action claiming that viewers bought the exhibition because they were defrauded into thinking that it would be a fight. But in the end, most pay-per-view buyers got what they wanted. Tyson–Jones was a reasonable representation of a fight.

There will be more Mike Tyson events in the future as Triller seeks to build its "Legends Only" franchise. Tyson has floated the idea of fighting exhibitions against Tyson Fury and Anthony Joshua. One can imagine a scenario in which Mike says that he's ready for a "real" fight and enters the ring against a no-hope opponent with the promise that, in later bouts, he'll seek to avenge one or more of his professional losses.

It speaks to the sad state of boxing today that the biggest headlines the sport generates in the mainstream media are about Mike Tyson. It's sad that an exhibition between two long-past-their-prime boxers will be the sport's biggest pay-per-view event in 2020.

Boxing has failed its fans. It has consistently fallen short by not giving the public fights that the public want to see. It offers unsatisfying match-ups, so viewers turn instead to paying $49.99 for the equivalent of a one-on-one basketball game between David Robinson and Hakeem Olajuwon.

"Boxing," Anthony Joshua has said, "should be about less talk and more action."

Joshua–Pulev
and the Heavyweight Mix

On December 12, 2020, Anthony Joshua of England outclassed Kubrat Pulev of Bulgaria en route to a ninth-round stoppage to retain his World Boxing Association, International Boxing Federation, and World Boxing Organization heavyweight belts. It was Joshua's first fight in the United Kingdom since September 2018 and the first major sanctioning body heavyweight title fight since the coronavirus lockdown began.

Joshua was born in Watford (fifteen miles northwest of London) in 1989 to Nigerian parents who divorced when he was twelve. After attending boarding school briefly in Nigeria, he returned to England and found trouble in the streets, culminating in an arrest for the possession of eight ounces of cannabis with "intent to supply"—a charge that carried with it a maximum sentence of fourteen years in prison.

After pleading guilty to a lesser offense and performing court-mandated community service, Joshua dedicated himself to boxing. In 2010, no less an authority than Tyson Fury (then twenty-two years old with a dozen professional victories on his résumé) sparred with Anthony and told commentator Steve Bunce, "He's red hot. I thought I have got to take it easy because he is only an amateur and he probably won't spar again if I go mad. He rushed out at me and threw a one-two, left hook, and I slipped and slide. And bash, he hit me a big uppercut right on the point of the chin. If I had a weak chin, I would have been knocked out for a month. He is very very very good and young, only twenty. Watch out for that name, Anthony Joshua."

Two years later, Joshua won a gold medal in the super-heavyweight division at the London Olympics. Since then, he has carried himself with class, both in and out of the ring. As Tony Parsons wrote, "He is a warrior and a gentleman. In the toxic trash-talking world of boxing—now amplified a million times on social media—he insists on treating his opponents with respect before and after the fight."

"I'm a real person," Anthony told Andrew Nagy of *GQ*. "I make mistakes. I'm not perfect. I'm trying, though. I really am. I'm working on myself every day."

There was a time when Joshua was The Man in the heavyweight division. On April 29, 2017, he climbed off the canvas to knock out Wladimir Klitschko in a thrilling encounter before ninety thousand screaming fans at Wembley Stadium in London. Thereafter, he consolidated the WBA, IBF, and WBO titles. But there were moments after the Klitschko fight when Joshua looked tentative in the ring. Some fighters walk through fire to win and are stronger for the experience. Others, having been badly hurt once (as Joshua was against Klitschko), are less confident.

On June 1, 2019, Joshua (then 22–0 with 21 knockouts) was beaten into submission at Madison Square Garden over seven rounds by Andy Ruiz (a 20-to-1 underdog). Six months later, they fought again; this time in Saudi Arabia. Ruiz, a shade over six feet tall, weighed in for the rematch at 283 pounds. He was so out of shape that his back was jiggling.

Joshua jabbed and moved ("ran" if one is being less kind) for most of the fight en route to winning a lackluster unanimous decision. This wasn't a young Muhammad Ali outboxing a young Mike Tyson. Bart Barry summed up matters nicely when he wrote, "It was fat guy versus a nervous one and it failed all expectations. Trust yourself, dear aficionado. Trust your gut on this one. A pundit writing or saying that [Ruiz–Joshua II] was anything better than woeful does so with the same integrity as a waiter embellishing the daily specials or a flight attendant thanking you for loyalty to her airline. Saturday was just awful."

"The belts can be your best friend or your best enemy," Joshua said when Ruiz–Joshua II was over. "It just depends on you as a person. Trust me. It's not all fun."

Later, Joshua would look back on 2019 and observe, "The pressure that I went through last year was tough, but it made me mentally stronger. I grew a thicker skin. Just because I took a loss from Ruiz, I don't think that's enough to change someone. Every fighter trains hard, but it's character that separates us, and I've got a lot of character."

The brings us to Joshua–Pulev. The fight had originally been scheduled for October 2017, but Pulev was forced to withdraw because of a muscle injury. Their 2020 confrontation was postponed several times because of COVID-19 issues and eventually slated for December 12 at the O2 Dome in London. Then, on December 2, Matchroom (Joshua's promoter) announced that the bout was being moved to the smaller SSE Arena at Wembley. One thousand fans were allowed to attend. Tickets were priced from £100 to £1,000.

Pulev came into the contest with a 28–1 (14 KOs) record. But he's thirty-nine years old (eight years older than Joshua) and had been maneuvered into position as the IBF mandatory challenger by picking over the carcasses of aging heavyweights who were long past their prime. In his one previous title bout, he'd been knocked out in 2014 by Wladimir Klitschko (the final knockout of Klitschko's ring career).

Bulgarians have won sixteen Olympic gold medals in wrestling, twelve in weightlifting, and four in boxing. But their success in professional boxing has been negligible. Bob Arum (who co-promotes Pulev) beat the drums for his fighter, declaring, "I think Pulev is gonna beat Joshua. I really do. Look, Andy Ruiz is a good kid. He fought most of his fights for us. But the fact that he could knock out Joshua says volumes about Joshua. And the rematch that they had, I mean, that doesn't count. Ruiz wasn't in any kind of shape. He came in fat and Joshua was reluctant to engage with him. So, I really think Pulev, who's a big tough Bulgarian, is gonna knock Joshua out."

Pulev echoed that theme, saying, "We waited a long time for this fight. In 2017, I had a problem and that's why I said to my trainer we must go for the win, not to fight now but fight a couple of years later. I knew the fight would come one day. I'm here now, ready to fight and win. This fight is for all of Bulgaria. Nobody from my country has ever been heavyweight champion of the world. That is why it will be so good for my country and my people. Bulgarian fans will be really happy."

Joshua weighed in for the bout at 240.8 pounds, Pulev at 239.7. That was a good weight for each fighter. There was some aggressive back-and-forth posturing at the weigh-in (which the promotion hoped would pump up pay-per-view buys). But after the weigh-in, the fighters fist-bumped and Pulev told Joshua that he liked and respected him.

The fight itself was short on drama. My notes on the bout read as follows:

Round 1—A feeling-out round. Joshua a bit more active. Neither fighter doing much.

Round 2—Joshua picks up the pace a bit. Pulev doing nothing to score points and not seeking to engage.

Round 3—Joshua right hand stuns Pulev. Anthony goes for
the kill. Big uppercuts. Pulev turns his back and stumbles
into the ropes. Referee calls it a knockdown. Joshua pum-
meling Pulev, drops him again with an uppercut. Pulev
survives the round.

Round 4—Pulev hanging tough, but that's all he's doing.

Round 5—Pulev is game but he can't compete at Joshua's
level. It's target practice for A.J.

Round 6—Pulev throwing his right hand with a bit more
conviction.

Round 7—Joshua taking his time. He has a stationary target
in front of him.

Round 8—Pulev's most competitive round so far. But he
needs a KO to win and he's not a power puncher.

Round 9—Series of uppercuts drop Pulev. A right hand fin-
ishes him. KO 9.

So . . . what comes next?

Let's start with the fact that, at present, Tyson Fury is the number
one heavyweight in the world. Joshua–Ruiz I was about dethroning a
king. Wilder–Fury II was about crowning a new one. Fury established his
supremacy in the heavyweight division with his seven-round demolition of
Wilder on February 22, 2020.

Wilder had a contractual right to a third fight against Fury with a designated purse split between them prior to Fury defending his title against
another opponent. But Fury now says that, since Fury–Wilder III didn't
occur within a contractually mandated five-month window, he's free to
fight whomever he wants. That makes Fury-Joshua likely.

Fury–Joshua wouldn't be a crossover fight in the United States. If the
two fighters walked through the heart of any city in America, few people
other than hardcore boxing fans would recognize them. And that number
wouldn't increase by much if Wilder was walking with them. The most
common reaction from passersby would be "maybe they're basketball
players."

But Fury–Joshua, even if it took place in the Middle East (which Bob

Arum, who co-promotes Fury, says is likely), would be a huge event in the United Kingdom.

If Fury beat Joshua, he'd be the UNDISPUTED heavyweight champion of the world. And if Joshua beat Fury, he'd have all the belts (although there would still be the nagging question of how Anthony would fare against Wilder).

Meanwhile, Joshua is a breath of fresh air in boxing. For starters, he refuses to engage in what has become the unfortunate ritual of fighters demeaning their opponents. "When you disrespect another fighter," Anthony says, "you disrespect the sport. You shouldn't do that to other athletes. 'He's shit; he's this; he's that.' It reflects badly on boxing, calling people bums. There's a way to do it. 'He's a good fighter, but I'm better!'"

Joshua is a very good fighter. He has a hurting right hand and a concussive uppercut. He's still a work in progress. But unlike Wilder, he's progressing. He was a bit overrated before his loss to Andy Ruiz. He might be a bit underrated now.

And let's not forget: Joshua has the memory of standing in the ring, looking down at the multitudes after defeating Wladimir Klitschko to become King of the World. The power of that moment is near unimaginable. He wants that feeling again. Against Tyson Fury. With a roaring crowd. For the right to be called King of the World and King of England.

Hall of Fame promoter Russell Peltz has lamented, "Boxing isn't the sport I fell in love with anymore." But fighters like Canelo Álvarez remind us of why boxing at its best is still great.

Canelo Álvarez, Callum Smith, and DAZN

Earlier this year, Norm Frauenheim wrote, "Canelo Alvarez is fighting for history. But history, like profit, has been suspended for who-knows-how-long because of COVID-19. Alvarez is lucky. He was a wealthy man before the virus appeared and spread its deadly appendages like a weapon of mass destruction. Over just three fights in his rich DAZN deal, he earned $97.5 million. Canelo doesn't have to fight, unlike most in the prize-fighting profession. But if money isn't a motivation anymore, Canelo's immense pride is. For Alvarez, history isn't complicated. It's simple. Julio Cesar Chavez is the defining face of Mexico's fabled boxing history. He was when Canelo was born in 1990. He has been ever since. Canelo had begun his monumental pursuit of supplanting Chavez. His run at history was underway. Now, a pandemic-altered landscape includes a potential dilemma for Canelo. History or profit? Money or legacy? Canelo's claim on legacy is hard to make, much less sustain, when he's not fighting. Inactivity opens the way to a skepticism that's hard to counter. Canelo has to fight. But the world is operating on a different a timetable these days. Tick-tock, we're all on the pandemic clock."

On December 19, 2020, Álvarez resumed his quest for greatness and reasserted his claim to the #1 pound-for-pound ranking in boxing today with a dominant twelve-round victory over Callum Smith at the Alamodome in San Antonio. There were numerous twists and turns in the road he followed to get there.

On October 17, 2018, it was announced that DAZN, Canelo, and Golden Boy (Álvarez's promoter at the time) had entered into a contractual relationship to stream Canelo's next eleven fights on DAZN platforms throughout the world with Canelo being paid a minimum of $365 million. With certain exceptions, DAZN would pay Golden Boy $40 million for each fight card headed by Canelo, and Golden Boy would pay Canelo $35 million of that. This would leave Golden Boy with $5 million plus the live gate and other revenue streams to pay Canelo's opponent, each of the undercard fighters, the host site, and other promotional expenses. What was left over would be Golden Boy's profit.

Thereafter, Bernard Hopkins sagely observed, "Canelo has the money on paper. But he doesn't have it in the bank yet."

Then DAZN got buyer's remorse and took a position of dubious legal merit.

The contractual relationships amongst Canelo, Golden Boy, and DAZN required that Canelo fight one "premier" fighter during each corporate year. DAZN took the position that Danny Jacobs and Sergey Kovalev (who Canelo fought on DAZN) weren't premier fighters and that, unless Golden Boy delivered a third fight between Canelo and Gennady Golovkin, the promoter would be in breach of its contractual obligations. DAZN also listed several fighters other than Golovkin who would qualify as premier opponents. But these names were so impractical as to suggest bad faith on the network's part (e.g., Conor McGregor and Oscar De La Hoya).

On September 8, 2020, Canelo filed a lawsuit against DAZN and Golden Boy. Most likely, he would have prevailed in court. But litigation is expensive and would have put his career on hold with no guarantee that he'd be able to collect whatever judgment he won. On November 6, it was announced that the case had been settled and Canelo was free of any future obligations to Golden Boy or DAZN.

The settlement formally terminated Golden Boy's lucrative contractual relationship with Canelo. But that relationship had been on shaky ground for some time. And Golden Boy had no realistic choice but to accede to the settlement because Golden Boy CEO Oscar De La Hoya had significant personal financial exposure in the litigation, and Golden Boy needs the license fees it receives from DAZN in conjunction with other fighters to navigate boxing's perilous pandemic-swept waters.

When Canelo's free agency became a reality, he had multiple suitors. No one offered a long-term $35 million per fight guarantee. But he wasn't going to go poor either.

Canelo had fought on Showtime multiple times before leaving the network for HBO. Most notably, he'd battled Floyd Mayweather in a 2013 megafight on Showtime PPV. Shortly after Canelo's lawsuit against DAZN and Golden Boy was filed, Showtime Sports president Stephen Espinoza told *Forbes*, "We're proud of the time we spent with Canelo. We did some important fights in his career and we helped launch him as a pay-per-view attraction in the United States. We'd love to be in business with him again. We're obviously going to respect his existing contracts. We're not going to run afoul of that. If there's a time when he's available, we'll be very aggressive. We have a lot of offer. As soon as there's some clarity, we'd love to have the discussion."

After Canelo's lawsuit was settled, Al Haymon entered the sweepstakes, offering Canelo a three-fight deal for $75 million. The first fight would have been against Caleb Plant. One of the next two opponents would have been Jermall Charlo at a 166-pound catchweight. Álvarez said he'd fight Plant for $25 million but didn't want to commit to three fights at those numbers.

Then, on November 17, Canelo tweeted that his next fight would be against Callum Smith on December 19 and that (to the surprise of many) the fight would be streamed on DAZN. The promoter would be Matchroom Boxing, which promotes Smith and, more significantly, has an intricate financial relationship with DAZN. Multiple sources say that Canelo and his team received approximately $25 million for the fight. About $5 million was allocated for Smith's services.

Smith, a Liverpool native, is thirty years old (the same age as Canelo). Over the years, he'd compiled a 27–0 (19 KOs) ring record and collected the WBC "diamond" and WBA "world" super-middleweight belts. There was a time when he was touted as a potential star. But he'd yet to beat a fighter of note other than a 2018 stoppage of a shopworn George Groves in the last fight of Groves's career. Most recently, Callum had won a lackluster decision over John Ryder.

Tickets for Canelo–Smith went on sale on November 25 (one day before Thanksgiving). Buyers were advised that there would be limited capacity at the 72,000-seat Alamodome with up to 15,000 fans seated in socially distanced clusters. Ticket prices ranged from $2,005.50 down to $80.50. Buyers who went to Ticketmaster on the first day of sales saw a pop-up window that advised, "Prices may fluctuate based on demand at any time." One day before the fight, some prices had been cut in half.

The mix of glitz and glamour normally associated with a Canelo fight week was absent from the scene. "You don't see the people," Canelo noted. "You don't see the flags. You don't see everything that surrounds fight week. But for the most part, it's very similar to what I do. I stay in my room, focus, take care of media, all of that; stay focused and get ready for what's coming."

Smith, for his part, observed, "I'm in the position I've always wanted to be since I was a little boy. I want to test myself against the biggest names in the sport, and Canelo certainly is that. Four weeks notice for the biggest fight possible isn't ideal. However, given the times that we're in, I kind of expected to get it at late notice. And I wasn't sitting around doing nothing. I've been in the gym. I have been training. I'm a winner, and I don't take fights [just] for a payday."

Each fighter weighed in at 168 pounds, but there was a huge disparity in height between them. Smith, at six feet, three inches, is a tall super-middleweight. Canelo is six inches shorter. Canelo's fight against Sergey Kovalev had given Callum what he thought was a blueprint for beating Canelo. Jab, use your superior height and reach to keep him at bay, pile up points, and—this is the hard part—take Canelo's punches when they land and don't get tired.

Despite holding two 168-pound belts, Smith walked to the ring and was introduced first. That reflected the relative status of the two fighters. The crowd was overwhelmingly pro-Canelo, a 5-to-1 betting favorite.

My notes on the fight read as follows:

Round 1—A feeling-out round with Canelo moving forward. Smith not throwing his jab.

Round 2—Smith throwing a little more but Canelo still stalking. Neither fighter landing much.

Round 3—Canelo still stalking, closing the gap. Smith very cautious, not fighting tall.

Round 4—Canelo backing Smith up against the ropes, landing solid blows.

Round 5—Smith trying to fight more aggressively. But Canelo is hard to hit and hits harder.

Round 6—Smith a bit more effective because he's staying off the ropes. But Canelo's body shots are taking a toll.

Round 7—Canelo patient, cutting off the ring well and
landing.

Round 8—Canelo asking questions, and Smith has no
answers. When Smith lands, Canelo comes back harder.

Round 9—Both men landing their best punches so far. But
Canelo is landing more often and harder. Much harder.

Round 10—Canelo putting a beating on Smith with hurting
body blows.

Round 11—Smith fighting courageously but his cause is
hopeless.

Round 12—Canelo looking to finish with a knockout. Smith
has never been knocked off his feet before and hangs
tough until the end.

I gave Canelo every round. Two of the judges (Steve Weisfeld and
Rafael Ramos) scored it 119–109. Steve Morrow had it 117–111, which
is a bit hard to fathom.

"I reached the top of the mountain and now I've been knocked off it,"
Smith acknowledged in a post-fight interview. "He's got everything."

"I showed what I am," Canelo offered.

He certainly did. Canelo keeps getting better as a fighter. He has "man
strength" now and is hitting harder than before. He's also wiser and has
added wrinkles to his defense. He's the best fighter in the world.

What does Canelo's victory over Smith mean for boxing?

Among other things, it fits within the narrative of what's happening
at DAZN.

Two years ago, DAZN announced its intention to change boxing's
business model. It pledged "an end to pay-per-view" and promised to
deliver pay-per-view quality fights to subscribers in the United States for
the modest sum of $9.99 a month (later increased to $19.99 per month
or $99.99 for a one-year subscription). It signed Canelo and Golovkin to
multifight deals for close to $500 million, contracted with Golden Boy and
the World Boxing Super Series for additional fights, and gave Matchroom
CEO Eddie Hearn in the neighborhood of $125 million a year to deliver
more boxing.

That got everyone's attention. Then things soured.

DAZN's anchor sport in the United States is boxing. But its primary sport worldwide is soccer. In 2019, soccer was the most-watched sport on DAZN in the network's nine markets, logging in at 314.6 million hours. Boxing (22.6 million hours) ranked fifth, behind soccer, baseball, motor sports, and football. And 90 percent of DAZN's business is outside of the United States.

Meanwhile, DAZN overestimated the demand for boxing in the US market. It has been plagued by a poor business model and has not used its resources efficiently in buying content. Fighters have been signed pursuant to poorly drawn contracts (e.g., DAZN failed to lock in a third fight between Canelo and Golovkin). And Matchroom has failed to deliver content commensurate with the license fees that it has paid to fighters.

"Eddie Hearn," one observer noted, "spent DAZN's money like it was DAZN's money." For example, Matchroom signed Tevin Farmer to a four-fight deal worth approximately $2 million plus the fee that Matchroom paid to Farmer's promoter, Lou DiBella.

DAZN won't reveal the number of current subscribers that it has in the United States. But the network spent close to $10 million in license fees for a February 29, 2020, card headlined by Mikey Garcia vs. Jesse Vargas. One informed source says that this card engendered a meager 20,000 new subscriptions, most of which were not renewed.

In March 2020 as COVID-19 spread, DAZN suspended the payment of rights fees for events that were postponed and other content that wasn't delivered to its platforms in nine countries around the world. This led to claims of breach of contract lodged by Major League Baseball and other content providers. Meanwhile, boxing ground to a halt.

The pandemic improved DAZN's short-term balance sheet in America because it brought the network a modicum of relief from some of its financial obligations. Also, many subscribers didn't take the steps necessary to cancel their monthly subscriptions. But the lethargy of subscribers is not a good business model. And given DAZN's contractual history with Major League Baseball, Canelo, and others, some content providers will be reluctant to engage with the network in the future—particularly since DAZN lacks a broad platform to attract prospective viewers. Visibility and trust are important concepts.

The bottom line is that, to date, DAZN has spent hundreds of millions of dollars in the United States to build what is essentially a niche boxing channel. It should also be noted that DAZN jumpstarted the trash-boxing carnival with its streaming of Logan Paul vs. KSI on November 9, 2019. But it was bypassed when the big money started rolling in with Mike Tyson and Roy Jones.

Meanwhile, the leadership team at DAZN has been changing. On June 29, 2020, it was announced that Simon Denyer was leaving his role as chief executive officer of DAZN Group (which oversees DAZN's global operations) and would be replaced by James Rushton, who previously had been DAZN's chief revenue officer. John Skipper remained as executive chairman of DAZN Group.

Now, a source says, key decisions at DAZN are being made by Ed McCarthy (DAZN's chief operating officer in London and a lawyer by trade who formerly worked for Access Industries). Access Industries is Len Blavatnik's holding company. Blavatnik is a Ukranian-born billionaire with UK and US citizenship who has funded DAZN from its inception.

"McCarthy is the new number-one guy," the source says. "Skipper has been marginalized and [executive vice president for North America] Joe Markowski can no longer sign off on significant decisions without approval from above."

Canelo vs. Callum Smith served as the launching pad for two changes in DAZN's economic model.

The first change was long in coming. After a false start this spring occasioned by the pandemic, DAZN rolled out a worldwide English-language app that it had originally intended to introduce in conjunction with a planned May 2 fight between Canelo and Billy Joe Saunders. The app, which DAZN says is available on most internet-connected devices, was announced as having an initial monthly price point in new markets of £1.99 ($2.70) or less. This leads to the question of whether, at some point, DAZN will close down its network in the United States and America will be just one more country with access to the English-language app. Also, one has to ask how much boxing will contribute to making DAZN's new app a success. Consider the fact that India has 1.34 billion people, but there were only 2,000 buys for the rematch between Deontay Wilder and Tyson Fury in all of India. There's a reason these markets are untapped.

The second change is more intriguing. On December 15 (four days before Canelo–Smith), DAZN announced that the fight would be available in the United States through traditional pay-per-view channels for $69.99. Purchasers would also receive a four-month subscription (January through April 2021) to DAZN.

According to ProSportsMedia.com, distribution of the pay-per-view was facilitated by In Demand (which reaches 55 million homes through cable systems like Comcast, Cox Communications, Charter Communications, AT&T, and Verizon). The distributors will receive a cut of revenue from the initial purchase and also "share in the money brought in from new DAZN subscribers who choose to keep paying for the service after their four-month trial expires."

The transition to a pay-per-view hybrid is a major change in strategy for DAZN and an acknowledgment that its previous "pay-per-view is dead" mantra is no longer operative.

Supporters of DAZN's pay-per-view gambit say it shows that network executives are constructively evolving in their thinking and that the plan will encourage buyers to sample DAZN during the first four months of 2021. They also believe that the $69.99 price point will reinforce the value of DAZN's one-year subscription offer.

But there were—and still are—potential problems. Apart from possible technological issues, it's virtually impossible to market a pay-per-view fight on four days' notice. Further to that point, when a promotion makes a deal with a cable system to carry a pay-per-view event, the system generally commits to marketing in support of the event (which wasn't feasible on a large scale here).

Many consumers, even if they knew about the Canelo–Smith pay-per-view option, didn't know how to place an order. And people who did know were probably savvy enough to know that they could buy a one-month subscription for $19.99 and then cancel instead of paying $69.99.

Also, there's the question of whether this is a stand-alone move for Canelo's fights or DAZN will offer similar pay-per-view bundles for other fighters in the future. And will DAZN at some point charge regular subscribers extra for big fights the way ESPN+ charges subscribers extra for major UFC cards? DAZN might say now that this won't happen. But this is the same network that, for two years, assured the public that "pay-per-view is dead."

If DAZN is to succeed in the United States, it has to show subscribers that it's worth having all the time.

What will happen to DAZN?

As recently as a year ago, everyone in the boxing industry had its eye on DAZN to see what would happen next. Now DAZN is often little more than an afterthought in conversations about the future of boxing. For the near future, Len Blavatnik will probably keep supplying the funds necessary to keep it afloat. According to the latest Bloomberg Billionaires Index, Blavatnik is worth $33 billion ($8 billion more than in 2019). Currently, he's said to be considering an effort to recoup his investment in DAZN through the sale of public stock. Alternatively, he might keep DAZN USA alive, build DAZN's other platforms throughout the world, and cut his losses down the road by selling the entire network to an entity that wants to get into sports video streaming worldwide without having to start from scratch.

That said, the numbers for DAZN only add up (for the short term, at least) as long as Blavatnik is willing to keep losing money. And billionaires don't like throwing good money after bad. They throw good money after good. That's one of the reasons they're billionaires. To date (like the institutional investors in Premier Boxing Champions), Blavatnik hasn't gotten his money's worth out of DAZN.

Putting a positive spin on things, DAZN can say, "Look, 2020 was a challenging year for everyone and it accelerated some long-term trends like more people cutting their cable cord and signing up for streaming services. Media models change quickly today. We're in the right place at the right time. And don't forget, Netflix has seen an extraordinary rise in the value of its stock despite having a lot of red ink on its balance sheet."

But Netflix has built a huge platform while DAZN has had little subscriber growth. And streaming video is not a formula for guaranteed success.

The Walt Disney Company is at one end of the spectrum. When Disney+ launched in November 2019, Disney said that it hoped to reach 90 million subscribers by 2024. Then, on December 10, 2020, the company announced that Disney+ had amassed 86.6 million worldwide subscribers. Disney stock jumped 13.6 percent the following day. By contrast, HBO Max (another big-name streaming service) is struggling.

And by the way, subscribers can get a bundled package of Disney+, ESPN+, and Hulu for $12.99 a month (which is 35 percent less than the monthly cost for DAZN).

But let's put the business end of things aside in closing and return to Canelo Álvarez. Canelo is the brightest star in today's boxing firmament. He has been fighting professionally for fifteen years. The list of fighters he has beaten compares favorably with the victims on Julio César Chávez Sr.'s ring ledger. Canelo's quest for the most exalted place in Mexican ring lore is not quixotic.

Curiosities

Following tradition, I've included a non-boxing "bonus piece" in Broken Dreams.

I Didn't Watch the Super Bowl
This Year

If football is our national religion, then the Super Bowl is the holiest day of the year. More than one hundred million people in the United States watched Super Bowl LIV on February 2, 2020. That's more people than went to a church, temple, or mosque that week. The game is one of the few unifying events left in America.

With the exception of Super Bowl VI (more on that later), I'd watched every Super Bowl ever. I didn't watch the Super Bowl this year. Let me explain.

I'm a football fan. My memory of NFL Championship games dates to 1956 when I was ten years old and the New York Giants routed the Chicago Bears at Yankee Stadium 47–7. Two years later, the Baltimore Colts beat the Giants in a 23–17 overtime thriller that boosted the NFL to a new level of popularity and is often referred to as "the greatest football game ever played." I listened to it on the radio.

The radio?

Yeah. The radio. The NFL had a policy back then of blacking out all home games to boost attendance, even a sold-out championship game. Television revenue was secondary to ticket sales in those days.

In 1960, the American Football League was created. Its owners had deep pockets, which led to an expensive bidding war for players. Six years later, being rational men of business, the warring owners reached a meeting of the minds and joined their respective enterprises together. However, the NFL–AFL merger wasn't complete until 1970. Until then, the leagues maintained separate identities, with teams from each league meeting only in what was known as the "AFL–NFL World Championship Game."

The first of these championship games was played on January 15, 1967, in the Los Angeles Memorial Coliseum. The leagues had used different footballs during the regular season (the AFL ball was slightly more passer friendly). So whichever team was on offense was allowed to use the ball it was familiar with in that inaugural encounter. The contest was telecast jointly by CBS (which had a contract with the NFL) and NBC (the AFL network) and blacked out within 75 miles of Los Angeles. Ticket prices ranged from six to twelve dollars. There were 33,000 empty seats. A 30-second commercial cost $42,000. The Green Bay Packers throttled the Kansas City Chiefs 35–10, after which Green Bay coach Vince Lombardi told the media, "I don't think that Kansas City compares with the top teams of the NFL. That's what you wanted me to say, and I said it."

I was in my senior year of college and watched the game with a classmate at his parents' apartment. They had a large color television, which wasn't that common in those days. One year later, the Packers vanquished the Oakland Raiders 33–14. I took a break from studying for first-year law school exams and watched the game in a student lounge.

Then came Super Bowl III—the game that changed everything.

The Packers had been dethroned as NFL champions by the Baltimore Colts. That set the stage for an encounter that rivals the 1958 Colts–Giants contest in historical importance. The New York Jets, led by quarterback Joe Namath, were 18-point underdogs in what had been rebranded as the "Super Bowl." Three days before the game, Namath attended a luncheon at the Miami Touchdown Club and boldly predicted, "We're gonna win the game. I guarantee it." On Sunday, the Jets did just that, dominating the Colts en route to a 16–7 triumph. Everyone who watched that game remembers it. The following year, the AFL Kansas City Chiefs toppled the mighty Minnesota Vikings 23–7. Parity between the leagues had been achieved.

The early Super Bowls stand out in my mind, probably because football mattered to me more then than it does now. I missed one game. On January 16, 1972, the Dallas Cowboys shut down the Miami Dolphins en route to a 24–3 triumph. I was working as a litigator at a Wall Street law firm and was called into the office with several other associates to prepare papers for an emergency court session scheduled for the following day. The consensus is that if you had to miss a Super Bowl, that was the one to miss.

Over the years, there have been boring Super Bowls but also some very good games and memorable Super Bowl moments. The best of these include:

Super Bowl XXIII (January 22, 1989)—Joe Montana leading the San Francisco 49ers on a 92-yard scoring drive in the closing minutes en route to a 20–16 triumph over the Cincinnati Bengals.

Super Bowl XXV (January 27, 1991)—The New York Giants besting the Buffalo Bills 20–19 when Scott Norwood's last-second field goal attempt went wide right.

Super Bowl XXXII (January 25, 1998)—Denver 31, Green Bay 24 in a contest highlighted by Broncos quarterback John Elway's "helicopter spin" for a crucial first down late in the game.

Super Bowl XXXIV (January 30, 2000)—Time expired with the Tennessee Titans trailing the St. Louis Rams 23–16 and the ball on the Rams 1-yard line.

Super Bowl XXXVI (February 3, 2002) and Super Bowl XXXVIII (February 1, 2004), which ended with game-winning field goals by Adam Vinatieri of the New England Patriots against the St. Louis Rams and Carolina Panthers.

Super Bowl XLII (February 3, 2008)—David Tyree's "helmet catch" in the closing minutes of the Giants' 17–14 victory over the previously unbeaten New England Patriots.

Super Bowl XLIX (February 1, 2015)—Malcolm Butler's game-saving interception sealed a 28–24 Patriots win over the Seattle Seahawks.

Super Bowl LI (February 5, 2017)—Tom Brady rallied the Patriots from a 28–3 deficit and 16 points down in the fourth quarter to beat the Atlanta Falcons 34–28 in the first overtime Super Bowl ever.

Super Bowl LII (February 4, 2018)—Philadelphia 41, New England 33 in a shoot-out that went down to the wire.

But over time, personal moments became more important to me than the game itself.

Football fans remember Super Bowl XLVI (February 5, 2012) as one of the best. The Giants had squeezed into the playoffs with a 9–7 regular season record before beating the Falcons, Packers, and 49ers to advance to the Super Bowl. There, against New England, they rallied from a 17–9 deficit to score the winning touchdown with 57 seconds left on the clock.

I don't remember much about the game itself. I watched it with a friend named Yvonne Silverman, her husband, her brother, and a longtime family friend at the Silvermans' apartment. Yvonne was dying of brain cancer. Once one of the smartest, wittiest, most verbal people I've known, she was unable to speak. She sat in a chair for the entire game. Michael (her husband) put a plate with food cut into small pieces beside her. She was able to lift food off the plate with her hand and put it in her mouth. During the second half of the game, Michael put some fudge that I'd brought on the plate.

Yvonne sat mute for four hours. The fudge seemed to be to her liking. She ate several pieces. When the game was over and I leaned over to kiss her good-bye, she said very clearly, "Thank you for the fudge." Those were the only words she spoke that afternoon and the last words she ever said to me. That was my Super Bowl XLVI moment.

I've never been to a Super Bowl. When I was young, it seemed like it would be a really cool thing to do. Now I think the hassle might outweigh the gain. I haven't watched the Super Bowl pre-game show for decades.

In recent years, the collegial aspects of watching the Super Bowl with friends has meant as much to me as the game itself. I invite a half-dozen people to my apartment and put out a deli spread.

The halftime shows bore me. In the early years, they were filler. At the first AFL–NFL World Championship Game, the University of Arizona Symphonic Marching Band, Grambling State University Matching Band, Anaheim High School Drill Team, and trumpeter Al Hirt performed. The following year, the Grambling Band had the field to itself. At Super Bowl III (the "Joe Namath Super Bowl"), viewers were entertained at halftime by the Florida A&M University Marching Band and various Miami-area high school bands. The first big star to perform during a Super Bowl halftime was Ella Fitzgerald at Super Bowl VI. As late as Super Bowl XXIII, various South Florida dancers and an Elvis Presley impersonator were featured.

Everything changed with Super Bowl XXVII when Michael Jackson took center stage. Big names have been the rule since then. Diana Ross, James Brown, Stevie Wonder, U2, Sting, Paul McCartney, the Rolling

Stones, Beyoncé, Bruce Springsteen, Madonna, Katy Perry, Lady Gaga, and quite a few more.

I don't care about the commercials, although some of them (most notably, Apple's *1984*-themed Super Bowl XVIII commercial) have earned plaudits.

I draw a distinction between the Super Bowl as an event and the Super Bowl as a game. Insofar as the latter is concerned, it's a football game between two very good teams that's exponentially more important than it would otherwise be because of the stakes involved.

I identify with Dallas Cowboys running back Duane Thomas (the Marshawn Lynch of his day when it came to media relations). Prior to Super Bowl V, Thomas responded to a reporter who called the Super Bowl "the ultimate game" with the rejoinder, "Then why are they playing it again next year?"

Jerry Izenberg of the *Newark Star-Ledger* is the dean of American sportswriters and one of two journalists who covered each of the first fifty-three Super Bowls. Jerry Green of the *Detroit News* is the other.

This year, Izenberg didn't go to the Super Bowl.

"I've been writing about sports for more than sixty years," Izenberg told me recently. "And for sixty years, I heard people say, 'The legs are the first thing to go.' I didn't think that applied to 89-year-old sportswriters, but my legs are the reason I'm not going this year. There's just too much walking around. Am I sad? A little bit. But I'm at peace with not going.

"I've had mixed feelings about covering the Super Bowl for a long time," Izenberg continued. "The first few Super Bowls, you could walk into the players' hotel rooms, sit on the bed, and talk with them about anything you wanted. Most of them were happy to talk with you. Now, every time I write about the Super Bowl, I feel like I'm helping promote one of the most overhyped, overblown, overwatched, overvalued spectacles in America. I have a lot of respect for the game of football and the men who play it well. I draw a distinction between my attitude toward the league, which is a study in arrogance, and the players and coaches and other people involved, some of whom are great guys."

Jim Lampley called NFL games for NBC and hosted Super Bowls for both NBC and ABC.

"In my teenage years," Lampley recalls, "very few things were as important to me as watching the Super Bowl. But I relinquished that commitment long ago. For me, the game has lost its majesty and magnetism. Part of that is the oppressively commercial nature of it all. And part of it is what the game represents in American culture today and the way I fit into the culture"

Robert Lipsyte has been writing about the role of sports in American society since the 1960s. If Izenberg is the dean of American sportswriters, then Lipsyte is a tenured professor.

In a recent article for the *National Memo*, Lipsyte outlined the ways in which he thinks that the NFL today mirrors some of the more troubling aspects of contemporary American life. Among the negatives he listed are the normalization of brutality, controlling the media, unfair hiring practices, and crushing dissent.

"Watching the Super Bowl," Lipsyte concluded, "is casting a vote for the values that have helped bring us the show most dangerous to our survival as a civilization, the Trump administration."

In recent years, the playing of the National Anthem at football games has become a flashpoint for debate.

Whitney Houston's rendition of the anthem at Super Bowl XXV (January 27, 1991) was the most memorable to date. Other anthem singers have included Barry Manilow, Neil Diamond, Billy Joel, Garth Brooks, and Mariah Carey, There was no anthem in 1977. Instead, Vikki Carr sang "America the Beautiful."

Prior to a 2016 NFL pre-season game, Colin Kaepernick knelt during the playing of the National Anthem. What began as a protest against the inappropriate use of force by a minority of police officers against people of color and the inadequate response of the criminal justice system to these incidents grew to encompass other matters of concern to the minority community and others. Thereafter, Kaepernick's protest was twisted by his detractors into a statement of disrespect for the United States and members of the American military who put themselves in harm's way overseas.

Dallas Cowboys owner Jerry Jones has been the most vocal NFL owner in chastising Kaepernick, warning his players, "If you do not honor and stand for the flag in the way that a lot of our fans feel that you should, then you won't play."

Jones played football at the University of Arkansas and was co-captain of the Razorbacks' 1964 national championship team. He has long said that his experience on that team was a foundation stone for his successful business career. Did Jones's African American teammates get a similar boost from their playing days at Arkansas? Not exactly. What do I mean by "not exactly"? Well, Jones didn't have any African American teammates. The Southwest Conference (of which Arkansas was a member) didn't allow Black players back then.

Looking at the official Dallas Cowboys website, there's a group photo of the 2019–20 Dallas Cowboys cheerleaders. There are thirty women in the photo. Only two appear to be African American.

The Anthem at both the AFC and NFC championship game this year was sung by people of color after a huge American flag was unfurled on the field. One doesn't have to be a cynic to note that this is a league whose workforce is roughly 70 percent African American but whose thirty-two teams currently have a total of three Black head coaches.

And let's reflect for a moment on the Washington Redskins. Unlike "Blackhawks" and "Braves," "Redskins" is a derogatory term. Want proof? Use the term "Redskins" in a sentence that doesn't carry a negative connotation and is unrelated to the National Football League.

I feel disaffected by a lot of what's happening in America today. As the regular NFL season wound down, I began to think about not watching the Super Bowl this year.

A single vote doesn't matter in a presidential election. We vote because we're part of something much larger than ourselves and because each of is making a statement regarding our individual values. When I contribute financially to a major charity, I know the money I send is just a drop in the ocean of its annual funding. But I'm making a statement and choosing to be part of a larger whole.

By not watching the Super Bowl, I'd be making a statement to myself by separating myself from the culture for a day.

Would I miss a Malcolm Butler moment if I didn't watch the Super Bowl this year? Maybe. Would it matter if I did? No.

Also, it occurred to me that this year's Super Bowl was being televised by FOX. And I'm not particularly fond of FOX.

Super Bowl LIV shaped up as a competitive matchup between two exciting, very good teams. Kansas City would be going to the game for the first time in fifty years. San Francisco last won the big one in 1995 but made it to Super Bowl XLVII seven years ago. The 49ers quarterback on that Sunday in 2013 was Colin Kaepernick.

Among the betting propositions posted online for this year's game were an over-under on the temperature at game time, whether or not a player would be arrested in Miami after the game, and whether Jennifer Lopez would "show butt cleavage" during her halftime performance. As I said, the Super Bowl has become a cultural touchstone in America. It's also the day when there's more gambling and (Robert Kraft, take note) more sex trafficking in the United States than on any other day of the year.

As for what I'd do while the game was in progress; the opening kickoff was scheduled for 6:30 p.m. Eastern time. That ruled out going to a museum, and it would be too cold to take a walk in the park. The best way to insulate myself from the game would be to stay home.

To fill the time, I watched *The Irishman* on Netflix. All 3 hours, 30 minutes of it, about the same length as the Super Bowl. Instead of Patrick Mahomes, Jimmy Garoppolo, and Travis Kelce, I fixed my attention on Robert De Niro, Al Pacino, and Joe Pesci.

Like the NFL, the *The Irishman* was violent. Instead of paying homage to the American flag, the mobsters professed allegiance to the Catholic Church. My telephone rang several times, but I didn't answer it or go online for scoring updates.

After *The Irishman* ended, I read a back issue of the *New Yorker*. At 10:30, I went online to check on the game, which logistics dictated would be over by then.

It had been a good game. The teams were tied 10–10 at the half. San Francisco led 20–10 midway through the fourth quarter. Then Kansas City rallied for three late touchdowns and a 31–20 victory. The Chiefs' explosion for 21 points in a 5-minute, 1-second span is now part of Super Bowl lore.

Do I regret not watching the Super Bowl this year? No. But I expect that next year I'll invite friends over for a deli spread and watch the game again.

"As a magician," Russ Anber says, "I'm talking to the audience and my hands are doing something else. That can be difficult, like giving instructions to a fighter between rounds while you're closing a cut. Your mind has to be in two places at once."

Russ Anber: The Magician

Go to YouTube. Type in "Russ Anber magic." Click on several of the videos that come up and you'll see a guy with a deck of cards. Or maybe he'll be manipulating three metal cups and some tiny balls.

"I've seen that guy before," you might say to yourself. "Wasn't he in Vasyl Lomachenko's corner?"

That's right; he was. And the corners of Oleksandr Usyk, Artur Beterbiev, Jean Pascal, Eleider Álvarez, Badou Jack, Callum Smith, Liam Smith, Mick Conlan, and Sergio Martínez.

Russ Anber was born in Montreal in 1961. When he was eleven, his family moved to a town called Sainte-Adele, fifty miles northwest of the city. His father ran a business that manufactured metal attachments for belts, motorcycle helmets, and sports equipment. His mother was a stay-at-home mom.

Anber was captivated by the boxing competition at the 1976 Montreal Olympics. The release of *Rocky* later that year further fueled his fire. Thus motivated, he embarked upon a short-lived amateur boxing career that consisted of three fights before the age of eighteen.

"It was nothing to brag about," Russ recalls. "The first two fights were at 118 pounds, and I won a decision in both of them against the same opponent. The third fight was on short notice at 126 pounds. That one is a bad memory. I was a late replacement. I wasn't ready and I was in over my head. They stopped it after the first round."

That was the end of Anber's sojourn as an active fighter. But he was hooked on boxing. He hung around. He made friends. At age eighteen, he worked Vinnie Curto's corner when the Massachusetts middleweight decisioned Marciano Bernardi in Montreal.

Things flowed from there. Since then, Anber has worked as a trainer and cutman. He has been behind the microphone as a TV commentator for the Canadian Broadcasting Corporation at six Olympic Games. In 2003, he founded Rival Boxing (a boxing equipment manufacturer). Until two years ago, he owned a gym.

Anber grew up fluent in English (his first language) and French. He has developed a good working knowledge of Spanish. He considers himself an old-school trainer. His heroes are men like Eddie Futch, Ray Arcel, and Angelo Dundee. He prides himself on his ability to work with an amateur, build a foundation under him, and guide the fighter to world-class status, as he did with Otis Grant and David Lemieux. He has also carved out a niche for himself as one of the best hand-wrappers in boxing.

Wrapping a fighter's hands is an art and a science. In boxing, as in many other athletic endeavors, specialization is now common. Many trainers no longer wrap hands or close cuts when they work a fight at the highest level. Anber learned to multitask on his way up the ladder. His skills are very much in demand.

"The hand evolved as a grip, not a club," Russ explains. "The smallest bones in the body are in your hand, and many of these bones are fragile. The key to a good handwrap is to protect the hand so the fighter can form a fist without straining and things are at just the right tension so everything is held in place without interfering with circulation in the hand."

As for Anber and magic. . . .

Magic is a universal language. Like boxing, it requires learning the mechanics of the craft, constant repetition, and dexterity with the hands. A magician's hands are as important to him as a fighter's hands are to the fighter.

"And each fighter and magician has his own personality," Anber adds. "With the great ones, whether it's boxing or magic, their personality comes out."

How did he get involved with magic?

"I was fifteen," Russ remembers. "And I got a job working in a sporting-goods store as a ski technician. Another kid who got hired at the same time was working in the tennis department and started dabbling in magic. He agreed to show me how one of his tricks was done on the understanding that I'd practice it. We were two kids with a dream. I wanted to succeed in some way in boxing and he wanted to be a magician."

"I'm not a great magician," Anber acknowledges. "My repertoire is simple. Most of it is with a deck of cards. I also do cups and balls. I'm not a stage performer. I do tricks for the fighters I work with and friends."

Who are the magicians that he admires most?

"The king has to be Dai Vernon," Russ says. "And if I was going to put three more faces on the Mount Rushmore of Modern Magicians, it would be Frank Garcia, Harry Lorayne, and Paul Harris."

What about Harry Houdini?

"Houdini performed card tricks, but he wasn't particularly skilled at them," Anber answers. "His claim to fame was as an escape artist, not a magician in the way we think of magicians today."

Asked for more thoughts on magic, Russ volunteers, "The toughest audience I ever performed for was Vasily Lomachenko and his father. They had no interest in being entertained. No, let me correct that. Their entertainment was in trying to figure out how I did the tricks. That was all they wanted to do. A few times, they figured them out. But most of the time, they couldn't."

"And this might surprise you," Anber adds. "Wladimir Klitschko is a very good amateur magician. He's the best magician I know in boxing."

So . . . if Anber had to choose between working the corner for a major championship fight or performing onstage in a major magic show, which would he choose?

"I'm not good enough to perform in a major magic show," Russ answers. "So I'll stick with what I do well and choose boxing."

And by the way . . . the fourteen-year-old kid who worked with Anber at the sporting goods store and wanted to be a magician someday was named Alain Choquette. He's now one of the most famous magicians in the world.

Fistic Nuggets

What was it like to be Muhammad Ali? Millions of words have been written about that subject. Here are a few more.

Ali loved magic and fancied himself an amateur magician. One afternoon, I was with him at Tannen's Magic Shop in midtown Manhattan. The shop was founded in 1925 and was the oldest continuously operating magic emporium in the United States. After a while, Lonnie Ali glanced at her watch and said, "Muhammad, it's getting late. We'd better go now or we'll have trouble getting a cab back to the hotel."

"Don't worry about it," Ali told her. "The police will take care of it."

So we stayed in the store until 5:30. Then we went out onto the street. As Lonnie had predicted, there were no cabs.

A passerby did a double-take. There was a request for an autograph. Several more people stopped. Soon there were twenty. And before long, more. The crowd spilled off of the sidewalk onto the street. Traffic was completely blocked.

A police car arrived to see what the problem was. It didn't take long for the officers to figure out that the only way to reopen the street was to put Ali in the police car and drive him back to his hotel.

"I told you," Muhammad told Lonnie afterward. "I knew the police would take care of it."

★ ★ ★

ESPN's ten-part series *The Last Dance* chronicled Michael Jordan's greatness as a basketball player and showed him against a series of rivals. One of these rivals was Reggie Miller, the Indiana Pacers superstar known for trash-talking with adversaries as diverse as Jordan and New York Knicks uberfan Spike Lee.

I saw a different side of Miller at an HBO party before a fight in Las Vegas. I was talking with Ann Wolfe, known to HBO viewers as James Kirkland's trainer and one of the most ferocious punchers in women's boxing. Earlier in the year, she'd scored a devastating first-round knockout of highly touted Vonda Ward—a six-foot, six-inch, 18–0 fighter who'd played basketball at the University of Tennessee.

Wolfe came from particularly hard origins. "My father was a murderer and a drug dealer," she once reminisced. "He loved me but that doesn't change what he did." She'd dropped out of school in seventh grade and later acknowledged, "I could write my name but I couldn't read at all. I lived in a house with no running water, no heat. My whole life, everybody picked on me."

Boxing was her salvation.

"I love boxing because it's the only thing I've ever done in my whole life that I was good at," Wolfe told one interviewer. "A lot of people don't like me to say it, but I truly like to knock people unconscious, out cold and flat on their back or stomach. I'll fight you till I die and it's over."

"This is a savage, murderous sport," Wolfe said on another occasion. "We're punching each other in the damn head. If you ain't trying to kill somebody, why the hell are you punching people in the head until you make them unconscious?"

But Wolfe had a charming side. And at times she was like a kid. Now, at the HBO party. . . .

"Omigod!" she exclaimed. "At that table over there. It's Reggie Miller."

So I looked. And yes, it was Reggie Miller in conversation with a friend.

"Omigod!" Wolfe said again. "He's my favorite player."

"Would you like to meet him?" I asked.

"Omigod! [that was her third "omigod"] Yes."

I'd never met Reggie Miller before. But with nothing to lose, I brought Wolfe over to his table.

"Excuse me, Mr. Miller. I apologize for intruding. But this is Ann Wolfe. She's a huge fan of yours and just wanted to say hello."

Then the unexpected happened. Miller stood up.

"I know who you are," he said with a warm welcoming smile. "I saw what you did to that basketball player. That was amazing. All props to you."

Wolfe looked as though she'd died and gone to heaven. They chatted for a minute or two. Then, not wanting to overstay her welcome, she excused herself.

"He was so nice," she told me afterward. "He made me feel like I'm somebody."

★ ★ ★

All fighters are nervous in the twenty-four hours leading up to a fight. And the condition often takes its greatest toll when a fighter is trying to sleep the night before the fight.

In 1996, Michael Grant, then a young heavyweight on the rise, asked Vernon Forrest, who was five years away from his career-defining victory over Shane Mosley, how he dealt with the problem.

"It's simple," Forrest responded. "I'm 18-and-0 with 15 knockouts. So if I'm lying in bed thinking about the other guy, I say to myself, 'Hey, he's lying in bed right now thinking about me. And I'm a lot happier right now than he is."

★ ★ ★

A cautionary tale for those who would invest in boxing.

Steve Lott (who worked for years with Bill Cayton and Jim Jacobs) was in Las Vegas when Craig Hamilton (who co-managed Michael Grant with Cayton) asked Steve if he'd like to join him at the blackjack table.

"Do you see all those guys playing blackjack?" Steve responded. "Most of them are playing now just to get even. I'm already even."

Think about that before investing in boxing. If you like the action, fine. But the action can be very expensive. And most investors don't get back to even.

Issues and Answers

This was among the most important articles I wrote in 2020.

An Email from a Reader

On March 22, 2020, I posted an article on Boxing Scene titled "Muhammad Ali and the Coronavirus." Some reader comments in the Boxing Forum were favorable. Others were not:

* "Who gives a shit what Ali would have thought. He doesn't think, he's gone."
* "This is the dumbest article I ever read in my life. WTF does Ali have to do with the coronavirus pandemic?"

I received several emails telling me that it was unfair to speculate as to what Ali might have thought about the coronavirus. Lonnie Ali and the Muhammad Ali Center in Louisville disagreed with that criticism and posted the article on the Ali Center website.

I also received an email that read, "Who cares what a dead nigger would have thought about the coronavirus."

There is a virus spreading across America that has nothing to do with COVID-19. Racism has existed since the dawn of civilization. Like other plagues, it returns in more virulent form from time to time.

I think we can assume that the writer of the "nigger" email is a bigot and proud of his (or her) bigotry. There have always been people like that. Once upon a time, open expressions of bigotry were common. Then those utterances became unacceptable to most Americans. They might have been bandied about in back rooms and bars. But they were denounced by people of conscience. I'm not talking about "political correctness." I'm talking about basic decency.

Now, once again, people are reinforcing each other in their prejudices. There's a boldness to the hate that's creating an environment that older generations saw when Andrew Goodman, Michael Schwerner, and James Chaney were murdered in Mississippi and Matthew Shepard was murdered in Wyoming. Neo-Nazis are coming out of the closet. People are proud of their bigotries.

I get emails from readers on a regular basis. Many of them are well thought out, including some that disagree with me. On one occasion, a reader took me to task for a column I'd written and made his points so well that I helped him get his email published as a column. That led to a two-year stint as a paid columnist for a website until he went on to other things.

I also get emails from people who tell me that Barack Obama was born in Kenya and was responsible for 9/11 because he was aware of the plot and did nothing to stop it. This ignores the fact that George W. Bush was president on September 11, 2001. Obama was an Illinois state legislator at the time and didn't become president until January 20, 2009.

Chatrooms reach a wider audience than person-to-person emails. Letters to the editor of a publication must meet certain standards to be published. Chatrooms are often guided by the mantra "anything goes."

Some chatroom comments are intelligently expressed. Whether or not I agree with them, they represent a point of view that, like mine, deserves to be heard. But I'm astounded by the ignorance of some of the people who comment. They say whatever they want to say without knowing the facts and without regard to accuracy or truth.

"Everyone knows that Hauser is on the take from Arum. . . . Everyone knows that Hauser hates Arum. . . . Haymon must have paid Hauser to write this article. . . . Hauser hates successful Black people."

On March 14, 2020, three days after the National Basketball Association announced that it was canceling all games until further notice and one day after a Top Rank fight card at Madison Square Garden was canceled, I posted a column on The Sweet Science about the burgeoning coronavirus pandemic and its impact on sports.

Two days later, using a pseudonym, a reader went into the "fight forum," attacked reports about the coronavirus as "a LIE," and grouped me with "leftist treasonists all too happy to be a part of this disruption to our economy. The real viral outbreak," the comment continued, "is TRUMP DERANGEMENT SYNDROME, aka TDS!! Look at how it's destroying our country."

The comment was removed from the forum because of a website policy that precludes posting certain types of statements (including inaccurate information that threatens public safety or health).

I later learned the identity of the person who had posted the comment. He actually writes occasionally for the website in question. I'd met him once before. He thinks I'm a "leftist treasonist." I think he's an ignorant coward who hides behind the anonymity of posting on social media.

Last Sunday (May 31), I posted an article—again, on Boxing Scene—titled "Which Active Fighters Deserve to Be Called Great?" I quoted Larry Holmes as saying, "What makes a fighter great is the opponents he beats." I then added, "Boxing's current business model deprives elite fighters of the opportunity to prove and improve upon their skills by fighting other elite fighters. Except on rare occasions, the best no longer fight the best. We don't know what most of today's top pound-for-pound fighters would do if faced with an abundantly skilled opponent who asks questions of them that they haven't been asked before. Instead, we're left to speculate as to which fighters might someday be great or might have been great if only they'd fought the best."

Manny Pacquiao, I concluded, definitely deserves to be called "great." I also listed nine other active fighters—Terence Crawford, Vasyl Lomachenko, Mikey Garcia, Gennady Golovkin, Oleksandr Usyk, Naoya Inoue, Román González, Tyson Fury, and Canelo Álvarez—and voiced the opinion that, based on his accomplishments to date, Canelo is the most deserving of the group.

The first "comment" posted in response to the article began, "thomas huaser the fraud!" (either the poster couldn't type or he couldn't spell; I'm not sure which) and accused me of writing "fake news."

Another correspondent complained, "Hauser doesn't even mention Inoue here." Actually, I did.

A third rocket scientist let it all hang out: "What a rubbish article. No wonder Hauser hasn't written a book since 2004. And this clown is going to be in the HOF [Hall of Fame] himself? Shows you what a joke that is."

This is typical of the "say anything you want without regard to facts" approach. For the record, I've published twenty-three books since 2004. This includes fifteen collections of articles about boxing (published annually by the University of Arkansas Press), five collections of essays on subjects ranging from race relations to the Beatles, and three novels. One of the novels was about Charles Dickens. Rocket Scientist might not have heard of Dickens, but he was a famous English author.

My point is this. If you disagree with me, fine. You're just as entitled to your opinion as I am to mine. But get your facts right. And don't debase the dialogue with stupid, unfounded accusations.

Let's state the obvious. Discussions about which active fighters today are "great" are insignificant when set against America's current national trauma. But boxing forums offer a window onto what exists at present in other realms of social media. A lot of people use social media responsibly. But too often, their voices are drowned out.

There have always been ignorant, mean-spirited people on both sides of the dialogue. But now these people have a platform, and standards for discussion have dropped

It's getting harder and harder to stand up to the mob. Bullies are often the loudest kids in the schoolyard and make the most noise. Shouting louder than anyone else and saying outrageous things gets attention. The default mode for too many people is to criticize and attack.

But it's more than a loss of civility. Too many people say anything they want without regard to truth. The "facts" are whatever they want them to be. The crux of what they write is often a crude attack based on race, religion, or sexual orientation. And too many people support whatever the speaker says as long as their own biases are reaffirmed.

This behavior has been normalized. It trickles down from the top and oozes up from the bottom. Rather than bring us together, social media has divided us by algorithms that push divisive content to users who lose sight of how they're being manipulated. Anyone with any belief set can find a group of like-minded people on social media.

But there are also heartening examples of positive dialogue.

On May 17, I posted an article on Boxing Scene titled "What Will Fans See When Boxing Comes Back?"

A week later, I received an email from a reader. I've taken the liberty of excerpting it here.

"This is an interesting article," the email began, "and I do not want to comment too much due to the fact I have to check into a few facts."

That in itself was a refreshing start. Fact-check rather than—as we used to say before guns became a political flashpoint—shooting from the hip.

Then the letter evolved into something very different from the average reader email that I get: "Deception and corruption and just dirty dealing are being done to American workers right now. Those that work in retail in this country and are being sent back to work or told, 'If you do not return, there will be no unemployment insurance for you. If you decide not to return to work under whatever conditions we deem acceptable, you will have no pay.' That means to some of us, NO FOOD NO SHELTER. That means being thrown into deep poverty. Deep poverty eats away at your pockets rather rapidly. Then it eats away at your insides. Not just from lack of food but the inability to continue to take the humiliation that comes with being out of work and broke in this country. You become the enemy. You are no longer a citizen. You would have had to experience it to know it, TH.

"I am not looking to school you or anyone," the email continued. "But this country has been exposed. This entire system has been exposed. And the whole sports world has been exposed. Those that blindly run toward the stadiums and the arenas are being fed a lie. If people cannot go without sports for a few years, I feel for them. And is it really sports that is important or is it just money? Sports used to be something that the average guy could identify with. Could relate to. Could afford to go to. He felt part of it. Now, more and more, I see the sports fan as a sucker. All he is is an irritant to be tolerated while the athletes perform. Let the games begin. Keep sports relevant. Then knock off this dying from a virus talk."

I've also thought a lot recently about an article I wrote in April 2008 titled "Hypocrisy at West Point." The article was critical of a policy called the "alternative service option" that had been adopted by the United States Military Academy in 2005.

The purpose of the alternative service option was to resurrect the football program at West Point. In the five years prior to its adoption, Army's gridiron record was a pitiful 5 wins and 53 losses. The alternative service option released cadets who had "unique talents and abilities" (i.e., were good enough to play in a major professional sports league) from their commitment to serve five years of active duty in the Army. I was highly critical of the option and wrote accordingly.

A boxing website is a strange place to spark a debate about United States military policy. But that's precisely what happened. "Hypocrisy at West Point" was discussed at length in service academy chatrooms. Then the debate rose to a higher level. In July 2008, the alternative service option was rescinded by the Department of Defense. It was reinstated earlier this year by Donald Trump.

Meanwhile, I was surprised by the outpouring of email that I received in response to the article—close to three hundred emails in all. The overwhelming majority were from service academy graduates.

I've always respected the service academies. To be admitted into these places, a young man or woman needs a high degree of intelligence, analytical ability, and motivation. Equally important, they are told, "For the rest of your life, you will be representing the academy. You should express yourself accordingly."

The emails that I received raised my respect to new heights. They were thoughtful. They were well written. They took the exchange of ideas to an even higher level.

They also educated me.

In "Hypocrisy at West Point," I'd made a thoughtless remark about the United States Military Academy motto. More than a few readers (many of whom agreed with my position on the alternative service option) took issue with that remark. And they were right. Thus, in a follow-up column titled "West Point Revisited," I closed with the following:

"A lot of thought went into the views expressed [by the service academy graduates] above. I want to add one last thought of my own to them. My previous article contained a reference to the United States Military Academy motto: 'Duty, Honor, Country.' General Douglas MacArthur, in his Farewell Speech to the Corps of Cadets at West Point, referred to 'those three hallowed words' as 'an expression of the ethics of the American soldier' and 'a great moral code.' The reference I made to the motto was disrespectful and inappropriate. I apologize for it."

Several days later, I received another email, this one from a 1985 United States Military Academy graduate who wrote, "Sir, Both your original and follow-up articles were forwarded by a fellow graduate of West Point. I read them both. As a military man, I am skeptical of the intentions of the media in general when it comes to my chosen profession of arms. But I do not have to agree with a man to read and learn from his work. I only have to respect him. Your concluding thought in the 'West Point Revisited' article told me all I need to know about you. You are an upright man who can respect the military and the ideals to which we hold ourselves. Therefore, I can respect you and your point of view."

That's how issues of public interest should be debated and discussed.

Investigative reporting is an important check on government.

Politics, Problems, and Power at the New York State Athletic Commission

Part One

The New York State Athletic Commission is important. Fights at Madison Square Garden and Barclays Center are within its domain. Although its budget is shielded from scrutiny by an arcane financial structure (not even the commissioners and executive director know the actual numbers), it appears as though the NYSAC has the second-largest operating budget of any state athletic commission in the country.

Over the years, the New York State inspector general has conducted multiple investigations of wrongdoing at the commission. The most publicized of these investigations occurred after heavyweight Magomed Abdusalamov suffered severe brain damage in a 2013 fight at Madison Square Garden. The subsequent report of the inspector general (which covered a wide range of issues, many of which were unrelated to Abdusalamov) documented numerous instances of incompetence and corruption at the NYSAC. Ultimately, the State of New York paid $22 million to Abdusalamov and his family to settle claims alleging substandard medical protocols and improper conduct by NYSAC personnel.

The NYSAC has long been a favor bank for powerful economic interests and a source of employment at various levels for the politically well connected. There have been periods of good oversight, most notably during the tenure of David Berlin, who served as executive director of the commission from May 2014 through May 2016. Then Berlin was jettisoned because too often, his commitment to good governance was at odds with political expediency.

The New York State Athletic Commission falls within the jurisdiction of New York's Department of State. This places it under the control of Governor Andrew Cuomo. The Department of State hires and fires key NYSAC personnel.

Some conscientious, dedicated public servants work at the NYSAC. But too often, political connections take priority over performance. This applies to some—not all—fulltime jobs at the commission, as well as the selection of fight-night officials such as inspectors, referees, and judges.

Now, at the start of 2020, the commission is failing to deal constructively with multiple issues that threaten fighter safety and ignoring a situation that might become a significant financial scandal.

Multiple sources say that Assistant Executive Deputy Secretary of State James Leary is the primary liaison between Governor Cuomo's office and the NYSAC. "Jim is a competent attorney and very much a part of the political system," a lawyer who knows Leary says.

Another attorney who has worked with Leary and NYSAC executive director Kim Sumbler adds, "Everything of importance at the commission is now approved at or above the Jim Leary level. Kim can take small steps but that's all."

There's also an obsession with secrecy at the NYSAC that at times is bizarre. Let a simple example suffice.

In September 2018, Theresa D'Andrea was assigned by the Department of State to the position of fulltime counsel for the NYSAC. D'Andrea had no apparent legal expertise relating to combat sports. She had to feel her way through the nuts-and-bolts issues inherent in her job on a day-to-day basis. Her precise duties at the commission were unclear, although several commission employees reported that she was responsible for recording RSVPs for a January 4, 2019, office holiday party that were sent to almost one hundred commission personnel. This seems like an inefficient use of state resources for an attorney whose salary was listed by the state as $123,000 a year.

On October 23, 2019, this writer was told that D'Andrea was no longer with the NYSAC. To confirm this information, I emailed Mercedes Padilla (the official spokesperson for the commission). The email to Padilla read in full: "Dear Mercedes, Is Theresa D'Andrea still counsel for the NYSAC? Thank you. Thomas Hauser."

The following morning, Padilla emailed back, "Yes, she is."

I followed up with, "Are you certain? Several people at the weigh-in yesterday said that she had left the position."

Padilla responded, "Hi Tom, We do not comment on personnel matters."

Does anyone think that's an appropriate response from a government agency?

There have been an increasing number of complaints from commission employees about absentee leadership.

The New York State Athletic Commission is located at 123 William Street in Manhattan (one of New York City's five boroughs). Kim Sumbler's Facebook page lists her as living in Ontario (which, for the uninitiated, is in Canada, not New York). The Office of the Inspector General has been told (and is satisfied with the explanation) that Sumbler works at home and out of a Department of State office in Buffalo. Director of Boxing Matt Delaglio and Director of Mixed Martial Arts Ed Kunkle (both of whom are well regarded within the combat sports community) carry the ball in New York when Sumbler is absent from the NYSAC office.

The NYSAC has five commissioners who, in theory, are charged with making policy for the commission. But the commissioners rarely, if ever, discuss issues of importance. In some instances they aren't even aware of them. One of the commissioners—Dr. James Vosswinkel—attends fights, employee training sessions, and other commission-related events on a regular basis. The other four commissioners are largely uninvolved.

Many of the commission's per diem employees are poorly trained. It doesn't help for an inspector to watch a fighter's hands being wrapped in the dressing room before a fight if the inspector doesn't know what to look for.

One of the most counterproductive practices at the NYSAC today is that there are times when an employee is "written up" by a supervisor for a breach of protocol or other misdeed, but the supervisor is told to not discuss it with the employee. The logic behind this practice is that confronting the employee directly would risk alienating the employee. An alienated employee might complain to a political backer or take legal action against the commission, but it's good to have a record of misdeeds on file in case the employee sues the NYSAC later on. The ill-advised nature of this practice is evident in that (1) the complaint against the employee might be unfounded, but the employee isn't given the opportunity to rebut it, and (2) if the employee isn't told that a problem exists, it increases the likelihood that the employee will make the same mistake again and again.

Poor judging and refereeing are also cause for concern in New York.

Two gross mismatches on an April 10, 2019, fight card at Sony Hall showed boxing at its worst. In the fifth bout of the evening, Alicia

Napoleon knocked Eva Bajic down twice in the second round. Each time, she punched Bajic after the knockdown but the referee seemed to not notice. In the next bout, Bakhodir Jalolov knocked Brendan Barrett down twice in the first stanza. Following the second knockdown, Jalolov punched Barrett while Barrett was on the canvas. Again, the referee let it pass.

Watching some of the NYSAC's lesser judges for an entire round can be a troubling experience. There are times when the fight is in one part of the ring and a judge is looking at another. On other occasions, the judges seem to be following the action but how they're processing it is unsettling.

June 1, 2019, was an important night for boxing in New York. In an early undercard fight, Josh Kelly was on the receiving end of a gift draw against Ray Robinson that left many fans shaking their heads. Then former Irish Olympian Katie Taylor (who, like Kelly, was the "house" fighter) was awarded a 96–94, 96–94, 95–95 decision over Delfine Persoon. Taylor has many fans, and deservedly so. But even her admirers questioned the decision.

Belfast native Carl Frampton (the 2016 Boxing Writers Association of America "Fighter of the Year") told BBC Radio 5, "The judges have got it wrong, and it is heartbreaking to see Delfine Persoon in tears. I thought she won that fight by miles. That was a disgraceful decision." Former WBA heavyweight beltholder David Haye added, "That is not the sight you want to see where someone has given everything in the gym but they do not get the decision because of the political power." Even Eddie Hearn (Taylor's promoter) acknowledged that he'd scored the fight a draw and conceded, "Quite a few people had Persoon winning."

There was worse to come. In the main event, Andy Ruiz dominated Anthony Joshua en route to a seventh-round knockout. At the time of the stoppage, two of the judges had Ruiz ahead by a meager one point and the third judge had Joshua leading by a 57–56 margin.

One week later, on the undercard of Gennady Golovkin vs. Steve Rolls, an even stranger scorecard was turned in at Madison Square Garden. In the third fight of the evening, Charles Conwell squared off against Courtney Pennington. Conwell clearly dominated the first half of the fight. Judge Ken Ezzo scored the first six rounds in his favor while judge Mark Consentino gave him six of the first seven. Alan Rubenstein inexplicably scored the first four rounds for Pennington.

Rubenstein's scorecard was so off the mark that, after the fourth stanza, a deputy commissioner was dispatched to ask him if he'd confused which fighter was which. That's hard to confuse, since the cards filled out by judges after each round clearly designate a "red" and "blue" corner. Rubenstein denied that he had confused the fighters. Pennington then rallied in the second half of the fight, winning three and two of the last four rounds on Ezzo's and Consentino's respective scorecards. But after being questioned about his scoring, Rubenstein scored all six of the final rounds in favor of Conwell.

Asked for comment on Rubenstein's scorecard, Lee Park (who at the time was the Department of State spokesperson for the NYSAC) responded, "We have no comment."

After the death of Maxim Dadashev from injuries sustained during a fight on ESPN+, ESPN commentator Teddy Atlas put the cost of poor judging in perspective.

"Anytime a fighter steps into the ring," Atlas declared, "they leave the ring with less of themselves. It's just a matter of how much less. That's why I can be so harsh sometimes in calling out the administrators of the sport when the judges don't do their job and they take a decision away from a fighter. We're not in baseball. We're not in a sport where, if you're robbed of a base hit, you get a chance to come up the next inning. We're in a sport where, if you're robbed of a win, you go back in the line and you may have to take thousands of punches more, many fights more, before you get back to that position where you can get out of the sport, where you can make the money, take care of your family, where you can achieve the things that you're in the sport to achieve. So every time one of the administrators, the so-called protectors of the sport, the judges and the officials, don't do their job properly, it puts a fighter at more risk than they should be."

There's a lack of common sense at the New York State Athletic Commission with regard to matters large and small.

At the small end of the spectrum, on March 17, 2019, Top Rank promoted a St. Patrick's Day card at Madison Square Garden. One of the undercard bouts saw Ireland's Paddy Barnes in the ring against Oscar Mojica. The NYSAC doctor assigned to Mojica's corner wore bright green pants and a green blouse in celebration of the holiday. Under normal circumstances, that would have been an acceptable fashion choice. But on St.

Patrick's Day, it was akin to a supposedly neutral official wearing a Paddy Barnes corner jacket while in Mojica's corner.

On a more troubling note, the NYSAC is mired in the Dark Ages when it comes to technology. For example, some trainers now use smartphones in the corner during a fight.

"I know for a fact that communications devices are being used in the corner in New York," promoter Lou DiBella said last year. "The trainer is there with a cell phone in his pocket and an earbud or Bluetooth in his ear. He gets information while the fight is going on, and sometimes it can give his fighter a competitive advantage."

The National Football League forbids the use of electronic coaching aids such as smartphones that might give one team or the other a competitive edge during the course of a game. Major League Baseball is currently dealing with an electronic cheating scandal and taking forceful steps to combat it.

Some state athletic commissions (such as California's and Nevada's) limit the use of smartphones in a fighter's corner during fights. The NYSAC has washed its hands of the issue.

Similarly, other states with significant boxing programs—Nevada, California, and New Jersey among them—utilize instant video review to correct miscalls by referees. New York does not. The folly of New York's position was made clear when Gennady Golovkin fought Sergiy Derevyanchenko at Madison Square Garden on October 5, 2019. In round two of that bout, a left hook from Golovkin landed cleanly and opened an ugly gash on Derevyanchenko's right eyelid. Harvey Dock (an excellent referee) mistakenly ruled that the cut had been caused by an accidental head butt. Because the New York State Athletic Commission doesn't allow for instant video review, Dock's ruling stood despite clear video evidence to the contrary. Had the fight ultimately been stopped because of the cut with Derevyanchenko leading on the judges' scorecards, the inequity of the result would have been enormous.

By way of contrast, thirteen days later, Artur Beterbiev fought Oleksandr Gvozdyk in Philadelphia. Late in round one, Beterbiev shoved Gvozdyk, who then tripped over Artur's foot and fell to the canvas. Referee Gary Rosato mistakenly called the incident a knockdown, which, at the time, loomed large. Gvozdyk had been winning the round, so the call represented a possible three-point swing on the judges' scorecards.

In New York, Rosato's miscall would have stood. But the Pennsylvania State Athletic Commission is run by Greg Sirb (one of the best boxing overseers in the country). Sirb quickly reviewed the video and, before the start of the second round, changed the call to "no knockdown."

Golovkin's October 5 fight against Derevyanchenko also highlighted how sloppy the NYSAC's oversight of fights can be.

Golovkin didn't come to the commission meeting one day before the fight when the gloves that the fighters would wear were selected. His trainer (Johnathon Banks) did and chose Gennady's gloves. Then, a half hour later, the NYSAC was told that Golovkin didn't like the gloves and wanted to switch to a pair that had been chosen by Nikita Ababiy (an undercard fighter). The change was approved by the NYSAC with the permission of the Derevyanchenko and Ababiy camps, and that was that. Until fight night.

On fight night, Ababiy found that the thumb on one of the gloves he'd gotten from Golovkin didn't fit comfortably and, shortly before he went to the ring, he had to reglove. Meanwhile—and more significantly—during Golovkin–Derevyanchenko, the padding in Gennady's left glove shifted and the punching area of his glove collapsed as though an indentation had been made by a half-orange. This is similar in principle to a glove splitting during a bout. The fight should have been stopped and the glove replaced. But the inspectors assigned to Golovkin's corner either didn't notice the problem or decided to let it pass.

After the fight, an NYSAC deputy commissioner examined—at least, in theory—Golovkin's gloves in the ring, and the lead inspector assigned to Gennady's corner filled out an "NYSAC Inspector Worksheet." The standard NYSAC Worksheet has a line that reads "Gloves Examined post-fight." In this instance, the "yes" box next to that entry was checked, but the glove irregularity wasn't noted.

The damage to Golovkin's glove was a health and safety issue. Possible implications included the loss of protection for Gennady's hands and increased damage to Derevyanchenko's face from punches. But that's the least of the health and safety issues facing the New York State Athletic Commission today.

Part Two

Nitin Sethi, a neurologist whose primary practice is affiliated with Weill Cornell Medicine (one of the best research and patient care centers in the world), is chief medical officer for the New York State Athletic Commission.

Dr. Sethi (who acknowledges that "no amount of boxing is good for the brain") devotes an enormous amount of time and energy to his part-time job with the commission. He's at the NYSAC for all the right reasons. It's not the money. It's not an ego trip. Sethi cares about boxing and its practitioners. In an October 2019 article for the *Journal of Combat Sports Medicine*, he wrote, "While ethical issues surrounding boxing have and continue to be passionately debated, the sport is here to stay and the passion and love for the sweet science is shared by millions around the world. Hence a more realistic goal for ringside physicians should be to help make this sport as safe as possible."

Sethi is a valuable asset to the NYSAC. One might take issue with some of his initiatives (such as extending the one-minute rest period between rounds to allow for an extended examination of fighters by a commission doctor). But he has been steadfast in his commitment to protecting the heath and safety of fighters, which, for too many in boxing, is little more than a rhetorical device.

One area where Sethi has excelled is in stopping fights when they should be stopped. A fighter's corner and sometimes even the referee might be concerned about whether the decision to stop a fight will cost them their next big payday. The ring doctor is concerned only with protecting the health and safety of the fighter.

This concern exposed Sethi to merciless, ignorant online attacks following UFC 244 at Madison Square Garden when he stopped the bout between Nate Diaz and Jorge Masvidal because of a horrific cut above Diaz's right eye. The attacks that followed included ethnic slurs and attempts to damage Sethi's reputation by posting fake patient reviews. Thereafter, neither the NYSAC nor the Association of Ringside Physicians supported Sethi as forcefully as they should have. But Sethi made the right call that night.

"I just did my job and stopped the fight when I was unable to guarantee the health and safety of the combatant going forward," he said afterward.

"My assessment was objective, based entirely on the medical facts in front of me at that time and based on my overall assessment of the fighter and not just the laceration. I am glad I did what I was there for. If I had not, I would have let myself down in my own eyes and those of people whom I respect very much."

But Sethi is limited in what he can accomplish at the NYSAC. Too often, the commission overlords play politics with medical issues.

"You'd think that, after the human tragedy of Magomed Abdusalamov and paying twenty-two million dollars to settle that case, the commission would do everything possible to clean up its act," one member of the boxing community notes. "But that hasn't happened."

Nowhere is this failure more evident than in the NYSAC's handling of issues relating to performance-enhancing drugs (PEDs). "We keep talking about improving our PED program," one frustrated commission employee says. "We talk about it, but we don't do it."

A fighter can lose his or her life in the ring. As Tris Dixon recently wrote, "There are few worse crimes in all of sport than allowing one person a physical advantage over another when the physical stakes are so high."

But the NYSAC's drug-testing program is fundamentally flawed. The commission takes a pre-fight urine sample from each fighter on fight night. For championship bouts, a post-fight urine sample is also taken. In today's world of micro-dosing, having fighters urinate into a cup on fight night without more is a grossly inadequate PED-testing program.

The New York State Athletic Commission has an outdated prohibited-drug list and refuses to incorporate the World Anti-Doping Agency's prohibited list by reference or separately list the substances banned by WADA. Thus, as things now stand, erythropoietin (EPO), blood doping, and meldonium—each of which is banned by every credible jurisdiction—are not banned by the NYSAC.

Neither Quest Diagnostics nor LabCorp (where the NYSAC sends blood and urine samples) is accredited by WADA.

Last spring, the New Jersey State Athletic Control Board "busted" two MMA combatants for illegal PED use. One of the fighters talked openly with New Jersey deputy attorney general Nick Lembo and told him that he'd been using the same substance for years in New York, so he assumed it wouldn't be a problem in New Jersey.

The case of Jarrell Miller is instructive with regard to the NYSAC's attitude toward banned performance-enhancing drugs.

On April 16, 2019, it was revealed that Miller (who had signed to fight Anthony Joshua at Madison Square Garden) had tested positive with the Voluntary Anti-Doping Association (VADA) for the banned substance GW1516. Two days later, VADA notified the NYSAC that a blood sample taken from Miller had tested positive for human growth hormone (a substance that, is banned by WADA but, inexplicably, not by New York). Then, on April 19, it was announced that a urine sample taken from Miller by VADA had come back positive for EPO (another performance-enhancing drug that's widely banned but not in New York). But the NYSAC refused to suspend Miller for the GW1516, claiming that it was unable to do so because he wasn't licensed in New York.

Pat English might be the best "boxing lawyer" in the country. He has represented Main Events for decades and is well versed in the federal and state regulations that govern the sweet science as well as the ins and outs of illegal PED use in boxing.

On April 29, 2019, English (who is on the legal committee of the Association of Boxing Commissions) sent a letter to the ABC executive board bemoaning the fact that "certain commissions are completely ignoring their responsibilities under the Professional Boxing Health and Safety Act" and "it appears as though some commissions do not understand the extent of their authority to issue suspensions."

English's letter went on to state, "It now appears that certain commissions are 'passing the trash.'" It then referenced "fighters who fail drug tests but are not placed on suspension" and declared, "An egregious example of this is the recent Jarrell Miller situation."

"Some commissions," English wrote, "have evaded their responsibilities by claiming that the fighter in question is not licensed in their state. The Miller situation is one of many examples. He was to fight in Madison Square Garden in June. The fight had been announced and Miller, a New York resident, had put in his renewal forms for his expired license. New York denied the license but it did not suspend Miller since he was not a licensee. This is circular logic and it misses the point. The suspension of a right to box is not synonymous with licensure. This is well established in other areas of law. If an individual's driver's license is suspended due to a

DWI conviction, the suspension does not end when his license expires. It continues during the period set forth by the court. Placing an individual on the suspension list is not limited by whether a fighter is currently licensed in a given state, and the failure to do so under appropriate circumstances is a failure to live up to a commission's responsibilities."

On April 30, 2019, ABC president Mike Mazzuli forwarded English's letter to NYSAC executive director Kim Sumbler with the notation, "You may want to use this with your attorneys. I do not disagree with Pat."

That same day, Sumbler responded to Mazzuli by email, writing, "As much as I don't appreciate his inference that NY is 'passing the trash,' I don't disagree with his argument and reasoning. I passed it up the chain for review."

Two minutes later, Mazzuli emailed back, "It was more than just Miller's suspension."

Sumbler concurred with a one-word reply: "True."

That afternoon, four of the five NYSAC commissioners convened for a prescheduled meeting. Commissioners James Vosswinkel, Philip Stieg, and Edwin Torres were present at the NYSAC office at 123 William Street in New York. Commissioner Donald Patterson and Kim Sumbler participated by telephone. Commissioner Ndidi Massay did not attend.

The commission voted to allow the executive director to approve the insertion of data-tracking chips made by Sportsmedia Technology Corporation in gloves during MMA contests.

Next, Sumbler read from a written statement noting that, "The commission staff has encountered scenarios where a professional boxer is wearing tassels around his or her shoe which fall off during the course of a bout and create a potential safety concern inside the ring or can distract the referee who now has to remove the fallen tassels from inside the ring."

In light of this perceived danger to the health, safety, and welfare of fighters, the commission then voted to approve protocols that regulate the wearing of tassels in combat sports.

There was no discussion of Jarrell Miller or performance-enhancing drugs. This is the equivalent of motorists drag-racing regularly down a city street and law enforcement authorities failing to halt the races, but saying that the cars involved can't hang fuzzy dice from rear-view mirrors unless the dice are properly attached.

The entire meeting lasted less than thirty minutes.

Two days later, on May 2 in a letter to the Association of Boxing Commissions executive board, Sumbler took issue with Pat English's April 29 letter and maintained, "The commission does not have any jurisdiction to suspend an applicant, but, rather, may only suspend an individual after he or she has received a New York State license." In making this statement, she relied on a single court case that had been decided twelve years earlier.

That elicited a same-day response from English, who wrote to Sumbler (with a copy to the ABC board), "The case you refer to appears to have been badly litigated on the part of the State [and] involves a suspension which probably should never have been issued since at least one other state and possibly two had looked at the same MRI and issued licenses. It is an opinion issued by the lowest level Court in New York which is not binding on any other trial Court involving very different facts."

English then added, "I see more than twenty years worth of work in the formulation of the Professional Boxing Health and Safety Act, the Muhammad Ali Act, mandatory adherence to the suspension list, and years of ABC work pushed backward by actions (or inactions) by some in situations such as the Miller situation, most often by folks who have no background whatsoever in fighter health and safety and sometimes by those with no understanding of the sport at all. That is, to me, morally repugnant. Kim, it is obvious to me that, while the letter was sent out under your name, you did not write it. It has the ring of someone trying to justify a position rather than attempting to find a solution towards a just result. Such people, to use 1960s phraseology, are part of the problem, not part of the solution."

On May 6, English sent another letter to Sumbler and the ABC executive board in which he pointed out, "Miller's Federal ID is issued by New York. The ID application form reads in part: 'Boxer agrees to abide by these terms and conditions [the Rules and Regulations of the New York State Athletic Commission] and any other rules set forth by the ABC and the Boxing Commission that issued the identification card.' By using PEDs, Miller obviously violated rules of the New York State Athletic Commission in violation of his signed application for an ID. The application form which Miller would have signed also states: 'Any false or misleading statements on this application may result in the Boxer being placed on the National Suspension list.' Frankly, if that does not give New York jurisdiction to suspend his Federal ID, I do not know what does. The language on the form signed by Miller is clear and unambiguous."

As I've written before, Jarrell Miller isn't the problem. He's a symptom of the problem. There are many elite fighters who are equally culpable of using banned performance-enhancing drugs. Miller was just less sophisticated than they are and got caught. But New York, which (unlike most states) has the resources to deal with boxing's PED problem, has made a conscious decision to not confront the issue in a meaningful way.

Contrast New York's handling of PED issues with the approach taken in recent years by the Nevada State Athletic Commission. In early 2018, the NSAC pulled down what was shaping up as the biggest fight of the year after Canelo Álvarez tested positive for clenbuterol. This past October, the NSAC indefinitely suspended Julio César Chávez Jr. (who was not yet licensed by the state) after Chávez refused to provide the Voluntary Anti-Doping Association with a urine sample that the Nevada commission had requested. It's not hard to figure out which of these two states—Nevada or New York—is making a serious effort to combat the use of banned performance-enhancing drugs in boxing.

So . . . what's really going on in New York?

One reliable source says that Kim Sumbler told him she's "hamstrung by the people above me" on the issue of performance-enhancing drugs. A second, equally reliable source says she told him that she has wanted to act more forcefully at times on the issue of PEDs but was told she couldn't do it. Sumbler declined to be interviewed for this article, as did James Leary and James Vosswinkel.

Who, then, is making PED policy at the New York State Athletic Commission? The commissioners aren't discussing PEDs in any meaningful way. The Medical Advisory Board isn't meeting (more on that shortly). The answer is that, right now, outside lobbyists are transmitting their wishes to the Cuomo administration, which then filters them down to the NYSAC in the form of directives through the Department of State.

If Jarrell Miller had been suspended, that might have resulted in litigation. And litigation would have run the risk of opening up a Pandora's box with regard to PEDs and the New York State Athletic Commission. Miller's

legal team might have focused on the fact that Jermall and Jermell Charlo
were allowed to fight at Barclays Center after "missing" VADA tests. It
might have argued that, had Miller's sample been collected by the NYSAC
and tested by Quest or LabCorp pursuant to current NYSAC protocols,
the GW1516 wouldn't have been detected. It might have drawn attention
to the gaping holes in the NYSAC's list of prohibited drugs.

The powers that be who actually control the NYSAC from above
(including lobbyists) don't want that. They're more concerned with their
own economic interests than the health and safety of fighters and the integrity of combat sports. An effective, vigilant program to curtail the use of
banned PEDs might drive big fights away from New York (as happened in
Nevada when the December 14, 2019, fight between Danny Jacobs and
Julio César Chávez Jr. was moved from Las Vegas to Phoenix).

The NYSAC medical staff has to take control of PED policy and do
what's right to limit the inevitable human damage that flows from illegal
PED use in combat sports. The commissioners won't do it. That was made
abundantly clear at the July 24, 2019, commission meeting.

Four commissioners attended the meeting: James Vosswinkel, Edwin
Torres, Donald Patterson, and (by telephone) Philip Stieg. Once again,
Kim Sumbler participated via internet hookup. Three other commission
personnel (including then-counsel Theresa D'Andrea) were physically
present.

One substantive matter was discussed. A urine sample taken from a
journeyman heavyweight named Tyrell Wright before a losing effort at
Madison Square Garden on October 27, 2018, had tested positive for nandrolone (an easily detected banned steroid). Wright had failed to attend
an administrative hearing on the matter, and the hearing examiner recommended that the commission impose a three-part penalty consisting of
(1) purse forfeiture, (2) a $1,000 fine payable to the NYSAC, and (3) the
revocation of Wright's license.

Appearing at the July 24 commission meeting, Wright apologized and
said that "a person I trusted" who had been with him as a physical conditioner "from day one" had given him "something I didn't want to take."
The commissioners were unmoved and imposed the recommended penalty.

The stunning thing about the process was that no one at the meeting
asked Wright for the name of the person who had given the nandrolone to

him. Government entities don't effectively combat heroin use by prosecuting addicts. They combat heroin use by prosecuting drug traffickers. Where
the use of illegal performance-enhancing drugs in boxing is concerned,
the suppliers are more of a problem than fighters. Presumably, Wright isn't
the only fighter that this physical conditioner gave a banned substance to
over the course of Wright's seven-year ring career. But the commissioners
made no effort to cut off the flow of illegal PEDs from this supplier to
other fighters.

The New York State Athletic Commission has a Medical Advisory
Board. The board has nine members. Five are necessary for a quorum.
The most recent board meeting was held on September 25, 2019. Nitin
Sethi chaired it. Four other members were present, either in person or by
telephone hookup.

Kim Sumbler began the meeting by saying that the NYSAC has excellent medical protocols. That took three minutes. The board members then
went into a closed executive session to evaluate the reappointment of current ring doctors and applications for appointment by two more doctors.
After the executive session ended, the renewals and new applications were
approved.

Next, the board voted to recommend to the five NYSAC commissioners that the NYSAC medical manual be revised to (1) eliminate "suspicion
of glaucoma" as a cause for denying a license to a fighter and require a
specific finding of glaucoma, and (2) require that a certain type of platelet
count for fighters be calculated once a year.

Dr. Anthony Curreri then asked a question about performance-
enhancing drugs, which Sumbler deflected, saying that the commission was
looking into the issue of banned substances. But she gave no particulars.

Exclusive of the time spent in "executive session" discussing the
appointment and reappointment of ring doctors, the entire meeting lasted
less than fifteen minutes.

That was the only meeting of the Medical Advisory Board in 2019.
The board has met twice in the past twenty-seven months. The first of
these meetings, which occurred on September 18, 2018, lasted 24 minutes.

This is not a system that does everything reasonably possible to safeguard the health and safety of fighters.

On the positive side of the ledger, James Vosswinkel has suggested that the NYSAC consider recommending or even mandating that its physicians take a course called Pre-Hospital Trauma Life Support given by the National Association of Emergency Medical Technicians in cooperation with the American College of Surgeons Committee on Trauma. No action has been taken by the Medical Advisory Board on this suggestion. But a dozen NYSAC physicians have taken the course and been certified.

However, there are more troubling issues on the negative side of the ledger.

Marcus McDaniel was shot three times in a 2016 drive-by shooting. Two of the bullets fractured ribs, punctured McDaniel's lung, ripped through his collarbone, and chipped his spine. The third lodged in his head.

On June 8, 2019, McDaniel fought Ali Akhmedov on the undercard of Gennady Golovkin vs. Steve Rolls at Madison Square Garden and was knocked out in the third round. McDaniel couldn't have an MRI before the fight because it might have moved the bullet in his head, so he was given a CT scan instead. As strange as it might sound, a bullet in the head doesn't necessarily disqualify a fighter from being licensed. A CT scan is considered an appropriate substitute for an MRI.

But—and this is a big "but"—when commission personnel reviewed their paperwork after the June 8 fight card, they couldn't find a New York license for McDaniel.

Marcus McDaniel (a fighter with a bullet in his head) was allowed to fight in New York without a New York license.

The commission then called Triple-G Promotions (the lead promoter for the card) but was told that it didn't represent McDaniel. Finally, it tracked down Les Bonano (McDaniel's promoter).

"Bobby Benton [McDaniel's trainer] filed all the forms with the commission," Bonano told this writer. "And I guess they lost them because, about a week after the fight, we were told that they didn't have a New York license on file for Marcus. So we filled out the forms again. Marcus signed them again. And we filed them again with the commission."

This is not good. What if McDaniel had been seriously injured in the fight? Think of the tragedy and the lawsuit that would have followed.

Moreover, sloppy administrative procedures and inadequate protocols at the New York State Athletic Commission extend far beyond lapses in paperwork. By and large, the men and women who run the commission wall themselves off from the boxing community. They don't attend press conferences. They rarely visit gyms. They stifle feedback from their own staff. There's a fundamental disconnect between the people in charge at the NYSAC and the "real world."

In a sport as dangerous as boxing, that's a recipe for disaster. Let a simple example suffice.

What precisely should a commission inspector do if a fighter collapses in the dressing room after a fight?

Calling a doctor would be a good start. Okay. How should the inspector call a doctor? Does the inspector leave the fighter unattended while he (or she) runs to ringside to look for a commission doctor? That could take a long time. Does the inspector telephone 911? Probably not since, pursuant to NYSAC regulations, there should already be paramedics and an ambulance on site. Does the inspector telephone someone at a designated number?

I've spoken with numerous inspectors and other "back of the house" NYSAC personnel. If there's a protocol in place, they don't know about it.

Part Three

On March 27, 2019, the *New York Times* published an investigative report that detailed a fundraiser for New York governor Andrew Cuomo. The report, which was featured on page 1 of the first section, began:

> The rooftop fund-raiser was meant to be a secretive affair, but word spread quickly among those with pending issues before the state. Lobbyists told their clients that the event would be a good thing to go to.
>
> After all, the dinner was being held a little more than two weeks before the New York State budget was due, and what better way to make valuable connections than to pay tribute to the guest of honor, Gov. Andrew M. Cuomo.
>
> Among those present were the vice president of a school bus company seeking tax breaks for the purchase of buses; a recycling company founder looking for a broadening of the 5-cent deposit law; and an affordable housing developer lobbying for real estate tax credits.

The fundraiser was held on March 14 on the 20th floor of the St. Regis Hotel, just off Fifth Avenue and a block from Trump Tower. The minimum donation per couple was $25,000.

The event, which was billed as a spring dinner with the governor, was strictly under the radar. It was not listed on Mr. Cuomo's calendar. The invitation was vaguely worded with the locale only provided in the RSVP.

A reporter who showed up at the fund-raiser was barred entry. The guests included senior Cuomo administration officials, including the state budget director. . . .

The fundraiser provided a vivid example of how things work in Albany's pay-to-play culture, where political contributions are often viewed by business leaders as a prerequisite for getting their perspective heard in the capital.

Four months later, on July 29, 2019, the *Times* ran a similar investigative report:

Months after landing its first job in nearly a decade on the New York City subway, a Long Island construction firm hosted an intimate fundraiser in its luxury suite at Citi Field for a special guest: Gov. Andrew M. Cuomo.

The firm, Haugland Group, had wanted to expand into the lucrative world of contracting for the Metropolitan Transportation Authority, the agency that oversees the subway and is controlled by Mr. Cuomo.

After securing a $23 million contract to clear clogged subway drains in October 2017, William Haugland and his son Billy, the company's leaders, sought to raise as much as a quarter of a million dollars for Mr. Cuomo's re-election campaign at the Citi Field event, according to a person with direct knowledge of the event.

Neither the family nor their companies had ever donated to Mr. Cuomo before.

Haugland Group was suddenly one of Mr. Cuomo's largest contributors as he ran for a third term. . . .

Another firm that cleared subway drains, Welkin Mechanical,

also donated to Mr. Cuomo. The campaign received the contri-
bution less than three weeks before the company won a nearly
$15 million contract in November 2017.

This is the environment in which the New York State Athletic
Commission exists. Money and political power dictate policy and policy
implementation at every level.

As noted in Part One of this series, the NYSAC doesn't have a budget
like its counterparts in most states. Its economic mysteries are folded into
the budget for the New York State Department of State. Thus, much of its
cost to taxpayers is hidden from public scrutiny and also from review by
the NYSAC commissioners and executive director.

On several occasions, the NYSAC and Department of State refused
a request by this writer for information stating the total annual cost of
operating the commission and a breakdown of these costs (e.g. salaries,
travel expenses, office space, etc). Finally, on February 8, 2019, I filed a
demand pursuant to New York's Freedom of Information Law to require
the production of the information.

But there was a problem. The New York State Department of State
(through the New York State Committee on Open Government) is the
entity that oversees administration of the Freedom of Information Law.
And the DOS refused to fulfill its legal obligation with regard to my request
for information about the NYSAC budget.

On March 19, 2019, I received an email from an assistant records
access officer named Cherise A. Watson that read, "Dear Mr. Hauser: This
is in response to your FOIL request of 'annual cost of operating the New
York State Athletic Commission.' It is taking significantly longer than
anticipated to review our records and respond to your request. Please be
advised that the Department of State needs additional time. The anticipated date of response is April 30, 2019."

On April 30, I received the same email with a different anticipated date
of response. That process repeated itself on May 29 and June 26.

Here I might add that Ms. Watson's June 26 email came one day after
Robert Freeman (director of the New York State Committee on Open
Government) was dismissed from his job after multiple complaints alleging
sexual harassment were filed against him and investigators found photos

of naked women on his state computer, in addition to sexually suggestive emails written by him on his state account.

On June 27, I filed an appeal in response to the failure of the Department of State to provide me with documents as required by law.

Finally, on July 26 (five and a half months after my Freedom of Information Law request), I received an email from the Department of State containing a one-page document that only partially responded to my request. For example, there is no reference in the document to the cost of office space allocated to the New York State Athletic Commission. Other entries seem to have been mischaracterized or are vague.

By way of example; Dr. Angela Gagliardi is assistant chief medical officer for the NYSAC. One source says that Gagliardi works from home, comes into the office one day a week, and coordinates medical matters for the NYSAC. She also attends weigh-ins and fights. In addition, Gagliardi has spent time in recent months contacting commission employees (including non-medical and per diem personnel) about the administrative requirement that all NYSAC business be transacted on Department of State servers rather than private email accounts.

According to SeeThroughNY, Gagliardi is an hourly employee who, in 2018, was paid at the rate of $77 an hour for a total of $174,855. If this information is correct—and if she never took a week off—Gagliardi worked approximately 2,271 hours in 2018 (an average of 43 hours, 20 minutes per week). Since $174,855 is more than the entire total listed for "per diem" employees by the Department of State in its production to me, I assume that either Gagliardi was classified in the document produced as a "fulltime employee," or the numbers provided by the DOS pursuant to the Freedom of Information Law are incorrect.

There are people assigned to the NYSAC who receive substantial salaries and who high-ranking commission officials have never met or even heard of. One such person is listed by SeeThroughNY as having been employed in 2015 as a "special assistant" in the "executive" category. Her "total pay" for that year was $105,550. David Berlin, who was NYSAC executive director at the time, says he has no idea who that person was.

More significantly, the New York State Athletic Commission and New York State Department of State appear to be countenancing false financial filings with the state that might lead to tax fraud.

Section 13 of the federal Muhammad Ali Boxing Reform Act is titled "Required Disclosures for Promoters." In part, it states, "A promoter shall not be entitled to receive any compensation directly or indirectly in connection with a boxing match until it provides to the boxing commission responsible for regulating the match in a State (1) a copy of any agreement in writing to which the promoter is a party with any boxer participating in the match; (2) a statement made under penalty of perjury that there are no other agreements, written or oral, between the promoter and the boxer with respect to that match."

This requirement is now being finessed in New York. For big fights, an official NYSAC bout contract with an artificially low purse is often filed with the commission by the promoter of record, and the fighter is paid more on the side from money that filters through some other mechanism, often through a party other than the promoter of record.

Meanwhile, section 206.12 of the NYSAC Regulations provides, "All contracts calling for the services of a professional in an authorized professional combative sport and entered into by licensed promoters, professionals or managers as one or more of the parties in such contracts shall be subject to Commission approval and must be filed with the Commission to be valid."

It appears as though this provision is being routinely circumvented with the silent assent of the NYSAC. The result is that there's a shell game going on with regard to fighters' purses. It's common practice for fighters in big fights in New York to be given two or more checks—one for the purse that's reported to the NYSAC and the other or others for the difference between that amount and the real purse.

The bout contracts and supporting paperwork are filed with the NYSAC by the promoter of record, who's not necessarily the driving promotional force behind the fight. In that regard, one of these promoters acknowledges, "Everyone is filing false paperwork on big fights. I file what I'm given."

For example:

* Gennady Golovkin's purse for fighting Steve Rolls in New York on June 8, 2019, was reported to the NYSAC as being $2 million. Dan Rafael of ESPN.com called that number "laughable" and reported

that Golovkin was "getting closer to $15 million." Four months later, the official purses reported to the NYSAC for Golovkin vs. Sergiy Derevyanchenko were $4 million for Derevyanchenko and $2.5 million for Golovkin.

* When Anthony Joshua fought Andy Ruiz at Madison Square Garden on June 1, 2019, Joshua's official paycheck based on his purse after certain deductions was $3.2 million, and Ruiz's was $1.3 million. In reality, Joshua received well into eight figures for the fight, and Ruiz's purse is believed to have been in the neighborhood of $6 million.

* Deontay Wilder's purse for fighting Dominic Breazeale on May 18, 2019, as reported to the NYSAC was $4 million. It's unclear how much Wilder actually contracted for to receive, but it's believed to have been at least $12 million.

Why are these discrepancies important? For starters, they set the stage for the possibility of underreporting with regard to New York State income tax. People can play games with the numbers and say things like, "Well, the bout contract was accurate. The other ten million dollars that so-and-so got was for personal appearances at corporate events or some kind of sponsorship (not taxable in New York)." But that's nonsense.

There are NYSAC employees who acknowledge (but not for attribution) that they know the purse filings are inaccurate.

One justification advanced in support of allowing this practice to continue is the claim that the purpose of the Ali Act and the New York State regulations is to "protect the fighter." Thus, if income is knowingly being underreported for tax purposes, it isn't relevant to these reporting requirements. But that's ridiculous. Filing false documents with the state is a crime. Knowingly underreporting income for tax purposes is a crime. And just as important: If false documents are being filed with the commission, how does the NYSAC know that the fighters are getting honest numbers?

Quite possibly, all appropriate New York State income taxes are being paid on fighters' purses. But this situation opens the door for abuse. It calls into question the integrity of the New York State Athletic Commission and also the integrity of the New York State Department of State. And as a related issue, the inaccurate purse filings for big fights are particularly irritating to referees and judges who, as per New York State Athletic

Commission Bulletin 2017-02, are supposed to paid a legally mandated percentage of the fighters' purses when they referee or judge a championship fight.

The bottom line is that the Cuomo administration, like many government entities on both sides of the political aisle, caters to and shields powerful economic interests.

For years, the application for a promoter's license in New York required applicants to list the name of each shareholder. This was designed to identify potential conflicts of interest and root out unsavory backers. In August 2018, the NYSAC removed the requirement that this information be listed. Why?

The nature of government is that, too often, regulatory agencies are run by entities that they're supposed to regulate. For example, in the Trump administration, the coal industry dictates policy to the Environmental Protection Agency. Similarly, crucial decisions at the New York State Athletic Commission are now being made by entities that the NYSAC is supposed to regulate. I'm not talking about small venues and small promoters. They don't make NYSAC policy. But large venues and large promoters with highly skilled lobbyists on retainer do.

Similarly, the NYSAC is often compliant with the wishes of the powerful to the detriment of good government. Here it's worth revisiting the case of Michael Bisping.

On November 4, 2017, Bisping tapped out while being choked by Georges St. Pierre at UFC 217 at Madison Square Garden. A left hook and series of forearm smashes had immobilized him. Then St. Pierre applied a naked chokehold that ended the bout.

Bisping appeared to temporarily lose consciousness. That night, he was placed on a thirty-day medical suspension by the NYSAC medical staff. Then, in mid-November, UFC contacted NYSAC executive director Kim Sumbler, told her that Bisping had been judged fit to fight by a neurologist in California, submitted supporting medical documentation, and asked that the suspension be lifted. The NYSAC complied with the request. On November 25, three weeks after enduring a beating in New York, Bisping was knocked out by Kelvin Gastelum on a UFC fight card in Shanghai. He did not fight again and, in May 2018, announced his retirement from MMA competition.

It now appears that Bisping, who at this point has a prosthetic right eye, was almost sightless in that eye when he fought St. Pierre in New York. During an October 15, 2019, podcast, he acknowledged, "My vision [in my right eye] was pretty much nonexistent since 2013. People always say, 'How did you fight with only one eye?' And I always say, 'With great fucking difficulty!'"

Reflecting on the situation with Michael Bisping, a high-ranking NYSAC official admits, "We don't hold big promoters to the same standards as small ones."

Asked for another example, the official says, "UFC is allowed to use a bottle of adrenaline that has already been opened for multiple fighters. Cutmen who work for other promoters' fighters have to use a new bottle for each fighter."

"The rules are different for UFC," another NYSAC official acknowledges. "They can do pretty much anything they want. The regular rule is that a fighter isn't allowed to eat anything after we take his pre-fight urine sample. If he does—and it's the same for women fighters—we take another urine sample. But UFC is allowed to come in and give snack bags to its fighters for them to eat without being retested."

Similarly, the Medical Standards for Combat Sports posted on the NYSAC website states, "The MAB [medical advisory board] and the Commission limit fluids at ringside only to authorized bottled water. Water must be in a sealed bottle and remain unopened until ringside."

Pursuant to this dictate, fighters are not allowed to ingest drinks with electrolytes after giving a pre-fight urine sample. But the NYSAC allows UFC combatants to use Bodyarmor Alkaline SportWater with "potassium-packed electrolytes." Perhaps that's because Bodyarmor is the "official sports drink of UFC."

And it doesn't stop there.

On November 1, 2019, Kelvin Gastelum weighed in for a UFC 244 match to be contested at Madison Square Garden against Darren Till. The contract weight was 186 pounds. It was widely known in the MMA community that Gastelum was having trouble making weight. Before stepping on the scale, he stripped down completely naked and a towel was lifted in front of him to shield his genitals from public view. Then, to everyone's surprise, his weight was announced as 184 pounds (two pounds under the contract weight).

But—and this is an elephant-sized "but"—video of the weigh-in shows Gastelum resting his elbow on his coach, Rafael Cordeiro, as he stood on the scale. And the NYSAC officials conducting the weigh-in missed it.

The incident brought back memories of another UFC weigh-in. Daniel Cormier fought Anthony Johnson in a cruiserweight title bout that was the main event on an April 8, 2017, UFC 210 card at KeyBank Center in Buffalo. The UFC cruiserweight limit is 205 pounds. Cormier stripped naked at the weigh-in and, with two defenders of public decency holding a towel in front of him, weighed in at 206.2 pounds. Then, literally 143 seconds later, he returned to the scale and weighed in at 205 pounds.

How did Cormier lose 1.2 pounds in 143 seconds? Video evidence shows that, on the second weigh-in attempt, Cormier was holding onto the towel and pressing downward, an age-old con used by amateur wrestlers in poorly regulated competitions to make weight. The following night, he won by submission over Johnson in the second round.

How did NYSAC make the same mistake twice?

In answering that question, one might note that weigh-ins for major fights in New York City are usually overseen by deputy commissioners Robert Orlando and George Ward. Orlando and Ward are retired New York City corrections officers. Each man has been with the commission for decades and knows all the tricks. But while on site and readying for the November 1 Gastelum–Till weigh-in, Orlando and Ward were advised by NYSAC executive director Kim Sumbler that they were being replaced at the scales by two less experienced commission employees who had been brought to New York City from upstate.

Six days after the fight, the NYSAC fined Gastelum and Cordeiro $1,000 and $200 respectively for "making contact" during the weigh-in. That's not even a slap on the wrist.

According to FollowTheMoney.org, Zuffa LLC (the parent company of UFC) has given more than $160,000 in direct campaign contributions to Andrew Cuomo. Various New York state legislators of both parties have also benefited from its generosity. And the company has spent millions more on lobbying.

The manner in which the New York State Athletic Commission does business today shows inadequate respect for combat sports and the fighters who risk their lives in the ring.

One week after posting "Politics, Problems, and Power at the New York State Athletic Commission," I had cause to write again about the NYSAC.

Ivan Redkach and the New York State Athletic Commission

With slightly more than a minute left in round eight of the January 25, 2020, fight at Barclays Center between Danny García and Ivan Redkach, Redkach bit García just below the left side of his neck while the fighters were in a clinch.

"I just felt something digging in my skin," García said at the post-fight press conference. "I thought a mosquito got me. I look over and he's biting me."

Referee Benjy Esteves didn't deduct points for the foul or issue a warning, so one assumes that he didn't see it. The Showtime commentating crew, which includes Al Bernstein and Paulie Malignaggi (two of the most knowledgeable observers in boxing), didn't see it either. After the round, a Showtime microphone picked up Ángel Garcia (Danny's father and trainer) bringing the incident to Esteves's attention. In an in-ring interview after the fight, García told Showtime's Jim Gray, "He said 'Mike Tyson' when he bit me."

On January 27, New York State Athletic Commission executive director Kim Sumbler signed a "Notice of Suspension, Imposition of Fine, and Purse Forfeiture." The document states—and the NYSAC subsequently announced—that the commission had (1) suspended Redkach for one year, (2) fined him $10,000 (the maximum allowable fine), and (3) confiscated his entire $300,000 purse. Where will the money go? The State of New York will keep it.

Biting, gnawing at an opponent—call it what you will—is indefensible. It can't be tolerated in boxing and demands punishment. But the NYSAC's handling of this matter to date is as inappropriate as Redkach's conduct.

There's a concept called "due process." Redkach is entitled to it. And he hasn't gotten it.

Who at the commission made this decision? The complaint was signed dument.

by Sumbler with apparent input from David A. Mossberg (an attorney with the New York State Department of State). But the NYSAC has refused to respond to an inquiry from this writer asking who specifically made the decision or what procedure was followed. We do know that Redkach hasn't been given an opportunity to explain what happened from his point of view.

In other words, the proceedings to date sound like something out *Alice's Adventures in Wonderland* where the Knave of Hearts is put on trial for allegedly stealing tarts baked by the Queen.

"Let the jury consider their verdict," the King said.

"No, no!" said the Queen. "Sentence first, verdict afterward."

There's no official ring registry for biting in boxing. Most famously, Mike Tyson was disqualified after biting off part of Evander Holyfield's ear in their 1997 rematch. Eight years later, Tyson bit Kevin McBride on the nipple before being knocked out in an ignominious end to his storied ring career. Two years before Tyson–Holyfield, Andrew Golota bit Sampson Po'hua on the side of the neck. In 2019, Kash Ali was disqualified after biting David Price just below the chest in a fight in Liverpool. Adrian Dodson bit Alain Bonnamie on the chest in round twelve of a 1999 fight in England and was disqualified.

García–Redkach wasn't Mike Tyson biting off part of Evander Holyfield's ear. To treat it as though it were is ridiculous.

It doesn't appear as though Redkach was trying to injure García in any significant way. He didn't spit out his mouthpiece (as Tyson did against Holyfield). He didn't break the skin or leave an ugly, bite-marked-shaped welt as was the case in the other biting incidents referenced above. Did Redkach really say "Mike Tyson," or was García joking (as he did at the post-fight press conference while talking about Redkach's "brand new veneers")? If García's corner hadn't brought the incident to the attention of Benjy Esteves after round eight, and Danny hadn't referenced the bite in post-fight interviews, it's doubtful that the NYSAC would have even known about it.

The notice served on Redkach by the NYSAC says that, following the fight, García was examined by the commission's chief medical officer, "who observed impressions that appeared consistent with bite marks on Mr. García's left anterior base of the neck/upper torso."

"Consistent with," not "diagnostic of."

Moreover, since no one alleges that Redkach bit García more than once, that raises the question of whether these "impressions" (plural) were caused by a bite or the normal rigors of a fight.

In other words; punishment first, then we'll hold a hearing to find out what happened.

Once again, *Alice's Adventures in Wonderland*: "The King turned pale, and shut his note-book hastily. 'Consider your verdict,' he said to the jury in a low trembling voice."

"'Not yet, not yet!' the Rabbit hastily interrupted. 'There's a great deal to come before that!'"

Lou DiBella has promoted fight cards in New York for two decades.

"I used to promote Ivan Redkach," DiBella says. "I think he's a good person. Should he have bitten Danny García? No. Should he be punished? Yes. But for the commission to throw the book at him over this is the worst kind of hypocrisy. This is a commission that has made a conscious decision to look the other way when it comes to certain fighters who are using illegal PEDs. No one dies from being bitten on the shoulder in a boxing ring. Fighters can die from an opponent using PEDs. This is a commission that looks the other way while all sorts of illegal things like phony weigh-ins are going on. Has this commission ever suspended or fined a fighter for hitting another fighter who was on the canvas, for rabbit-punching, for a deliberate low blow? There are a lot of people who deserve to be punished by the New York commission for conduct that's a lot worse than what Ivan did, and the commission does nothing about them."

So . . . how should Ivan Redkach be punished?

A line has to be drawn to separate acceptable and unacceptable conduct. But the punishment should fit the crime. Also, one has to remember that Redkach's trainer and other members of his team are entitled to share in his $300,000 purse.

There might be instances where forfeiture of a fighter's total purse is appropriate. This isn't one of them. Based on what's publicly known at present, a $30,000 penalty (10 percent of Redkach's purse) coupled with a six-month suspension would be more than sufficient punishment.

Meanwhile, the commission's position in this matter has been further undercut by the fact that it gave Redkach a promoter's check for the full amount of his purse on fight night. And this check has already cleared. From the NYSAC's point of view, that's a textbook example of locking the barn door after the horse has been stolen.

Did the key commission personnel on site at Barclays Center on January 25 even know then that there had been a bite? If so, releasing the check speaks to sloppy administrative practices. If not, it speaks to the extent to which, despite sitting at ringside, they were oblivious to what was happening in front of them. Or maybe they didn't think it was such a big deal at the time.

The "Notice of Suspension, Imposition of Fine, and Purse Forfeiture" issued by the NYSAC provides that Redkach must pay the $10,000 fine within thirty days and forfeit the full amount of his $300,000 purse to the commission within forty-eight hours of the notice. Good luck on that.

Under New York State law, Redkach has the right to challenge the penalties imposed on him by the commission at a formal appeals hearing. He is expected to do so. This might lead to a negotiated settlement. The commission's most potent weapon in these negotiations would be the threat of keeping Ivan on suspension indefinitely and hoping that other states would honor the suspension.

Common sense dictates that the punishment the NYSAC is seeking to impose on Redkach is excessive. Three hundred thousand dollars? His entire purse? Come on! It's evocative of the croquet game in *Alice's Adventures in Wonderland,* once again highlighted by the irrational raging of the Queen of Hearts: "The Queen was in a furious passion, and went stamping about and shouting 'Off with his head!'"

Nine Days Later

Faced with widespread criticism for its draconian punishment of Ivan Redkach, the New York State Athletic Commission has stepped back from the brink.

With slightly more than a minute left in round eight of the January 25, 2020, fight at Barclays Center between Redkach and Danny García, Ivan bit Danny just below the left side of his neck while the fighters were in a clinch. It wasn't much of a bite. Referee Benjy Esteves didn't notice it. Nor did the Showtime commentating crew. Redkach immediately extended his right glove in a gesture of apology and the fight went on.

The bite was indefensible. So was the response of the New York State Athletic Commission.

Major League Baseball—to use a well-run sport as an example—suspends

players for PED abuse and domestic violence. By contrast, the NYSAC
generally looks the other way when these issues arise. When the Houston
Astros were caught in a cheating scandal, their general manager and manager lost their jobs. But when Kelvin Gastelum and his trainer orchestrated
a phony weigh-in prior to UFC 244, the NYSAC was content to fine them
$1,000 and $200 respectively.

Suppose a baseball player charges the mound and throws a punch that
does no damage? Can anyone imagine MLB fining him a full year's salary
and suspending him for an entire year? Of course, not. But on January 27,
the New York State Athletic Commission (1) suspended Redkach for one
year; (2) fined him $10,000 (the maximum allowable fine); and (3) confis-
cated his entire $300,000 purse.

The absurdity of the NYSAC's action against Redkach was detailed in
an earlier article by this writer. Suffice it to say here that the commission
acted without properly investigating the matter and in contravention of
Redkach's due process rights.

Moreover, the punishment was based in large part on a belief that
turned out to be false. The commission appears to have relied heavily on a
flippant remark made in the ring by García after the fight to the effect that
Redkach said "Mike Tyson" when he bit him. In my February 4 article, I
raised the question, "Did Redkach really say 'Mike Tyson' or was García
joking?"

The NYSAC should have asked that question before embarrassing
itself. On January 30, García acknowledged during an interview on DAZN
that Redkach never said "Mike Tyson":

> Q: The guy said "Mike Tyson" when he bit you, right?
> García: Nah, I just said that. I was trolling. I was trolling
> for sure.

On February 13, the NYSAC came to grips with the absurdity of its
position and wiped some of the egg off its face. Faced with the threat of
legal action, it reduced Redkach's suspension to six months and agreed that
Ivan could keep his $300,000 purse. The $10,000 fine will stand. That's an
equitable resolution and begs the question: "What were NYSAC executive
director Kim Sumbler and Jim Leary (who funnels directives to Sumbler
from above) thinking when they imposed the original punishment?"

Paulie Malignaggi, Showtime, and the Dialogue on Race

Part One

On July 30, 2020, it was reported that Paulie Malignaggi—an analyst for *Showtime Boxing* since 2012—had been dropped from the network's commentating team. Technically, Malignaggi wasn't fired. Rather, Showtime will no longer use him on telecasts and not renew his contract when it expires at the end of the year.

In reporting on Malignaggi's termination, the media has focused on comments that Paulie made during an April 22 interview with IFL-TV. But the issues surrounding his departure from Showtime go far beyond any one interview. Interviews with multiple industry insiders lead to a more complete and nuanced picture of what transpired.

Malignaggi was a good fighter. He was always willing to go in tough and compiled a 36–8 record during a fifteen-year career that saw him win world titles at 140 and 147 pounds. He was lacking in power (only 7 knockout victories in 44 bouts) but had a fighter's heart.

People tend to forget how heroically Malignaggi performed against Miguel Cotto in Madison Square Garden on the eve of the 2006 Puerto Rican Day Parade. Paulie was getting beaten up. Badly. By a bigger, stronger, future Hall of Fame fighter who was at his peak. But he didn't just try to survive. He never stopped trying to win and went the distance, absorbing a brutal beating but winning four rounds on two judges' scorecards and five on the third.

Afterward, Arturo Gatti commended Malignaggi for his courage. "I'm proud that you're Italian," Gatti told him.

Paulie has permanent nerve damage in his face as a consequence of the Cotto fight. "Pain is temporary," he says. "Pride is forever."

Most people who know Paulie like him. He's also an exceptionally good TV analyst.

Malignaggi's termination by Showtime resulted not just as a consequence of the IFL interview but from an accumulation of incidents.

Paulie is Paulie. He says what he thinks and wears his emotions on his sleeve. That has always been part of his appeal. He isn't a traditional corporate soldier. Nor is he one to calm troubled waters. Sometimes he'll cannonball into them. Over the years, he has brought a lot to the table for Showtime—including occasional problems.

Showtime management felt that Malignaggi crossed over the line of propriety on several occasions.

When Adrien Broner showed up at the kickoff press conference for his 2013 fight against Malignaggi, he taunted Paulie by appearing with and commenting upon a woman that Malignaggi had previously dated. That elicited a heated response from Paulie, who told reporters. "There are girls who are close to you and girls that we call weekend pussy. Jessica was weekend pussy. That means Jessica could fuck anybody she wants. And when I got time on the weekends, I could do whatever I wanted to do and she loved it. She loved getting hit [role playing] when we slept together. As a matter of fact, Adrien, if you fucked her, you already know that. Weekend pussy is exactly that. The only weekend pussy Adrien gets is the kind he pays for. He doesn't understand what it's like to be good looking and get regular pussy and the weekend pussy and you don't pay for none of it. It just comes to you. That's my life."

This wasn't the image that Showtime wanted for its commentating team.

"I shouldn't have called her weekend pussy," Paulie acknowledged afterward. "I got mad. What I should have said was that this is a woman who's a very bad representative of what women can be. But after everything I'd gone through [including an apparently spurious claim by the woman that she'd gotten pregnant by Paulie], it ticked me off when Broner and this woman made my private personal life public and did it in such a dishonest way."

Then Malignaggi went to war with Conor McGregor over comments regarding a sparring session between them that took place before McGregor's 2017 fight against Floyd Mayweather. That led to ongoing verbal warfare and an ugly incident at the Mayweather–McGregor weigh-in when Paulie was being taunted by some of Conor's fans and offered to fight them on the spot. Things got heated and security was thin.

"I wish I'd never gone to spar with McGregor," Malignaggi said later. "They treated me like shit when I was there. Then they lied and dumped shit on my reputation afterward. But I did go spar with him and you can't undo the past. And I still have to deal with it. You should have seen the social media after I sparred with McGregor. His idiot fans calling me a faggot, a little Dago, things they wouldn't have the courage to come up to me on the street and say to my face. And they don't just put it on their sites. They put it all over my social media pages. I can post a photo of me at the beach and, a day later, there's all sorts of ugly shit attached to it."

Regardless, Showtime management felt that the weigh-in incident put other Showtime personnel in harm's way.

Two years later, Malignaggi lost his composure and dignity at the kick-off press conference for a Bare Knuckle Fighting Championship bout that he was about to engage in against Artem Lobov (a friend of McGregor's). In addition to calling MMA fans "a piece of shit community," he told Lobov, "You're a piece of shit and I'm gonna treat you like the dirtbag that you are. After I beat the shit out of you, I'm gonna spit on you. I'm gonna take out my dick after I knock your teeth out and piss in that toothless mouth of yours. You got five weeks to live, motherfucker."

"You have to put the press conference in context," Paulie explained afterward. "There's a whole back story that people don't understand. I grew up in a not very nice place. And I'm not talking about the neighborhood. I'm talking about what my life was like and the abuse I took. I went into boxing to get away from that place and to deal with the anger that I had inside me in an acceptable way. This is bringing out a side of me that I thought I'd left in my past. It's a response to the lies and humiliation and pain to me and my family and everything else that this guy and his piece-of-shit friend Conor McGregor caused to be dumped on me."

That said, from Showtime's point of view, this wasn't how the network wanted its commentators to be seen by the public. And in addition, Premier Boxing Champions (which supplies most of Showtime's boxing content) was unhappy with comments that Malignaggi had made regarding one of its flagship fighters, Deontay Wilder.

Still, the powers that be at Showtime were empathetic with Malignaggi.

They understood that he was transitioning from being a brash-talking fighter to a network spokesperson and that the process would take time, particularly during the years when he was still fighting and those roles overlapped.

Then politics became a factor.

Malignaggi wholeheartedly—and sometimes stridently—supports Donald Trump. He kept his political opinions off of Showtime's boxing telecasts but engaged in heated social media debate on a wide range of issues. Some of his thoughts— dealing with issues like single parenthood in the Black community and the shooting of Ahmaud Arbery—involve racial issues.

On April 22, Malignaggi was interviewed by IFL and asked about Devin Haney's comment: "I will never lose to a white boy in my life. Can't no white boy beat me."

In response, Paulie talked about boxing being dominated sequentially by Irish American, Jewish, Italian American, Black (he didn't mention Hispanic), and now Eastern European fighters. Then the conversation turned to the issue of a double standard and what would have happened if a white fighter had said, "Can't no Black boy beat me."

As part of his response, Paulie opined, "I don't believe there is racial oppression in 2020, in this century. I believe there has been, sure. But I don't believe there's any racial oppression today. I believe it's all made up. The whole hypothesis of racial oppression is way exaggerated in this century."

The interview was conducted more than a month before George Floyd's May 25, 2020, death beneath the knee of Minneapolis police officer Derek Chauvin. But even for it's time, it was an ill-considered comment.

Initially, Malignaggi's statement about the absence of racial oppression didn't cause much of a stir. A few podcasts and websites referenced it, but that was all. Showtime Sports president Stephen Espinoza and executive producer David Dinkins Jr. called Paulie and asked that he tone things down, and he agreed to do so. Then, on May 25, George Floyd was killed and the landscape changed.

On July 14, Nick Cannon was fired by ViacomCBS from the comedy improv show *Wild 'N Out* after making racist anti-Semitic comments during a podcast. Cannon's remarks were widely viewed as being more offensive than anything Malignaggi had said. But there were questions as to why Cannon (a Black man) lost his job while Paulie went unpunished. The issue was brought to the attention of executives above Showtime Sports on the corporate ladder. Finally, as Showtime's August 1 return to boxing approached, Espinoza and Dinkins called Paulie again and said, "We have to clean this up."

Conversations with multiple sources provide the details of what happened next. Malignaggi said that he would issue a statement apologizing "if my comments offended anyone." Espinoza responded that this ritualized public apology wasn't good enough; that there could be no "if" in the statement. Paulie then asked for a chance to write the statement himself.

The statement that Malignaggi drafted acknowledged having offended some people and that his words might have been been construed as insensitive and even ignorant. He talked about having viewed things through the prism of bad experiences that he'd had in his own life and that, in doing so, he'd failed to empathize with the experiences of others. He also talked about the need for people on all sides of the divide to engage in a healthy dialogue, pledged to do his part in pursuing that goal, and promised to choose his words more wisely and carefully in the future.

Espinoza sent back a revised draft that was similar in content but had two phrases that Malignaggi was uncomfortable with:

1. The Espinoza draft contained the statement that Paulie was "sorry" his recent statements had offended many people. Paulie wanted to change that to an acknowledgment that his statements had offended many people and that he regretted not having chosen his words more wisely. From Malignaggi's point of view, a statement saying that he was "sorry" might have been interpreted as the abandonment of his personal beliefs.
2. Malignaggi had written that his words "may have come off" as insensitive and ignorant. Espinoza wanted to shift the "may" so that Paulie acknowledged that his words had come off as insensitive and "maybe even ignorant."

Malignaggi then sent Espinoza and Dinkins a note requesting that they meet halfway on the issues. Rather than meet halfway, Espinoza telephoned Paulie and told him that Showtime had decided to terminate his employment. Informed sources say that the decision-making process reached above Showtime Sports, but that final responsibility for the decision rested with Espinoza. These same sources say that it was a difficult decision for Espinoza given his personal fondness for Malignaggi and his respect for Paulie's work as a commentator. But after discussions with Malignaggi, the feeling was that, despite his written words, Paulie's mind was insufficiently open to other people's experiences and that he was less willing to listen and learn than would be necessary for him to continue in a role as a representative for Showtime.

Espinoza and Malignaggi agreed on a quiet parting. But the following day, Paulie's termination was reported on Boxing Scene in an article by Keith Idec. Malignaggi felt that the leak was an attempt by Showtime to undermine his credibility and value as a commentator and hinder his ability to find work with another network. Espinoza was equally exasperated by the leak. In reality, the information was divulged by a representative of Premier Boxing Champions.

Part Two

Other factors were involved, but Paulie Malignaggi's termination as a commentator by Showtime was intertwined with the issue of race.

The balance in America tilts toward white privilege. This doesn't mean that every white person has an easy life and every Black person is disadvantaged. But there are segments of American society that prove each day by their conduct that white lives matter more to them than Black lives matter. For centuries, people with this belief have controlled the levers of power in American society. The situation is more equitable now than in the 1950s when the Civil Rights Movement began to gather momentum. But we have a long way to go before reaching the goal of equal opportunity. The problem didn't disappear when Barack Obama was elected president.

People of goodwill struggle with the issue of race on an individual and corporate level. The lines keep shifting. And they shifted a lot with the death of George Floyd.

It took a gruesome video of Floyd's death after 8 minutes and 46 seconds beneath Derek Chauvin's knee for the National Football League to abandon its policy of allowing individual teams to punish players who knelt during the playing of the national anthem. A person could get whiplash from the pivot that NFL commissioner Roger Goodell made on that issue. The Aunt Jemima brand—a staple for the Quaker Oats Company for more than a century—has now been "retired." Diversity, Equity, Inclusion is the new corporate mantra. The reexamination of attitudes toward race is permeating every level of American society.

Paulie Malignaggi didn't grow up with much privilege in his life. He has been in survival mode for many of his thirty-nine years.

Malignaggi was born in Brooklyn in 1980. His parents were Italian immigrants. When he was several months old, the family moved back to Italy. Six years later, having had a second child, they returned to the United States. This time, Paulie's father stayed for a few weeks and went back to Italy alone. Twelve years passed before Paulie saw his father again.

"I didn't have a nice growing up," Malignaggi said years ago. "For a while, my mother, my brother Umberto, and I lived with my mother's parents in Brooklyn. Then my mother found an old Italian couple who let us live with them in a dilapidated old house. We were on welfare. I remember going into stores and getting dirty looks because we paid with food stamps. And I didn't know any English when we moved back to Brooklyn. That was hard."

When Paulie was nine, his mother remarried and moved with her sons to New Jersey. There was physical abuse. "From the start," Malignaggi remembers, "our step-father beat us [Paulie and his brother]."

Eventually, Paulie and Umberto were thrown out of the house. For the next two years, they slept on their grandparents' couch in Brooklyn. Paulie enrolled in high school but wasn't much of a student. Before dropping out, he cut classes, got into fights, and was involved with petty crime.

"I had problems; no doubt about it," Malignaggi acknowledged. "I acted out. I was turning into the wrong kind of person. I had this anger in me. I was bitter. I was losing my conscience. Some of the kids I hung out with then are in jail. Some straightened out. One is dead."

White privilege?

It's important to distinguish between insensitivity on issues of race and being a racist. A racist is someone who discriminates or feels prejudice against people of another race, or who believes that one race is superior to another. Malignaggi doesn't think that way. He has good one-on-one relationships with people of color—more than most white people do.

He also knows about police brutality. Paulie once got into a street fight with a guy who turned out to be an undercover cop, was arrested, and, while handcuffed, was beaten by three cops.

"I know it happens," he says. "I went through it myself."

He watched videos of George Floyd's death before coming to the conclusion, "What that cop did was wrong. There was no excuse for it."

Malignaggi could have salvaged his career at Showtime by offering to say something along the lines of "events in recent months have opened my eyes" or "events in recent months have changed my thinking." That was the road traveled by the lords of the NFL, NBA, and MLB, whether motivated by a sincere change of heart or as an economic imperative. But fighters are often reluctant to back down. And maybe Paulie's eyes haven't been opened.

White privilege manifests itself in many forms. Yes, Malignaggi had a hard life growing up. But it might have been harder had he been Black. Would Paulie have made the same purses as a fighter if he'd been Black? By way of comparison, anyone who thinks that Arturo Gatti would have made as much money as he did if he'd been Black is living in a dream world.

Let me make two biases of my own clear at this point: (1) I deplore Donald Trump and everything that he represents; (2) I've known Paulie for nineteen years and I like him.

In my view, a lot of what Malignaggi says and thinks (particularly about Trump) is misguided. That means, by definition, he feels the same way about a lot of things that I say and think.

I'm troubled by the fact that, too often today, intelligent dialogue between people on opposing sides of the political spectrum has given way to shouting by internet mobs who hurl invective from their safe haven behind computers. I also think that the practice of people calling other people "racist" with impunity and without substantiation is dangerous.

That said, Showtime has the right to present itself to the public in a certain way. It can't discriminate in employment on the basis of race, religion, or sexual orientation. It can choose its spokespeople and set guidelines for how these people conduct themselves in public.

A television commentator represents the network that he or she works for at all times. The public at large identifies the commentator with the network.

This isn't a First Amendment issue. Showtime isn't the government. Paulie has the right to speak his mind on political and social issues.

Showtime has the right to say, "Your public comments are inconsistent with our values. We no longer want you to represent us."

Sports commentators speak out on issues related to their sport all the time. But comments regarding politics and race have long been treacherous terrain.

In 1988, CBS fired Jimmy Snyder (known as "Jimmy the Greek") from *NFL Today* after an interview on another network in which he made statements regarding what he viewed as the genetic superiority of Black athletes.

Former all-star pitcher and ESPN baseball analyst Curt Schilling was fired by ESPN in 2016 because of social media posts with regard to transgender rights. He had been previously suspended for one month after a Twitter post that compared "extremist Muslims" to Nazis.

In 2017, Jemele Hill was suspended by ESPN from her role as a host on *SportsCenter* for two weeks after two tweets, the first of which referenced Donald Trump as a white supremacist, and the second of which suggested that Dallas Cowboys fans boycott the team's advertisers as a protest against owner Jerry Jones's threat to punish players who knelt during the playing of the National Anthem.

On June 2, 2020, Grant Napear (a play-by-play commentator for the Sacramento Kings for thirty years) was dismissed from his job when DeMarcus Cousins asked on Twitter for Napear's thoughts regarding Black Lives Matter after the death of George Floyd and Napear tweeted back, "ALL LIVES MATTER . . . EVERY SINGLE ONE!!!"

If there's an argument against the proposition that all lives matter, I'm unaware of it. But in these ugly times, it has become a code phrase in some circles for a repudiation of the idea that Black Lives Matter.

We've come a long way since Game 5 of the 1981 NBA Finals when play-by-play commentators Gary Bender and Rick Barry were discussing a photo of Bill Russell (the third member of the announcing team) that was taken during the 1956 Summer Olympics. Barry, in an act of monumental insensitivity and stupidity, referenced the "big watermelon grin" on Russell's face. Russell, one of the most dignified athletes ever, was not amused.

Should a media organization have policies that are more restrictive, less restrictive, or the same as other companies'? The line is drawn in different places by different companies and for different professions. But as a practical matter, it's generally drawn in favor of the employer. The employer sets the guidelines, sometimes in response to principle and sometimes in response to economic pressure from the marketplace. It's a subjective standard, not an objective one. "Tread carefully" and "be responsible" are nebulous guidelines.

MSNBC chooses one type of representation. FOX News chooses another. Either way, no one suggests that, if a TV commentator walked around in public wearing a swastika, the network couldn't terminate his or her employment. Or wore a T-shirt emblazoned with the words "I hate all white [or Black] people."

ESPN has wrestled with these issues and publicly released social media guidelines for its employees. In part, these guidelines state,

> ESPN is a journalistic organization (not a political or advo-cacy organization). We should do nothing to undermine that position. We are committed to inclusion, tolerance and that which makes us different. But we must remember that public comments on social platforms will reflect on ESPN and may affect your own credibility as a journalist. At ESPN, we have a shared responsibility to one another that accompanies the ben-efits we collectively and individually enjoy. Everything we post or comment on in social media is public. And everything we do in public is associated with ESPN. Think before you tweet, post or otherwise engage on social platforms. Understand that at all times you are representing ESPN, and social sites offer the equivalent of a live microphone. Simple rule: If you wouldn't say it on the air or write it in a column, don't post it on any social network.

Referencing Paulie Malignaggi's termination, Stephen Espinoza told *The Athletic*, "We have very high standards that we expect of announcers and of everyone who represents our brand."

That's a laudable sentiment. But lest anyone think that Showtime has made a great statement of principle with regard to Malignaggi, keep in mind that the network has made no public statement as to why Paulie has been dismissed and no effort to clarify what its principles are.

Also, Showtime is the network that lent its prestige to the characteri-zation of people as "cunts," "pussies," and "faggots," and used misogynistic, homophobic statements by Floyd Mayweather and Conor McGregor as a marketing tool to engender pay-per-view buys for their 2017 fight. Indeed, Showtime went so far on that occasion as to post videos of McGregor simulating sexual intercourse with a microphone strategically placed between his legs as "a little present for my beautiful, Black female fans."

Showtime has offered to pay Malignaggi for the rest of his contract (which runs until the end of this year), but only with a non-compete clause for the duration of the contract and with limits regarding what Paulie can say publicly about Showtime and a variety of issues.

Malignaggi has worked for Sky TV in the past but always on a fight-by-fight basis. They never had a multi-bout contract. It's possible now that Sky and other networks will be reluctant to hire him.

Meanwhile, a lot of people will miss Paulie's voice on Showtime's boxing telecasts. "It is disappointing," Espinoza said. "We certainly have a lot of affection for Paulie, and he's developed into a very good analyst. It's always difficult when you have to part ways."

As for Malignaggi, he's declining to talk publicly about the matter, but does say, "I'm unhappy about the way things have played out. But I'll always be grateful to Stephen for giving me the opportunity to show what I could do as a commentator and helping me become a better commentator."

Paulie had it made and threw away much of what he had on principle. Some people might see that as admirable. But one has to question the principle.

We all need correction and guidance during the course of our lives. Ideally, Paulie will think things through and come to a more nuanced understanding of what constitutes racial oppression in the twenty-first century. Personal growth and forgiveness are honorable concepts. Perhaps someday he'll be behind a microphone again for Showtime. These times cry out for reconciliation.

In that regard, one might look to a thought that Paulie himself voiced earlier this year on *The Ak and Barak Show*: "When you calm down, you have to be able to understand the difference between constructive criticism and hating criticism. You know? And you have to be able to take the constructive criticism and build yourself and get better."

Red Smith, the Pulitzer Prize–winning sportswriter, once wrote, "It takes a special talent to be a disgrace to boxing."

Boxing Dishonored:
The Backstory on Estrada vs. Adkins

Seniesa Estrada squared off against Miranda Adkins in the third fight of the evening on DAZN's July 24, 2020, return to boxing.

Estrada, age twenty-eight, has a 19–0 (8 KOs) ring record and is the WBC silver female light-flyweight champion. She can fight.

Adkins, a 50-to-1 underdog, was born and raised in Kansas. She began training in martial arts at age thirty-nine and is now forty-two years old. BoxRec.com listed her record as five wins with five knockouts in five fights. Her first four opponents had been making their pro debut. She fought one of them again in her fifth outing. None of them has ever won a professional fight or lasted past the first round against a fighter other than Adkins. At present, they have a composite ring record of 0 wins and 8 losses.

Against Estrada, Adkins evinced no idea of what to do in a boxing ring and never threw a punch. She got hit with six of the seven punches that Seniesa threw. The slaughter ended seven seconds after the opening bell with Adkins lying unconscious on the canvas.

The fight card was promoted by Golden Boy, which arranged for Adkins's services through John Carden. According to BoxRec, Carden has been a boxing promoter since 2006 and has promoted shows in Missouri (23), Kansas (15), Iowa (1), and Nebraska (1). In recent years, Kansas has been his promotional base.

Carden's company—Carden Combat Sports—promotes itself with the tagline "The Legacy Continues." Many of its fights resemble toughman or toughwoman contests.

Carden is Adkins's promoter and de facto manger. They appear to have been married in Pololu Valley, Hawaii, on May 25, 2019, and listed Bed Bath & Beyond as their online bridal registry. Social media posts by Adkins earlier this year suggest that the couple has since separated.

The most recent fight card promoted by Carden Combat Sports took place in Abilene, Kansas, on June 6, 2020. There were thirteen bouts—eight regular boxing matches, two bareknuckle fights, two kickboxing fights, and one MMA contest.

The Rules and Regulations of the Kansas Athletic Commission require fighters to submit a negative report from an HIV test taken within six months preceding their scheduled fight. That's all. No MRI. No blood or urine test for performance-enhancing drugs. The Rules and Regulations further state, "A physician whose sole purpose is to conduct physical examinations of applicants [fighters] shall not be required to be licensed by the commission." One physician (chosen by the promoter) is assigned to each fight card.

Two weeks before the June 6 event, the fighters were asked to fill out coronavirus participation questionnaires. At the weigh-in, their temperature was taken. That was the only coronavirus "testing" required by the Kansas Athletic Commission, whose website states, "For promoters, Kansas has never been more open for business or ready for promotions to come into the state. The commission has gone to great lengths to make our process as easy as possible and have developed several initiatives designed to help make our state more promoter-friendly."

Charles Jay is one of the best investigative journalists in sports. Between 2002 and 2005, he wrote 175 articles about boxing under the title "Operation Clean-Up."

Two years ago, Jay wrote a penetrating investigative piece that explored a 2016 fight in Missouri between a club fighter named Bryan Timmons and a young man named James Kindred. It was, Jay wrote, "perhaps the most egregious and despicable thing I have ever heard of in boxing, and I've been in and around the industry for over thirty years."

As recounted by Jay, John Carden, who then ran a promotional company called Legacy Boxing, was promoting an April 16, 2016, fight card at the No Place Bar in St. Joseph, Missouri, and needed an opponent for Timmons, a thirty-five-year-old local club fighter with a 3–7 ring record who had lost four fights in a row. Carden's solution was to book thirty-three-year-old James Kindred, who had never boxed as an amateur or pro, as the opponent. There is no evidence that Kindred had even sparred in a gym.

At the weigh-in (where Kindred appeared without representation), Carden was advised by Dave Callaway and his son Joey (local residents who Carden later described as "good friends" of his) that Kindred was intellectually challenged and should not be in a boxing ring.

More specifically, as Jay wrote, "Kindred is what is known as a 'special needs' individual; someone referred to in some circles as 'intellectually-challenged' or, by those not of a politically-correct nature, 'mentally retarded.'" Indeed, Kindred was so cognitively challenged that he had been allowed to compete at the 2014 Special Olympics.

"James Kindred wanted to be a fighter," Jay wrote. "Just like some of the guys he's seen on television. The thing is, a perfectly reasonable argument can be made that he had no understanding whatsoever about what he was about to get into. Boxing is an activity where an opponent is throwing punches at you in an aggressive manner. It is hard enough to engage in this if you have not had gloves on in a competitive situation. But there is something that is absolutely essential, and that is the very specific understanding of the potential dangers that are involved. Such a thing might be referred to as the 'reality of consent.' As someone certified to be involved in Special Olympics competition, there is every reason to believe James Kindred did not possess the capacity for this."

So what happened when Carden was advised of Kindred's status?

"One would expect," Jay wrote, "that there might have been surprise and/or shock on the part of Carden, and that he would have scrapped the fight (he had thirteen scheduled) or at least sought some counsel by way of the boxing commission which had regulatory and medical personnel on hand."

But he didn't. And as Jay explained, "No one from the commission ever bothered to do the logical thing a reasonable person might do when they want to find a 'fighter' who has no professional or amateur experience, which is to perform a simple Google search. Yours truly, upon first hearing the name 'James Kindred,' was able to find his Special Olympics page through Google in less than a minute."

Fight night arrived. Then fate intervened. A local woman (Jay withheld her name to protect her privacy) was at the fights. She was friendly with Bryan Timmons and his wife. She was also a longtime Special Olympics volunteer. The woman asked Timmons's wife who Timmons was fighting and was told that it was James Kindred. The woman knew Kindred from her work with the Special Olympics and advised the Timmonses of the situation. Bryan's first instinct was to withdraw from the fight. He and the woman went over to Kindred to tell him, and Kindred started crying. He said that this was his dream and he didn't want people to say there was something he couldn't do.

Timmons then did something extraordinary. "I didn't want to fight him," he told Jay. "But I didn't want him to feel not good enough and was scared he would try again and who knows what?"

So Timmons went in the ring, pulled his punches, and went through the charade until the referee called a halt to the "fight" fifty-seven seconds into the second round.

"In the end, I'm glad it was me," Timmons said. "I hated it at the time, but he could have got real hurt had it been someone else."

Yeah. Kindred could have wound up unconscious on the ring canvas like Miranda Adkins.

I spoke this week with Tim Lueckenhoff, executive director of the Missouri Office of Athletics. "I had no clue at the time that he [Kindred] was a Special Olympian," Lueckenhoff said. "He passed all the pre-fight medicals including the psychological exam. The doctor who examined him didn't pick up on the intellectual problem. Technically, it's not against the law for someone with special intellectual needs to fight in Missouri, although we don't approve of it."

Then Lueckenhoff added, "Unfortunately, John Carden does a lot of shows that aren't what you'd want them to be. As far as he's concerned, it seems to be all about putting bodies in the ring without regard for the skill level or safety of the fighters. He promoted a number of shows here. And then, after this one [the Kindred fight card], we suggested that he promote somewhere else. Most of his shows since then have been in Kansas, although he did co-promote one here with Darrell Smith last year [Miranda Adkins's second fight against Shania Ward]. That one was pretty bad. The opponent didn't know what she was doing and looked like she just wanted to get paid and go back to Kansas."

That brings us to the July 24 confrontation between Seniesa Estrada and Adkins. Internet writers have heaped adjectives on the butchery, calling it "brutal . . . ugly . . . repulsive . . . appalling . . . gross . . . revolting . . . disgusting."

How did it come about?

Adkins was a late replacement for Jacky Calvo, who was slated to fight Estrada but suffered a knee injury two weeks before the bout.

"We wanted to do right by Seniesa and get her a fight," Golden Boy matchmaker Robert Diaz told this writer. "So we started calling around right away. It was hard because there's a limited number of women in her weight class; very few top fighters are willing to fight on short notice; and we're in the middle of a pandemic. Then a booking agent I called [Diaz declined to say which one] told me about Miranda. She wasn't ideal. Her age worked against her and the opposition she'd fought was extremely limited. But she was an undefeated professional boxer. So I called John Carden. We made the deal and he flew to Los Angeles with Miranda. I'll take the blame. My goal was to get a fight for Seniesa. The most important thing now is that Miranda is okay."

The fight was changed from ten to eight rounds in light of Adkins's limited experience. It could have been scheduled for eight seconds and wouldn't have gone the distance.

Clearly, the California State Athletic Commission should have been more vigilant. But there's no need to beat up on CSAC executive director Andy Foster because he's already beating up on himself.

"It's fair to criticize me," Foster said this week. "I didn't think Adkins would win. But Golden Boy brought the fight in, and I looked at her record. Five knockouts and five wins in five fights. The WBC had approved her as the opponent for one of its title fights. And even if a fighter hasn't beaten a quality opponent, if they've knocked out everyone they've fought, they might be able to fight. What can I say? I should have checked it out further. I got duped by her record and made a mistake."

DAZN wasn't responsible for making the fight. It streamed the entire card and was focused on quality control for the main event. That said, it was disheartening to hear blow-by-blow commentator Todd Grisham celebrate the knockout and triumphantly proclaim, "One of the quickest knockouts in women's boxing history. You witnessed it live here on DAZN."

John Carden is also to blame. He's an experienced boxing guy. Adkins might not have fully understood the peril she was facing. It's possible that she had never even been hit hard in the head by a world-class professional fighter before. But Carden knew what Adkins was getting into against

Estrada. One assumes that the $10,000 purse paid to Adkins weighed heavily in the decision-making process at his end.

Estrada's purse was $75,000. She did her job and showed no joy in the slaughter.

Boxing needs more vigilant regulation. Without it, malignancies will continue to spread.

The sports memorabilia business is often best characterized by the warning "caveat emptor."

The Ali–Kopechne Letter

On July 18, 1969, United States senator Ted Kennedy was driving a car on Chappaquiddick Island in Massachusetts when he lost control of the vehicle. The car plunged off a bridge into a pond. Kennedy survived the accident. His twenty-eight-year-old passenger—Mary Jo Kopechne—drowned. Compounding his wrongdoing, Kennedy sought to cover up his involvement in the tragedy. He subsequently pled guilty to a charge of leaving the scene of an accident and received a two-month suspended jail sentence. His behavior before the accident was inappropriate. His behavior after the accident was deplorable.

On May 2, 2020, SCP Auctions sold a letter that it says was written by Muhammad Ali to Joseph Kopechne (Mary Jo's father). The letter, which was written by hand on an 8.5-inch-by-11-inch sheet of white paper, is dated July 31, 1969. It was Lot #319 in the SCP Premier Spring Auction catalog and, in its entirety, reads as follows:

> Mr. Joseph Kopechne
> Berkeley Heights, N.J. 07922
> Regarding Edward M. Kennedy: Cocksmith
>
> Dear Mr. Kopechne = Assert yourself in the interests of the good name of your daughter. Get yourself a good lawyer and sue that no good son of a bitch, Edward M. Kennedy, for everything he's got. His intent from start to finish was a forced illicit sexual intercourse and rape of your daughter, and since the accident [there was a line break here necessitating the hyphen] was based thereon, he should be prosecuted and tried for murder. There were no mitigating circumstances. His TV speech was written for him by a dozen lawyers and speechmakers, and was not his own. The cheap two-bit hypocrite!

Sincerely,
Muhammad Ali
Cassius Clay

The letter was accompanied at auction by the original hand-addressed envelope postmarked July 31, 1969, in Los Angeles.

The SCP catalog advised prospective bidders, "The letter comes straight from the Kopechne family. A letter of provenance from Mary Jo's cousin, William Nelson, is included. On July 18, 2019, the 50th anniversary of Mary Jo's death, the Kopechne family felt it was time for this controversial letter to finally be exposed to the public."

Georgetta Nelson Potoski was one of Mary Jo Kopechne's cousins. William Nelson is Potoski's son.

Including the 20 percent buyer's premium, the letter sold at auction on May 2 for $12,545.

But it is authentic?

The letter was offered to Heritage Auctions for consignment in spring 2019. But Heritage had doubts about its authenticity and declined to put it up for auction. Then, in July 2019, Potoski and Nelson issued a joint statement announcing the existence of the letter to the *Times Leader*, a publication that describes itself as the "flagship of The Times Leader Media Group, a collection of print and digital products that cover the Scranton/Wilkes-Barre metropolitan area."

Thereafter, Gray Flannel Auctions put the letter up for auction. But the bidding closed on January 23, 2020, without the $5,000 minimum having been bid. Then SCP got involved.

SCP Auctions was founded in 1979 and is one of the largest auctioneers and private sellers of sports memorabilia and cards in the United States. Its past sales have included a Babe Ruth game-worn road jersey ($4,415,000), a set of three documents from 1857 titled "Laws of Base Ball" ($3,263,246), and a T206 Honus Wagner tobacco card graded PSA NM-MT 8 ($2,800,000).

Where boxing is concerned, in November 2012, SCP auctioned off "The Angelo Dundee Collection" for more than $1,300,000. The gloves worn by Cassius Clay in his first fight against Sonny Liston and by Muhammad Ali in his first fight against Joe Frazier were included in the Dundee auction. Each pair sold for $385,848.

But SCP has not been free of controversy.

Craig Hamilton is the foremost boxing memorabilia dealer in the United States. Over the years, he has been retained by Sotheby's, Christie's, Heritage, and numerous other auction houses to document and authenticate memorabilia prior to auction.

Six years ago, Hamilton reviewed the 2014 SCP Summer Premier Auction. Fifty-nine boxing-related items had been sold. Some of them were cause for concern. For example:

* A pair of "Jim Jeffries fight worn Everlast boxing shoes, circa 1910" sold for $1,200. But as Hamilton noted, "The problem with that is, Everlast didn't make boxing equipment in 1910. They started making it in 1917, long after Jeffries's career was over."
* A pair of "Willie Pep fight worn Everlast boxing gloves circa 1942" sold for $1,320. But as Hamilton pointed out, "These gloves were stamped '24 14,' which indicates that they're 14-ounce gloves. Pep wore 6-ounce gloves in fights."
* A "fight worn boxing robe" from Gene Tunney circa 1926 sold for $15,052. "How do they know that Tunney wore this robe in a fight?" Hamilton asked. "Over the years, I've looked at every film of Gene Tunney in the ring that I could find. I have 200 to 300 photos of Tunney in the ring before and after fights. And I've I never seen him standing in the ring wearing a robe. Every image I've seen shows him wearing a towel over his shoulders, not a robe."

"I'm not saying that SCP is dishonest," Hamilton said at the time. "But there are times when its authentication procedures are a bit sloppy."

That brings us to the Ali–Kopechne letter.

SCP says that the body of the letter and two signatures ("Muhammad Ali" and "Cassius Clay") were authenticated by PSA/DNA and Beckett Authentication Services. But apart from that issue, there's a question as to whether the thoughts in the letter represented Ali's thinking or the thoughts of someone else who dictated the letter to him. That's important because the SCP catalog goes much further than saying the letter is in Ali's hand. It ascribes the thoughts in it to him.

"Bold. Confrontational. Defiant. Valiant," the catalog description begins. "These words describe Muhammad Ali to a tee. He was the ultimate instigator, in and out of the ring. And while his showmanship in the heat of battle may have come off as arrogant to some, The Greatest of All Time was a very self-aware man, cognizant of his environment and principled in his convictions. He knew a little about fighting the establishment as well. Considered an outcast by the government, he took it upon himself to stand up for other sociopolitical injustices. Just two weeks after the notorious 1969 Chappaquiddick incident, which left Mary Jo Kopechne mysteriously dead at the hands of a privileged white Senator from America's most prestigious family, Ali aggressively came to the young lady's defense and handwrote this passionate letter addressed to her grieving father."

Indeed, the catalog copy goes so far as to state, "The Champ would not have added his original 'slave' name five years after converting to Islam unless he really wanted to pound home his passion for the message and make the Kopechne family absolutely certain that it was coming from him."

As noted earlier, the letter was offered to Heritage Auctions for consignment in spring 2019. But Heritage had doubts about its authenticity and, after consulting with Craig Hamilton, declined to put the letter up for auction. Among the points Hamilton made to Heritage in telephone conversations and in writing at that time were:

1. Ali would not have started a letter with the word "regarding."
2. Ali wouldn't have used a word like "cocksmith" or called Ted Kennedy a "no good son of a bitch." Nor would he have known Ted Kennedy's full name.
3. Ali wouldn't have known what words like "illicit," "mitigating," "assert," and "thereon" mean, let alone how to spell them.
4. Ali couldn't have spelled "hypocrite" or "Kopechne."
5. Ali wouldn't have known what a colon is.
6. It's improbable that Ali would have written "via air mail" on the envelope. Nor could he have spelled "Berkeley Heights" correctly.

Also, Hamilton doubted that Ali would have double-signed a letter like this in 1969 as "Cassius Clay."

Hamilton had no reason to question that the letter was sent to the

Kopechne family. But on May 22, 2019, he wrote to Chris Ivy (director of sports auctions for Heritage), stating, "The writing does resemble that of Ali. The issue is the content. There really is no way Ali decided to sit down, on his own, and write this letter. If he actually wrote it, someone had to dictate it to him and spell the words for him. Is it possible? You can never say never about anything. Unlikely, yes. It just isn't him. I couldn't write a letter saying I thought he wrote it. I leave open the possibility someone had him do it and helped him do it. That, in my view, is the only way it happened. He just was not capable of writing that letter independently. If you run it, in fairness to a buyer, I think you have to point that out."

In the interest of disclosure, I should add that Hamilton asked me what I thought of the Kopechne letter before he responded to Heritage. I was not paid for sharing my thoughts with him.

On May 3 of this year, speaking about the letter, Hamilton repeated his previously expressed reservations and told this writer, "The authenticators say Ali wrote it. If that's their opinion, okay. But then SCP should have put in an explanation saying that, while Ali might have written the letter, it's possible that he didn't create it."

But that's not what SCP did. Far from inserting a note of caution in the catalog, SCP doubled down on the import of the letter insofar as it purports to relate to Ali's state of mind at that time.

In that regard, Hamilton states, "They wanted to show that Ali created this out of some great anger and sat down and wrote this diatribe expressing all these thoughts he never expressed anywhere else, using all those words he probably didn't understand and certainly couldn't spell. I find it impossible to believe that it happened that way. Give me another example in Ali's entire lifetime when he sat down and wrote something that remotely resembled this letter in content or language."

It's possible that someone stood over Ali, dictated every word of the letter, and told him how to spell the big words. But that person would have had to tell Ali how to hyphenate "accident." And the big words look like they were written in a flowing hand which is inconsistent with someone dictating the spelling to the person who is doing the writing.

Also, the SCP catalog copy states in bold type, "A very significant addition to this letter that Ali included in the envelope was an invitation to an anti-Vietnam War demonstration held 8/17/1969 outside President Nixon's summer home in San Clemente, CA. This logically places Muhammad Ali in Southern California when the letter was written and mailed, meaning he must have flown into L.A. three weeks or a month before attending this peace rally in Orange County."

But an August 18, 1969, *New York Times* article about the rally makes no mention of Ali being in attendance. It's possible that a study of the historical record would reveal whether or not he was in Los Angeles on July 31, 1969 (the day the letter is dated and postmarked).

If not Ali, who would have gone to the trouble of creating this document in 1969 and mailing it to the Kopechne family? Someone who despised Ted Kennedy and wanted to make life as difficult as possible for him.

On May 4, this writer emailed Brendan Wells (SCP's auction director) and asked to speak with him regarding the letter. Wells requested that I send him my questions in advance, and I forwarded the following to him:

1. Other than the handwriting analysis by PSA/DNA and Beckett, did you take any steps to determine whether Muhammad Ali was in fact the author of the letter? And if so, what were these steps?
2. Prior to putting the letter up for auction, were you aware that Heritage Auctions declined to accept the letter for auction in 2019?
3. What is the basis for the statement in the auction catalog that Muhammad Ali attended the August 17, 1969, demonstration in Orange County?

That evening, Wells responded with a short email stating that the letter "passed Beckett and PSA/DNA" and that, "Out of respect to both the winning bidder and consignor (Kopechne family members), we will decline further comment" (parentheses in original).

It's hard to understand how answering questions regarding the authenticity of the letter would have been disrespectful to the Kopechne family and winning bidder.

There's no record I'm aware of that Ali spoke out publicly regarding Ted Kennedy's conduct in the aftermath of Chappaquiddick. I do know that, in later years, Muhammad spoke fondly of Kennedy. And there was a photograph of Ali and Kennedy together in the senator's office beside a pair of boxing gloves that Ali inscribed to Kennedy with the suggestion that the gloves might help him in the fight to knock out injustice.

So for now, let's give the final word to Khalilah Ali (known in 1969 as Belinda Ali). Belinda was Muhammad's second wife. They were married in 1967, two months after Ali was criminally convicted for refusing induction into the United States Army.

On May 5, this writer asked Khalilah about the letter.

"It's ridiculous," Khalilah responded. "Ali loved the Kennedys. He thought they were good people and he said they cared about Black people. There's no way he would have written anything like that because he didn't think it. And even if he thought it, let's be real. Ali didn't write letters like that. Ali couldn't write letters like that. This was a guy who had trouble getting through high school. He was smart in a lot of ways, but writing wasn't one of them. If he needed a serious letter, I wrote it for him to sign. But I never ever wrote a letter like this. I'll say it again. Ali didn't write stuff like this. Ali couldn't write stuff like this. It's absurd. Do you remember when Howard Cosell called Ali 'truculent,' and Ali said he didn't know what 'truculent' means? And now you're telling me that Ali knew words like 'mitigating' and 'illicit.' No, sir. No way. If Ali wanted to send something to this woman's father, he would have drawn a little heart on an index card and signed it 'Love, Muhammad Ali.' Except he wouldn't have known how to find the father."

This was a walk down memory lane.

The Best and the Most

I was a boxing fan before I was a boxing writer. In recent weeks with boxing on hiatus, I've had the opportunity to reflect on some of the best, most memorable experiences that I've had in the sweet science and others that I wish I'd had. Some of these thoughts follow.

The Best Fights I've Ever Been To

(1) Muhammad Ali vs. Joe Frazier I—March 8, 1971

I'd graduated from law school the previous year and was clerking for a United States district judge when I read in the *New York Times* that Muhammad Ali and Joe Frazier had signed to fight at Madison Square Garden. That day, I mailed a check for forty dollars (equivalent to $255 today) and a request for two mezzanine tickets (the least expensive seats in the house) to the Garden. The tickets arrived in the mail soon after. It's unlikely that tickets for a fight of that magnitude would be available at face value to an ordinary fan today. I went with a friend from law school. We sat in the last row of the mezzanine. Forty-nine years later, I remember moments from that night like it was yesterday.

(2) José Luis Castillo vs. Diego Corrales I—May 7, 2005

Great fights swing back and forth in terms of dominance. But let's be honest—they're also marked by brutal action. José Luis Castillo and Diego Corrales engaged in trench warfare round after round in a breathtaking fight at Mandalay Bay in Las Vegas. Corrales's left eye was hideously swollen. He was knocked down twice in round ten, spat out his mouthpiece after the second knockdown, and looked like a beaten fighter. But instead of ending the bout, referee Tony Weeks deducted a point from Corrales for removing his mouthpiece. That gave Diego 28 seconds to recover. Then everything changed. Both men threw right hands. Corrales's right hand got there first. Suddenly, Castillo was against the ropes, taking punches, glassy-eyed, his head wobbling like it was on a bobblehead doll. At that point, Weeks stopped the fight.

(3) Delvin Rodríguez vs. Pawel Wolack I—July 15, 2011

This was a quintessential club fight; the non-HBO version of Gatti–Ward I. It was contested at Roseland Ballroom, a small venue in Manhattan that no longer exists. There was no feeling-out process; just nonstop action between two fighters who willingly engaged for ten torrid rounds. By round seven, Wolak's right eye was swollen shut and useless. The only function it served was to make his head a bigger target. By the end of the fight, the entire right side of his face from his mouth to his hairline was misshapen, as though someone had shoved a tennis ball beneath the skin and painted the entire area purple. Rodríguez's face was less marked but he didn't look so good, either. No one begrudged either man the majority-draw decision of the judges.

The Best Fights I've Seen on Television

(1) Muhammad Ali vs. Joe Frazier III—October 1, 1975

Boxing fans are familiar with what happened on that hot, humid morning in Manila. The early rounds belonged to Ali. He outboxed Frazier, landed sharp, clean punches, and staggered Joe several times. Frazier kept coming forward. The tide turned in the middle rounds. Ali tired. Frazier rocked him with thunderous blows. Muhammad's arms came down, and Joe bludgeoned him against the ropes. In round twelve, Ali regained the initiative, wobbled Frazier, and measured him for more. One round later, a jolting right hand knocked Joe's mouthpiece into the crowd. Frazier was shaken but finished the round. In round fourteen, Ali resumed his assault. Frazier's left eye was completely closed. The vision in his right eye was limited. He was spitting blood. Ali's punches were landing cleanly. Joe couldn't see them coming. Frazier's trainer, Eddie Futch, stopped the fight after the fourteenth round. Associated Press boxing writer Ed Schuyler later recalled, "Everybody at ringside understood they were watching greatness. It was hell the whole way. I've never seen two people give more, ever."

(2) Sugar Ray Leonard vs. Thomas Hearns I—September 16, 1981

Ray Leonard was boxing's brightest star. The only blemish on his record was a close loss by decision to Roberto Duran, avenged five months later when he made Duran say "No más." Hearns was undefeated in 32 fights with 30 knockouts. Each fighter had an iconic trainer in his corner. Emanuel Steward with Hearns, Angelo Dundee with Leonard. The fight shaped up as a classic confrontation between boxer (Leonard) and puncher (Hearns). Except it didn't unfold that way. Rallying after a rocky sixth round, Hearns began controlling the fight with a nasty cobra-like jab. After twelve rounds, the area beneath Leonard's left eye was badly swollen. In the corner before the start of round thirteen, Dundee told his charge, "You're blowing it, son." And Ray dug as deep as a fighter can dig. In round thirteen, he battered Hearns around the ring after stunning him with a big right hand. In round fourteen, he closed the show. That night, Ray Leonard confirmed his greatness.

(3) Arturo Gatti vs. Micky Ward I—May 18, 2002

Gatti was the prototype for an all-action, blood-and-guts warrior. He'd been outboxed but never outslugged except for an outing against Oscar De La Hoya who bested him on both counts. Ward was a club fighter, albeit a very good one, with eleven defeats on his resume. When they fought each other at the Mohegan Sun Casino, fans quickly understood that they were watching a time-capsule fight. There were moments when the battle seemed to defy reality, marked as it was by unremitting punishment and an extraordinary ebb and flow. Ward was cut badly in round one and bled throughout the fight. In round nine, Gatti sank to the canvas from a vicious body shot, rose, took more punishment, turned the tide, and had Ward in trouble. Then Micky rallied, leaving Arturo out on his feet at the bell. Somehow, Gatti rallied again to win the tenth round. Ward prevailed by a narrow 95–93, 94–93, 94–94 margin. The two men faced off in the ring twice more. But neither of those fights (both of which Gatti won by unanimous decision) came close to the drama of their first encounter.

Great Fighters Who I'm Glad I Saw Fight at Their Peak

(1) Manny Pacquiao

There are great fighters (such as Sugar Ray Leonard and Larry Holmes) who I saw fight in person long after they'd passed their prime. In some instances, I've been privileged to see extraordinary craftsmen at their peak. I was at ten Manny Pacquiao fights. The first three—contested against Oscar De La Hoya, Ricky Hatton, and Miguel Cotto—saw Pacquiao at his best. The last—against Floyd Mayweather—was dreadful. I was in Manny's dressing room before and after his fights against Hatton and Cotto and also his fights at Cowboys Stadium against Joshua Clottey and Antonio Margarito. But it's his performance in the ring—not the hours spent in Manny's dressing room—that stands out most vividly in my mind. Pacquiao at his peak was one of the most exciting fighters I've ever seen and would have been competitive against the best in any era.

(2) Roy Jones

The first time I saw Roy Jones fight live, he knocked out Jorge Vaca in the first round at the Paramount Theatre at Madison Square Garden. He was six days shy of his twenty-third birthday. Greatness was stamped all over him. I was at ringside for fifteen of Roy's fights. On six of these occasions, I was in his dressing room before and after the bout. People have criticized the level of Roy's opposition. But he outpointed a twenty-eight-year-old Bernard Hopkins and a twenty-six-year-old James Toney. And on March 1, 2003, thirteen years after starting his career at 157 pounds, he outclassed John Ruiz to claim the WBA heavyweight crown. Jones's physical gifts—most notably, his speed and reflexes—separated him from other fighters. There was a time when you could have asked ten fighters, "Who's the best fighter in the world right now?" And without hesitation, every one of them would have answered, "Roy Jones."

(3) Mike Tyson

Mike Tyson's sixth pro fight was a third-round knockout of Larry Sims at the Mid-Hudson Civic Center in Poughkeepsie, New York, on July 19, 1985. I was there. I was also at ringside as Tyson's rise continued against Sammy Scaff, Mitch Green, and Reggie Gross. He was a scary, brutal, destructive force. I was in and out of boxing in those days. The only other time I saw Tyson fight live was his first-round destruction of Carl Williams in Atlantic City in 1989. Then he journeyed to Tokyo to meet his destiny in the person of James "Buster" Douglas. One of the sad things about Tyson is that all the craziness in his life has obscured how great a fighter he was when he was young. I'm glad I was able to witness the growth of that young fighter.

The Fights I Most Wish I Could Have Been At

(1) Joe Louis vs. Max Schmeling II—June 22, 1938

This was arguably the most important fight in boxing history. Joe Louis, the symbol of American democracy, vs. Max Schmeling, the darling of Nazi Germany. Schmeling had scored a shocking knockout upset over Louis two years earlier. Now Louis was ready to even the score. It was the clearest symbolic confrontation between good and evil in the history of sports and the first time that many people heard a Black man referred to simply as "the American." More than seventy thousand fans jammed Yankee Stadium. And on that night, Joe Louis was the greatest fighter who ever lived. He destroyed Schmeling, knocking him out at two minutes, four seconds of the first round.

(2) Gene Tunney vs. Jack Dempsey II—September 22, 1927

Jack Dempsey lifted boxing to unprecedented heights in the Roaring Twenties and redefined both the sport and business of boxing. Think about what it was like at Soldiers' Field in Chicago on September 22, 1927, when Dempsey sought to regain the heavyweight crown from Gene Tunney, who'd beaten him one year earlier. The staggering total of 104,943 fans rewrote boxing's record book, paying a live gate of $2,658,660 (equivalent to almost $40 million today). Then the bell rang, and Tunney prevailed in the famous "Long Count" fight.

(3) John L. Sullivan vs. Jake Kilrain—July 8, 1889

John L. Sullivan was America's first sports superstar and, other than presidents and a few military heroes, the most famous person in the United States. On that day, at 10:13 a.m., Sullivan and Kilrain "came to scratch" in a thirty-thousand-acre pine forest in Richburg, Mississippi. Imagine the scene. Their illegal bareknuckle fight was the last heavyweight championship contest ever fought under the London Prize Ring Rules. The weather was muggy, the temperature close to one hundred degrees. Two hours and sixteen minutes after the battle began, a thoroughly beaten Kilrain refused to come to scratch for the seventy-sixth round. An old era had come to an end. Modern boxing was about to dawn.

My Most Memorable Dressing Room Experiences

(1) With Billy Costello for Costello vs. Saoul Mamby—November 3, 1984

Over the years, I've spent the hours before and after fights in the dressing room with countless fighters. It's a privilege that I never take for granted. The first time that I did it remains the most meaningful for me. I'd been tracking WBC super-lightweight champion Billy Costello for months, spending five days a week with him while researching *The Black Lights* (my first book about boxing). We'd become friends. I don't use that term lightly. Now everything Billy had worked for was on the line. Fight day was an emotional rollercoaster. Thirty-six years later, images from those hours remain seared in my mind. Billy won a twelve-round decision. That was the most important thing about that afternoon.

(2) With Jermain Taylor for Taylor vs. Bernard Hopkins I—July 16, 2005

The stakes were incredibly high. Bernard Hopkins was undisputed middleweight champion of the world, unbeaten over the previous twelve years. Jermain Taylor was a promising young fighter with a ring résumé that was short on the type of experience deemed necessary to challenge "The Executioner." It was an ugly promotion. Hopkins constantly mocked Taylor, who he demeaned as a simple country boy from Arkansas. There was genuine hatred between Bernard and Lou DiBella (Hopkins's former promoter, who now worked with Jermain). I found myself emotionally drawn into it all. The fight was dramatic. Taylor surged ahead early, then tired and fought back courageously from the brink of being knocked out. Michael Buffer's reading of the scorecards was one of the most tense moments I've experienced in boxing. Taylor won a razor-thin split decision. I've never been in a dressing room, before or after a fight, quite like it.

(3) With Ricky Hatton for Hatton vs. Floyd Mayweather— December 8, 2007

A fighter's dressing room reflects his personality. Ricky Hatton's dressing room was always a madhouse. Booming music, nonstop motion. I always wondered why he wasn't exhausted by the time he left for the ring. Las Vegas had been buzzing about Mayweather–Hatton throughout the week. On fight night, the tension reached new heights. Luminaries as diverse as Ray Leonard and Tom Jones came into the dressing room to wish Ricky well before the fight. A recording of Mick Jagger singing "(I Can't Get No) Satisfaction" reverberated throughout the room. Hatton waged a spirited battle but was stopped in the tenth round. Afterward, Brad Pitt and Angelina Jolie stopped by the dressing room to offer condolences.

Dressing Rooms That I Wish I'd Been In

(1) Joe Louis vs. Max Schmeling II—June 22, 1938

I'm often asked why it's important to me to be in a fighter's dressing room before and after a big fight. The answer, apart from the fun of it all, is, "I'm writing for history. Think about what it would mean if someone had been in Joe Louis's dressing room before and after he knocked out Max Schmeling." Louis–Schmeling II is the only double entry on this list. Imagine the tension before and unbridled joy after that fight. That night, Joe Louis became a symbol of hope for all of America and entered the ranks of boxing immortals.

(2) Sonny Liston vs. Cassius Clay—February 25, 1964

I'm sure it was an extraordinary experience to be in Muhammad Ali's dressing room before any fight, with The Rumble in the Jungle and The Thrilla in Manila high on the list. But without Liston–Clay, the epic future bouts wouldn't have happened. The craziness, the excitement, the artistry and drama of Liston–Clay were the perfect launching pad for the man who, ten days later, changed his name to Muhammad Ali and ultimately would change the world.

(3) Jack Johnson vs. James Jeffries—July 4, 1910

Arthur Ashe said that, despite everything Muhammad Ali accomplished, Jack Johnson had a larger impact within the United States than Ali did. "Nothing that Frederick Douglass did," Ashe opined, "nothing that Booker T. Washington did, nothing that any African American had done up until that time had the same impact as Jack Johnson's fight against Jim Jeffries on July 4, 1910. It was the most awaited event in the history of African Americans to that date. Virtually every Black American knew that Johnson versus Jeffries was going to take place. They knew what was at stake and they also knew they could get the results almost immediately because of the advent of the telegraph. And when Johnson won, it completely destroyed one of the crucial pillars of white supremacy—the idea that the white man was superior in body and mind to all the darker peoples of the earth. That was just not true as far as anybody was concerned anymore because now a Black man held the title symbolic of the world's most physically powerful human being." I wish I could have been in Johnson's inner sanctum that afternoon to create a historical record of it all.

The Best Interviews I Had with a Fighter

(1) Muhammad Ali (1967)

Muhammad Ali appears in many of the categories on this list. That's partly because of his artistry as a fighter and importance as a social and political figure. And it's partly because of the relationship that I developed with him while working as his biographer and in later years. But my first interview with Ali came two decades before I started researching *Muhammad Ali: His Life and Times*.

When I was an undergraduate at Columbia University, I hosted a radio show called *Personalities In Sports* for the student-run radio station. Each week, I'd take a bulky reel-to-reel tape recorder into the field and interview the biggest names I could get. In March 1967, Ali was preparing to fight Zora Folley at Madison Square Garden. It was his final bout before his refusal to accept induction into the United States Army led to a three-and-a-half-year exile from boxing. John Condon (director of publicity for Madison Square Garden) arranged the interview for me. It took place in Ali's dressing room after a sparring session with Jimmy Ellis. I wasn't from the *New York Times* or any other news organization of note, but that didn't matter to Ali. He told me to turn on my tape recorder. We talked about Nation of Islam doctrine with some questions about the military draft, Zora Folley, and boxing in general thrown in. Ten minutes after we began, Ali announced, "That's all I'm gonna do," and the interview was over. I still have the tape.

(2) George Foreman (1988 and later)

On December 2, 1988, I was in Las Vegas with Muhammad Ali for the taping of a documentary titled *Champions Forever* featuring Ali, Joe Frazier, Larry Holmes, Ken Norton, and George Foreman. That gave me the opportunity to conduct interviews for my Ali biography. George had returned to the ring twenty-one months earlier after ten years away from boxing. Most people considered his comeback to be a quixotic quest or bad joke. Six more years would pass before he dethroned Michael Moorer to reclaim the heavyweight championship of the world. But in our conversation that day, I found him to be a thoughtful, insightful man.

"I don't think Muhammad's conversion was a religious experience," George told me. "I'll believe until the day I die that it was a social awakening that acquainted him with the Muslim religion. It was something that he needed at the time. The whole country needed it. Young people in particular were tired of walking around with a feeling of inferiority, and some of them were awakened socially by the call of the Muslims. Later on, what Muhammad believed began to turn more on religion. But at the start, I think it was something different."

That was the start of a relationship with George that has lasted for more than three decades. Over the years, we've talked in depth about family, religion, and other value-oriented issues. And it began on that day in Las Vegas.

(3) Ray Leonard (2010)

On May 1, 2010, I was in the media center at the MGM Grand in Las Vegas. Floyd Mayweather and Shane Mosley were scheduled to fight the following night. Leonard and Thomas Hearns were on hand for a mid-morning media sit-down to engender pay-per-view buys. When they were done and Ray was readying to leave, I approached him.

"We've never had the chance to really talk," I said. "I'd love the opportunity to sit with you sometime and discuss things in depth."

"How about now?" Ray suggested.

We talked for the better part of three hours. About boxing and much more.

Hall of Fame matchmaker Bruce Trampler says, "Most people who are serious about boxing understand that Sugar Ray Robinson was the best fighter ever. But as time goes by, more and more people are starting to believe that Ray Leonard was the best fighter since Robinson. People knew he was good, but not how good. His charisma overshadowed his talent."

Talking with Ray that day was special for me.

Fighters I Wish I Could Have Interviewed

(1) Jack Johnson

Jack Johnson's place in history is secure as a fighter and symbol of social injustice. But he was also an intelligent, complex, multifaceted man. I can imagine talking with him for hours about a wide range of subjects, not just boxing.

(2) Sugar Ray Robinson

I had a thirty-second telephone conversation with Sugar Ray Robinson in 1984. I'd just begun researching *The Black Lights* and wanted to know what it felt like to be acclaimed as the greatest fighter of all time. Bill Gallo (the boxing writer and sports cartoonist for the *New York Daily News*) gave me Robinson's home telephone number and told me to tell Ray's wife that Bill said it was okay for Ray to talk with me. So I called.

"Bill should know better than that," Millie Robinson told me. "Ray doesn't talk much these days." But I promised to be kind, and she put Ray on the line.

Robinson was sixty-three years old, aging badly and suffering from dementia. I asked him how it felt to be regarded as the greatest fighter of all time.

"It's the most wonderful feeling in the world," Robinson answered. "I can't say any more. I loved boxing, and every time I hear someone say 'pound for pound' . . ." His voice trailed off, then picked up again. "It's the most wonderful feeling in the world."

Robinson is the gold standard against which fighters are judged. And he became the standard bearer for a new kind of athlete, a superstar personality who demanded his due outside the ring as well as in it. I wish I could have talked with him. Really talked with him.

(3) Joe Louis

Joe Louis wasn't particularly verbal. As David Margolick wrote, "When you strip away all the layers of mythology and idealization, it's hard to say very much about the Louis who remains. He was dignified and decent, uneducated and inarticulate, though with an odd knack for reducing things to pithy truisms. For all of his violence in the ring, he was largely passive, affectless, even dull outside of it. He was not oblivious to the gargantuan impact he had on others. But like just about everything else, he took it all in stride. The hopes that people placed on his shoulders, enough to crush normal people, appeared to impose no particular burden on him. He had few deep feelings of his own, but he had an ability to generate intense passion in others. He was the perfect vehicle for everyone else's dreams."

There are very few in-depth interviews with Joe Louis on the public record. I would have loved to engage him in extended conversation.

And a Special Category

I met Don King in 1983. Since then, I've spent countless hours with him in public gatherings and private forums. I've written at length about the negative side of the Don King ledger. On the positive side, he was one of the smartest, most charismatic, hardest-working people I've known. And he forced America to accept him as he was on his terms. Don was Black and from the streets. He made no effort to hide it. To the contrary, he stuffed it in people's faces. We're not talking about an athlete, singer, or movie star who made his mark by entertaining people. We're talking about commerce, economic control.

Knowing Don King has enriched my life.

A clear line separates amateur and professional boxers in terms of their ring skills.

Should Amateur Records Count in Evaluating Greatness?

I received an email recently from a reader who asked whether a fighter's amateur record should be considered in evaluating whether the fighter was great.

It's a good question.

Three fighters stand at the pinnacle of amateur boxing. Hungarian middleweight Lazlo Papp (1948, 1952, and 1956) and Cuban heavyweights Teófilo Stevenson (1972, 1976, and 1980) and Félix Savón (1992, 1996, and 2000) each won three Olympic gold medals. Of the three, only Papp fought as a pro, compiling a 27–0–2 (15 KOs) record in a seven-year career that saw him win the European middleweight title.

Success as an amateur boxer is a factor in predicting greatness, just as success in the college ranks is a factor in predicting greatness for a football or basketball player. But there's a difference between being a great amateur and a great pro, starting with the level of competition.

There are no guarantees. JaMarcus Russell, Tim Couch, and Ki-Jana Carter were overall #1 picks in the NFL draft, and each had a mediocre pro career. The big question prior to the 1998 NFL draft was whether Peyton Manning or Ryan Leaf would be the overall #1 selection. The Indianapolis Colts scouts preferred Leaf but were overruled by the coaching staff, who insisted on drafting Manning. Leaf (who was selected by the San Diego Chargers with the #2 overall pick) was one of the most notorious "draft busts" of all time.

Cuba has a storied amateur boxing system that has produced more Olympic gold medal winners since Fidel Castro's rise to power in 1959 than any other country. Some of these gold-medal winners later turned pro. But none were "great" in the professional ranks.

Why not? People point to a range of factors. But the most important factor is that the demands of professional boxing are different from the demands placed on fighters in the amateur ranks.

Teófilo Stevenson might have been the most devastating amateur fighter ever. But he fought three-round fights against young men who weren't well schooled in avoiding his big right hand. Most of his opponents lacked bigtime power. Many had suspect chins.

Stevenson was a great amateur boxer. But he was competing against amateurs, not pros. We never learned if he had the physical skills and mental strength to succeed in the professional ranks.

Mark Breland was hailed in the 1980s as possibly the greatest amateur boxer of all time. He compiled a 110–1 record with 73 knockouts (the sole loss came on a 3–2 split decision) and won a gold medal at the 1984 Olympics. But he fell short of greatness as a pro.

Howard Davis had a great amateur career with 125 wins against 5 losses. He won a gold medal at the 1976 Olympics and was chosen over Teófilo Stevenson, Ray Leonard, and the Spinks brothers as recipient of the Val Barker Trophy, awarded to the outstanding boxer at the Montreal games. He also won a world amateur championship and two National AAU titles, defeating Thomas Hearns in the finals for his second AAU crown. But he failed in three world championship challenges as a pro.

Some great fighters have won National Golden Gloves, National AAU, and USA Boxing national championships. Ray Leonard, Evander Holyfield, Thomas Hearns, Roy Jones, Floyd Mayweather Jr., Michael Spinks, and Mike Tyson and are among them. But it's no sure predictor of success.

Over the past twenty years, twenty-seven men have won a National Golden Gloves super-heavyweight championship, National AAU super-heavyweight championship, or USA Boxing super-heavyweight championship. They are—drumroll, please—Steve Vukosa, T. J. Wilson, Jason Estrada, Lonnie Zaid, Malcolm Tann, Travis Walker, Raphael Butler, Mike Wilson, Gregory Corbin, Felix Stewart, Jonte Willis, Michael Hunter, Nathaniel James, Tor Hamer, Lenroy Thompson (a.k.a. Cam F. Awesome), Roberto Morban, Jonathan Hamm, Isaac Boes, Andrew Coleman, Stephan Shaw, Jermaine Franklin, Darmani Rock, Nkosi Solomon, Marcus Carter, Richard Torrez, Roney Hines, and Antonio Mireles. With all due respect for their accomplishments, there are no likely future Hall of Fame fighters there.

Fighters restart when they turn pro.

Sugar Ray Robinson is credited with an amateur record of 85 wins,

0 losses, and 69 knockouts. But his first pro fight was a four-round bout against Joe Echevarria—a fighter with a 4–17 pro record who would go winless in the last twenty fights of his career after facing Robinson.

Why did Robinson start his pro career that way? Because pro boxing is different from amateur boxing. There's a learning process that has to be assimilated. That involves fighting opponents who can punch harder and take a better punch than most amateurs; implementing new moves that a fighter has been taught in the gym; and learning to handle the pressure of fighting six, eight, ten, and twelve rounds.

Also, to be great, a fighter has to evolve physically and develop "man strength."

Look at the learning process that Cassius Clay went through after he turned pro.

There are no guarantees that amateur accomplishments will be matched in the pros.

Andre Ward (the last Olympic gold medalist in boxing from the United States) won his medal as a light-heavyweight at the 2004 Athens Olympics and had a great pro career. The three Olympic light-heavyweight gold medalists since Ward have been Zhang Xiaoping, Egor Mekhontsev, and Julio César La Cruz.

Some of the great Cuban fighters were young when they won their first Olympic gold medal. Teófilo Stevenson and Guillermo Rigondeaux were twenty. Joel Casamayor was twenty-one. We don't know how good they would have become as pros had they been put into a well-organized pro system at that time.

Vasyl Lomachenko won gold medals at the 2008 and 2012 Olympics. He turned pro in 2013 and went in tough from the start. Lomachenko lost a split decision to Orlando Salido in his second pro bout, defeated Gary Russell Jr. in his third, and is at or near the top of most pound-for-pound lists today. But Vasyl's claim to greatness rests not so much on his amateur credentials as on the fact that he fought and beat world-class opponents from the start of his pro career.

Do the electors consider a baseball player's minor league career when filling out their Hall of Fame ballots? Should a basketball player's accomplishments in high school count in evaluating greatness?

Greatness is a measure of what a fighter becomes in the professional ranks, not what he did as an amateur.

A fighter's amateur career is a building block for what he might be someday. But a fighter is measured by what he accomplishes as a pro.

In evaluating whether a fighter was great, the most important factor to be considered is who he beat. Muhammad Ali is heralded as a great fighter because he beat Sonny Liston, Joe Frazier, and George Foreman; not because he beat Zbigniew Pietrzykowski, Tony Madigan, and Gennady Shatkov at the 1960 Olympics.

Even a fighter's early professional bouts can be discounted in weighing greatness. Bernard Hopkins lost his first pro fight to Clinton Mitchell, who was also making his pro debut. Benny Leonard was knocked out in his pro debut by a 1–1 fighter named Mickey Finnegan. Henry Armstrong lost four of his first five professional outings.

If a fighter is a great pro, a stellar amateur career might give him a bit more cachet in evaluating his greatness. But then he wouldn't need it. How many people know or care that Joe Louis won the National AAU light-heavyweight championship in 1934?

As William Wordsworth wrote two centuries ago, "The Child is father of the Man."

Why Doesn't Boxing Attract More Young Fans?

Kids become sports fans at a young age and carry that passion with them throughout their lives.

Contrary to popular wisdom, boxing isn't an "old man's" sport. The average age of television viewers for boxing is younger than for Major League Baseball, NFL football, NASCAR, horse racing, tennis, and golf.

But boxing has an old look. Three of its most recognizable personalities in the United States are Don King (age 88), Michael Buffer (75), and George Foreman (71). And boxing doesn't attract young fans to the extent that other sports do.

By "young," I'm not talking about the 18-to-49 age demographic coveted by advertisers. I'm talking about age twelve and under, when lifelong allegiances to sports are formed. Except for inroads in the Hispanic community, boxing's fan base among pre-adolescent youngsters is minimal. That hurts it down the road in terms of total followers.

Years ago, boxing was ingrained in the fabric of America. Jack Johnson, Joe Louis, and Muhammad Ali had a huge impact on society. Fighters like Jack Dempsey, Rocky Marciano, and Sugar Ray Robinson were icons long before their ring careers came to an end.

That time is gone. Apologists for the sweet science say that, for decades, boxing has faced fierce competition from other sports to attract young fans. But all sports have competition from other sports, and many of them have succeeded where boxing has failed.

What's boxing's problem when it comes to attracting young fans? Actually, it has quite a few problems.

1. Kids don't play boxing like they play other sports, so they're less likely to become fans. Kids play baseball,

football, and basketball on the street, in backyards, in parks. Not so for boxing. A recent article in the *New York Times* reported that an estimated forty-five million children in the United States play sports on club teams and in youth leagues. Virtually none of these children box. A lot of them play soccer, which is why soccer now has the youngest TV-viewer demographic of any major sport.

2. Kids don't go to boxing matches as part of a community when they're growing up. They go to school football and basketball games and other events that make them feel as though they belong to a larger group.

3. It's hard for kids to identify with fighters because, except in rare instances, there's no home-state, let alone hometown, identification. Yes, Terence Crawford can put twelve thousand fans in seats in Nebraska. But the University of Nebraska football team can put ninety thousand fans in seats in Nebraska. And the Cornhuskers' record last year was five wins against seven losses.

4. There are no teams or leagues in boxing for kids to follow and keep them engaged on a regular basis. This also means there are virtually no rivalries that kids grow up with and experience year after year.

5. The most attractive fights (the ones that would be most likely to turn kids into fans) are on pay-per-view. Viewers have to spend money or break the law to watch them. It's ironic that boxing—the most egalitarian of all sports—is elitist in limiting access to its flagship events. "It's a rich man sport," George Foreman says. "Nothing we can do about it. The fact is that it's too expensive."

6. Boxing's most attractive fights are on TV too late at night for kids to watch them. In the 1970s and 1980s, good fights were televised on weekend afternoons on a regular basis. Now most big fights are contested well past kids' bedtime. World Series games don't start after midnight Eastern time. The Super Bowl and NBA Championship

games don't start after midnight Eastern time. Most college and professional football games are contested on Saturday and Sunday afternoons.

7. Most professional sports have programs that reach out to kids at an entry level, encouraging them to participate in and watch the sport. Boxing doesn't have that. Indeed, boxing, unlike most major sports, doesn't have a coordinated industry-wide strategy to attract fans at any level. There's no centralized organization that says, "We're in this together for the long haul, so let's invest in a unified way and build a fan base for the future." Instead, most people in boxing do what they can to advance their own narrow interests and trash everyone else.

8. The triggers for child awareness have moved from television to personal computers, tablets, and smartphones. Boxing has lagged behind other sports in exploiting this change. The NBA was promoting NBA.com long before other sports understood the power of the internet. The NFL has NFL.com and a host of sophisticated social media interactions as well as Fantasy Football. Boxing has a bunch of networks and promoters with competing websites that are run as though other networks and promoters don't exist. Similarly, sports video games introduce kids to sports and create new fans. EA Sports sells video games for a wide variety of sports, including the wildly successful *Madden NFL* video game series. The last boxing video game that EA Sports released was *Fight Night Champion* nine years ago.

9. Kids know when they're being entertained. Even stupid kids know when they're being entertained. And boxing doesn't entertain them. The average boxing card consists of blowout undercard fights that pit prospects against hopeless underdogs. Then there's a main event that's often the equivalent of a football game between Ohio State and Minnesota (or Ohio State vs. Akron if the kids are unlucky).

10. Kids get off on champions. Real champions. And boxing lacks recognizable champions. Instead, kids are told that a fighter is great because he's getting "X" dollars for his next fight and a fight is expected to do "Y" pay-per-view buys. Boxing fans know that Canelo Álvarez signed an eleven-fight, $365 million deal with DAZN. They know that Wilder–Fury II needed roughly 1.2 million buys for the promotion to break even and that it fell almost 400,000 buys short of that goal. How many fans know or care what LeBron James's salary is or how many viewers watched the NBA Championship Finals last year? Boxing has to restore legitimacy to the term "champion."

11. Athletes in major sports have endorsement deals with advertising campaigns built around them. Many of these ad campaigns are aimed at young viewers. These deals are virtually nonexistent in boxing.

12. Sports, unlike most forms of entertainment such as music and movies, are handed down from generation to generation. Boxing, alone among professional sports, uses bad behavior as a major marketing tool. This causes some parents to steer their children away from boxing as a spectator sport.

Boxing can do something about some of these issues. Others are beyond its control. Some of the issues relate both to children and older viewers. As a start, the powers that be might schedule some big fights when kids can watch them.

Jarrell Miller and Boxing's PED Problem

On June 27, 2020, it was revealed that, once again, Jarrell Miller had tested positive for a banned performance-enhancing drug. The test was administered by the Voluntary Anti-Doping Association (VADA) at the request of the Nevada State Athletic Commission soon after Miller signed to fight Jerry Forrest on a Top Rank card scheduled to be televised by ESPN on July 9.

A source close to the Nevada Commission says that the urine sample that tested positive was taken from Miller on June 16 and sent to the Sports Medicine Research and Testing Laboratory in Utah. The positive test result was reported by the lab directly to the Nevada commission.

The drug in question is GW1516 (a banned substance also known as Cardarine and Endurobol). It was developed in the 1990s to treat diabetes, obesity, and cardiovascular disease. Its use was largely discontinued in 2007 after it was linked to the development of cancer during trials on mice. It's not classified as an anabolic steroid, but is considered an anabolic compound and has anabolic properties because it helps build muscle mass. Essentially, it forces skeletal muscle to use fat rather than carbohydrates as an energy source and is also an endurance aid.

Samples taken from Miller on two later dates tested negative. A negative test result doesn't mean that a fighter hasn't used performance-enhancing drugs. It means that the fighter was clean on the day that a particular blood or urine sample was taken from him.

On June 29, as a consequence of the adverse test finding, Miller was temporarily suspended at the direction of Nevada State Athletic Commission executive director Bob Bennett. The full commission is expected to remove the "temporary" and suspend Miller at its next meeting. Absent a negotiated settlement between Miller and the commission, there will then be a hearing and the full commission will issue a final ruling on the matter.

This isn't Miller's first public encounter with a banned performance-enhancing drug. Nor is it his second. In 2014, he was suspended by the California State Athletic Commission after testing positive for methylhexaneamine following a Glory 17 kickboxing event. Several years ago, he was dropped from the World Boxing Council rankings because he refused to join the WBC Clean Boxing Program. Last year, he tested positive for GW1516, human growth hormone, and EPO prior to a scheduled June 1 heavyweight championship fight against Anthony Joshua at Madison Square Garden and was removed from the card.

When Miller tested positive prior to his scheduled fight against Joshua, the New York State Athletic Commission had an opportunity to send a message regarding the use of banned performance-enhancing drugs in New York. And it did.

The message the NYSAC sent was: "We don't care."

I've written at length about the NYSAC's dereliction of duty with regard to the use of banned PEDs in boxing. Suffice it to say here that, instead of acting as it should have with regard to Miller, the New York State Athletic Commission sent its dirty laundry to Nevada. Now the Nevada State Athletic Commission is cleaning it.

Miller underwent no PED testing for an entire year after his 2019 testing debacle in New York because the NYSAC walked away from its responsibilities. As soon as the Nevada State Athletic Commission was formally advised that Jarrell was scheduled to fight in Las Vegas on July 9, Bob Bennett asked VADA to test him. Miller had to have known that Nevada would test him. He probably didn't know that the test would be administered so quickly.

After the positive test result was announced, Miller told Fight Network, "I have never, ever willingly taken a steroid for performance-enhancing purposes. Did I take something for healing properties, for injuries? Yes, I have. But to win a fight and during a training camp? No, I have never done that. Nobody can be more outraged than me. I'm the one that's lost millions of dollars. I'm the one that's had his career on the line. But I have to think about it with a straight mind. I have to figure it out. Sit down with my team. Get everything in order and get everything done in the right way. It's sad. I'm angry about it. But like I said, there is an explanation for it, and me and my legal team are working on it."

So far, that's not much of an explanation.

What punishment should be meted out to Miller if the adverse finding is upheld?

Before answering that question, let's first give credit to Bob Bennett and the Nevada State Athletic Commission for making a sincere effort to tackle the issue of performance-enhancing drugs in boxing. Unlike the New York State Athletic Commission, the Nevada State Athletic Commission takes illegal PED use seriously. If Bennett had followed the New York formula, Nevada wouldn't have asked VADA to test Miller at all. And if a positive test result had come back, Nevada would have washed its hands of the matter and declined to license Miller without further pursuing the matter.

But let's keep things in focus. Miller is a symptom. He's not the cause of boxing's PED problem.

If you want a poster person for bad behavior with regard to performance-enhancing drugs in boxing, consider Travis Tygart (CEO of the United States Anti-Doping Agency). USADA conducted more than 1,500 tests for PEDs on professional boxers and reported only one positive test result to a governing state athletic commission. If Miller had been tested by USADA rather than VADA, his positive test result might have been "adjudicated internally" and never communicated to the Nevada commission.

What about the many physical conditioners who funnel PEDs to fighters? The managers and other team members who cover up for them? And the state athletic commissions in addition to New York that turn a blind eye toward the problem?

On April 29, 2019, attorney Pat English wrote a letter to the executive committee of the Association of Boxing Commissions with regard to the New York State Athletic Commission's handling of the Jarrell Miller matter. In that letter, English stated that the NYSAC was "completely ignoring" its responsibilities under the Professional Boxing Health and Safety Act. Three days later, English sent a similar letter to NYSAC executive director Kim Sumbler in which he declared, "I see more than twenty years worth of work in the formulation of the Professional Boxing Health and Safety Act, the Muhammad Ali Act, mandatory adherence to the suspension list, and years of ABC work pushed backward by actions (or inactions) by some in situations such as the Miller situation. That is, to me, morally repugnant."

English then took matters a step further and, as a member of the ABC legal committee, served as the driving force behind a change in ABC policy.

Fighters who apply for a federal identification card from now on will be required to fill out an ABC application form that states, "The use of performance enhancing drugs may result in the Boxer being placed on the National Suspension list. Boxer agrees that the following entities have the authority to place Boxer on the National Suspension list with cause and subject to due process: (a) The Commission issuing this ID. (b) Any Commission under whose jurisdiction an alleged rules violation has occurred if the Boxer is scheduled to fight in that jurisdiction, or (c) The ABC."

This gives the Association of Boxing Commissions the authority to suspend a fighter who tests positive for a banned performance-enhancing drug and will allow the ABC to fill the void when a commission (such as the NYSAC) fails to fulfill its responsibilities. Fighters will be bound to this new ABC policy as their old federal ID expires and they apply for a new one.

A five-person ABC committee has been set up to consider suspensions if and when the issue arises. The due process protocols that the committee will follow were drafted by English.

Jarrell Miller is a large target, figuratively and literally speaking. Given his past PED test history—and absent a satisfactory explanation for his most recent positive test result—a lengthy suspension would seem to be warranted. But the current situation is an indictment of the system, not just Miller. It's more important to reform delinquent state athletic commissions and punish illegal PED distributors than it is to reform Jarrell. Why should Jarrell Miller be banned from boxing while all of the facilitators and enablers go free?

Fistic Notes

Long before George Foreman was eating cheeseburgers and Andy Ruiz defied the body-shamers, there was "Two Ton" Tony Galento. But Foreman and Ruiz succeeded in the ring where Galento fell short. And unlike Foreman and Ruiz, Galento wasn't a nice guy.

Domenico Antonio Galento was born in Orange, New Jersey, on March 12, 1910. During a fifteen-year career that began in 1929, he compiled a 80–26–5 ring record with 57 KOs and 6 KOs by.

Listed as five feet, nine inches tall, Galento fought at 183 pounds early in his career. In later years, he tipped the scales at weights as high as 247 pounds. His stomach, it was written, "looked like a tidal wave of mud." To complement his lifestyle and supplement his income, he owned and operated a bar in Orange.

Galento was frequently belligerent and, speaking of whomever he was scheduled to fight next, often proclaimed, "I'll moida da bum." On a less charming note, he was a dirty fighter, known for the mantra, "I don't see anything wrong in sticking your thumb into a guy's eye."

The high point of Galento's career came on June 9, 1939, when he challenged Joe Louis at Yankee Stadium for the heavyweight crown. Louis was twenty-five years old and in his prime, having won his most recent three fights (including his fabled devastation of Max Schmeling) by knockout in the first round. Galento (who outweighed the champion by thirty-four pounds) was ranked by *The Ring* as its number-one heavyweight contender and was riding a wave of eleven consecutive knockout victories.

Galento had never been knocked down in a prizefight. That changed courtesy of a straight-right-left-hook combination from Louis in the second round. Then, surprisingly, a compact left hook to the jaw dropped the champion in the third stanza. In that moment, Galento reached what for him was summit of his ring career. But Louis had higher mountains to climb.

In round four, the Brown Bomber started landing at will. When Joe Louis landed at will, the opponent was in big trouble. With Galento staggering helplessly around the ring, referee Arthur Donovan stopped the carnage with 31 seconds left in the round.

Three months after losing to Louis, Galento returned to combat and knocked out Lou Nova in the fourteenth round of what is widely regarded as one of the ugliest, most foul-filled major fights of all time. In his next outing, he was stopped by Max Baer in seven rounds. Baer complained afterward that Galento, who was known for refusing to bathe in the days leading up to a fight, "smelled of rotten tuna and a tub of old liquor being sweated out."

The end years were hard for Galento. In 1977, suffering from diabetes, he underwent surgery to remove his left leg at mid-calf. In July 1979, his right leg was amputated. Later that month, he died from a heart attack.

It's considered poor form to speak ill of the dead. But one might quote Hall of Fame trainer Ray Arcel, who said of Galento, "Nobody liked him except maybe the guys who hung out in his saloon."

★ ★ ★

The annual awards bestowed by the Boxing Writers Association of America are an important trust. Being selected places a winner in the company of legends.

This year's nominees for Trainer of the Year are Teofimo Lopez Sr., Sugar Hill, Derrick James, Robert Garcia, and Eddy Reynoso. Typically, the honor goes to someone who has an elite fighter in his stable. Extra credit goes to a trainer who has developed a champion from scratch. Either way, as Don Turner (who was honored in 1996 for his work with Evander Holyfield) observed, "The fighter makes the fighter. The trainer only helps."

I would have added another name to this year's ballot for Trainer of the Year: Mark Breland.

One can argue that Breland doesn't belong on the ballot. Although he taught Deontay Wilder to leverage his right hand (which is powered by a gift of nature) and improved Wilder's jab. Deontay doesn't fight like a well-schooled fighter.

But there's another factor to be considered.

On February 22, 2020, Wilder was absorbing a brutal beating at the hands of Tyson Fury when Breland (Deontay's chief second) threw in the towel. Thereafter, Wilder accused Kenny Bayless of refereeing the fight as though he were drunk and participating in a conspiracy against him. He accused Fury of using loaded gloves. He said he lost because the outlandish costume that he wore for his ring walk was so heavy that it weakened his legs.

But Wilder's ugliest character assassination was reserved for Breland (widely regarded as one of the most decent people in boxing), whom he later dismissed as his trainer.

Knowing when to stop a fight is an important part of a trainer's job. There are too many "brave" trainers who don't know when to stop a fight. We've all seen examples of that and the tragedy that sometimes follows.

Wilder put the spotlight on Breland when he trashed and then dismissed him for doing his job. Breland deserves to be on the ballot for Trainer of the Year as a statement of principle and an acknowledgment that he did his job when it mattered most.

★ ★ ★

There's a natural (and appropriate) inclination to roll one's eyes when a world sanctioning body proposes a new weight division. But the World Boxing Council's plan to add a weight class between cruiserweight and heavyweight merits a fair hearing.

The first cruiserweight champion was Marvin Camel who won a March 31, 1980, decision over Mate Parlov to claim the WBC cruiserweight crown. At the time, the cruiserweight limit was 190 pounds. It was later raised to 200. The light-heavyweight limit (the next division down) has remained steady at 175 pounds.

WBC president Mauricio Sulaiman believes that the size of modern heavyweights has rendered current weight classifications obsolete and that a 220-pound heavyweight can't compete on equal terms with today's giants. Thus, he has championed the creation of a new division that would run from 200 to 224 pounds.

One can take issue with Sulaiman's plan. As Emanuel Steward noted, "a good 210-pound puncher can knock anyone out."

Speed and quickness also have to be factored into the equation.

Mike Tyson weighed between 215 and 220 pounds when he was at his best. After seeing how Anthony Joshua fared against Andy Ruiz, most knowledgeable observers would pick Tyson in his prime over the much-larger Joshua.

Evander Holyfield competed on even terms with larger men like Lennox Lewis and Riddick Bowe. Deontay Wilder weighed 212 pounds when he fought to a draw against Tyson Fury and 214 and 219 pounds when he twice whacked out Luis Ortiz.

Also, keep in mind that some fighters would dry out to make the 224-pound limit and come into the ring on fight night in the neighborhood of 240 pounds.

That said, today's athletes are bigger than their predecessors. Prior to the 1960s, not a single player in the National Football League weighed 300 pounds. Now there are college teams whose offensive and defensive lines average more than that. Jack Dempsey at his best weighed between 185 and 190 pounds. Rocky Marciano weighed 184 pounds when he knocked out Joe Louis and a half-pound more when he dethroned Jersey Joe Walcott.

Anyone who watched Oleksandr Usyk struggle against Dereck Chisora earlier this year understands the issue.

How should boxing handle the situation?

I'll accept the need for an additional weight class at the high end of the spectrum. But 224 pounds is too high. I suggest the following: light-heavyweight limit 175 pounds; cruiserweight limit 195 pounds; new-division limit 215 pounds.

Also, at present, there are eight weight divisions between 105 and 130 pounds. That's too many. Once upon a time ("when boxing was boxing," as the saying goes), the sweet science had eight weight divisions total. Boxing would be well served if today's bottom eight weight divisions were consolidated into six. But given the sanctioning bodies' lust for sanctioning fees, that won't happen.

Finally, for more than a century, there was something almost sacrosanct about the heavyweight championship of the world. Fights like the 1938 rematch between Joe Louis and Max Schmeling and the war of attrition between Muhammad Ali and Joe Frazier in Manila took on an almost mythological quality.

In recent decades, multiple sanctioning organizations with multiple heavyweight "champions" have tarnished the heavyweight throne. But the heavyweights are still boxing's glamour division. As of this writing, Sulaiman says that the new weight class will be named the "bridger" division to honor a six-year-old boy named Bridger Walker who (we are told) saved his four-year-old sister from a vicious dog. One might add that the new division will be a bridge between the cruiserweight and heavyweight divisions. Either way, it's an uninspiring name. But at least it doesn't divide the heavyweight division into "heavyweights" and "super-heavyweights." The "heavyweight champion" should always be The Man.

★ ★ ★

The pandemic has left boxing fans with a lot of free time on our hands and too few good fights to fill it. YouTube offers an endless stream of old and new fights to fill the void. But that's not all there is insofar the sweet science is concerned. Documentaries, interviews. You name it and YouTube has it.

Recently, I was on YouTube and came across an interview that Michael Kay conducted with George Foreman on the YES Network in 2004. It's forty-five minutes long and worth watching, particularly as it relates to some of Foreman's comments regarding the Rumble in the Jungle against Muhammad Ali:

* "One day, you're going through the airport, going to Africa, and everybody is afraid of you. Then, coming back from Africa, they're patting you on the back. 'It's all right. You'll be okay.' From praise to pity. I've never been so devastated in my life."
* "I beat this guy up and I beat him good. No one had ever stood up to my punching power. Then, seventh round, I hit him and I thought he was gonna fall. And he said, 'Is that all you got, George?' That was all I had, too."
* "Muhammad Ali was training to win the fight with me. I was training to kill him. I'm thinking, 'I'm gonna mount that head on my wall.' And he's thinking, 'I'm gonna win a boxing match.'"
* "I saw *When We Were Kings*. My kids are laughing. I'm thinking, 'That's not funny. I'm on the canvas, you know.' Every joke he tells, they're laughing. I found myself laughing with them."

★ "I've fallen in love all over again with Muhammad Ali. I think he
needed that victory back then a lot more than I needed it."

And there was a nice coda when Foreman told Michael Kay, "I'm so
happy about the way my life has gone, I wouldn't want to change anything
about it."

★ ★ ★

Eric Drath is a very good filmmaker. The release of *Macho: The Hector
Camacho Story* on Showtime this month (December 2020) demonstrates
that yet again.

Drath was born and raised in New York and interned at ABC News
while attending college at Columbia. He moved to Atlanta after gradua-
tion to work for CNN. Next came a stint at a startup network called FOX
News Channel. The irony of that pairing is not lost on him. Then the sweet
science entered his life.

"I wasn't a big boxing fan," Drath says. "But in the late nineties, a friend
invited me to go with him to some fights at Yonkers Raceway. We got there.
There was a boxing ring and, around it, a world I'd never known. I said to
myself, 'This is so cool. I want to know more about this.'"

The promoter that night was Joe DeGuardia. In due course, Drath left
FOX News to do publicity work for DeGuardia's promotional company.

"That," Eric recalls, "was when I learned that doing PR for a boxing
promoter was, 'Go get the van, pick up some fighters at the airport, take
them to the athletic commission to get licensed, make sure they have their
physicals, and send out a press release.'"

Eventually, Drath started a company called RingLink that got video
clips from promoters and charged the promoters a fee to transmit the clips
by satellite to TV stations. Then he got a manager's license and represented
a few fringe fighters. After that, he founded a company called Live Star
Entertainment that created satellite media tours for the music industry
and produced TV fights for various promoters. Most notably, Live Star
produced close to fifty Broadway Boxing shows for DiBella Entertainment
between 2008 and 2016.

Meanwhile, Drath had begun the process of carving out a niche for himself as a documentary filmmaker. Over the years, he has worked on subjects as diverse as Theodore Bikel and Pete Rose. But it began with boxing.

In 2006, Drath met Luis Resto at the Morris Park Boxing Gym in the Bronx. Resto (a former journeyman fighter) had been a key player in one of boxing's ugliest scandals. On June 16, 1983, he fought Billy Collins (an undefeated twenty-one-year-old prospect) at Madison Square Garden. Before the bout, Panama Lewis (Resto's trainer) removed some of the padding from his fighter's gloves. Collins suffered permanent eye damage during the bout, was unable to fight again, and died in a car crash nine months later. Resto and Lewis were imprisoned for their wrongdoing. Lewis was widely seen as the more culpable of the two.

"I liked Resto's story," Drath recounts. "Nobody else thought it was a good idea. But I scraped together some money, put together a rough cut, and gave it to a friend who gave it to a friend while they were standing together on the sideline during their daughters' high school lacrosse game."

The second parent standing on the sideline was Rick Bernstein (then the executive producer for HBO Sports).

"After that, I got a phone call," Drath remembers. "HBO made its own sports documentaries back then. But they liked it; they bought it; and they made some changes."

Assault in the Ring aired on HBO in 2008 and won an Emmy for Outstanding Sports Documentary. Drath was credited as its co-writer, director, and narrator. Then he pitched a documentary about Renee Richards to the network. But HBO passed on the project, so he sold it to ESPN, which televised the documentary after it premiered at the Tribeca Film Festival in 2011. Once again, Drath was the co-writer, director, and narrator.

Two more boxing projects for ESPN followed: *No Más* (2013), which focused on the second fight between Sugar Ray Leonard and Roberto Duran, and *Robbed* (2014), which told the tale of Ali–Norton III against the backdrop of violence occasioned by a New York City police job action.

That brings us to *Macho: The Hector Camacho Story*.

Initially, Drath conceived of *Macho* as an investigative report about Camacho's murder in Bayamón, Puerto Rico. Hector, who was involved with cocaine for most of his life, was shot four times on November 20, 2012, and removed from life support four days later. He was fifty years old when he died.

Then *Macho* evolved into a more complete biographical documentary with an emphasis on Camacho's ring career. The film would have been stronger with more exposition of what it meant—and still means—to be part of the underclass in Spanish Harlem where Camacho was raised and remains an icon. But it's put together well and has the advantage of a charismatic main character who lights up the screen when he's on camera.

Eric directed and narrated *Macho*. The film's most compelling moments deal with its subject's post-boxing life and include poignant footage of an unrecognizably fat Camacho as he neared age fifty.

Drath is one of the few directors who has made documentaries for HBO, Showtime, and ESPN. That leads to the question of how the experiences compared with one another.

"HBO was a tight organization that didn't want outside interference," Drath recalls. "They bought the film and in essence said, 'Okay, kid; you can stand outside the edit room while we finish it, and we'll show you what we're doing from time to time.' Showtime is the antithesis of that. They gave me notes but they also gave me the latitude to make the film I wanted to make. I loved the process. ESPN was somewhere in between. But it was an honor to work with all three of them."

And which of his documentaries does Drath like the most?

"I don't have a favorite," he answers. "I love the human element in documentaries. Each one I've been fortunate to make so far marks a different period of my life. And each one has that human element."

★ ★ ★

No one has a more passionate relationship with boxing than Hall of Fame promoter Lou DiBella. And no one is more critical of the business end of the sport. Interviews with DiBella often have the feel of a therapy session. Among the thoughts he has offered over the years are:

* "It's hard to get into boxing and not love it. And it's hard to get into boxing and not hate it."
* "I can't say that I enjoy the business but it's addictive. There's a part of me that wonders if I wouldn't be happier if I redirected away from it. But there's also part of me that loves the sport and loves the fighters

and thinks I can make money and have a positive impact on boxing at the same time."

★ "There are no rules in boxing. People get away with what they can."

★ "Boxing is a miserable business. Everything is a deal. People lie all the time and don't even consider it lying. Sooner or later, virtually everyone adopts a go-along mentality or they get crushed. If you stay in this business long enough, you're going to get fucked as many times as a porn star."

★ "The old saying 'what goes around comes around' doesn't apply to boxing."

★ ★ ★

Marco Antonio Barrera once said, "Boxing is filled with bad experiences."

Perhaps the worst of these experiences is the moment when a fighter knows that a fight is slipping away. And he's not just losing; he's getting beaten up. It's different from a sudden knockout. It's an inexorable progression. He knows he's in trouble. And he knows that his opponent knows it too.

The roar of the crowd accelerates his opponent's assault. This isn't about being outscored. It's not like playing tennis and being down 6–2, 5–0. It's about being punched in the face and body. Hard. Again and again. Losing is inevitable. The fighter no longer has enough in him to turn the tide. The question is, how much more of a beating will he take.

Sometimes the fighter has a discussion with himself: "Do I really want to do this anymore tonight?"

Maybe the old Irish proverb crosses his mind: "'Tis better to be a coward for a minute than dead for the rest of your life."

Or maybe he thinks something similar to what Jimmy Cannon wrote after Carmine Vingo was bludgeoned into a coma by Rocky Marciano at Madison Square Garden seventy years ago: "Men suffer unnecessarily and endure pain because they are too proud to quit. They accept suffering because to avoid it deliberately would be a renunciation of what a fighter is supposed to be. Even pointless courage has a splendor."

★ ★ ★

In the "golden age of boxing," Hollywood and the sweet science went hand in hand. *The Set-Up*, which premiered in 1949, is one of the better boxing movies from that era.

Robert Ryan plays Bill "Stoker" Thompson, an aging club fighter matched against an up-and-coming heavyweight prospect named Tiger Nelson on a seedy club fight card in Paradise City. Thompson's manager (Tiny, played by George Tobias) and trainer (Red, played by Percy Helton) have taken a bribe from a mobster named Little Boy (Alan Baxter) to ensure that Stoker goes down in the third round. Nelson has agreed to carry Stoker through the first two stanzas. Tiny tells Red that they'll divide the bribe money between themselves.

"What about Stoker?" Red asks.

"Why cut him in?" Tiny counters.

"Stoker can still punch," Red cautions. "If anything goes wrong—"

"Don't be a meathead," Tiny interrupts. "Nelson will butcher him. It's a hundred to one."

"That's just it. There's always the one."

The film is great fun. Most of the movie is set in the dressing room before the fight and then in the ring for the climactic battle. The drama builds nicely. The good guys are good and the bad guys are bad. The blood lust of the crowd is chilling. Black and white cinematography recreates the club fight atmosphere well.

Audrey Totter plays Stoker's long-suffering wife who wants him out of the fight game now. "I remember the first time you told me, 'I'm just one punch away from a title shot,'" she reminds him. "Don't you see? You'll always be just one punch away. How many more beatings do you have to take? Maybe you can go on taking the beatings. I can't."

The Set-Up was the #1 grossing film in the United States when it premiered in 1949. The *New York Times* called it "a sizzling melodrama" painted in "harsh realistic terms." Adding to that realism was the fact that Ryan boxed as an undergraduate at Dartmouth and was the school's intramural heavyweight champion for all four of his years on campus.

★ ★ ★

There's widespread awareness of the damage that results to fighters from head trauma. But there's another possible cause for many of these symptoms: post-traumatic stress disorder (PTSD).

Post-traumatic stress disorder is a condition in which a person has difficulty recovering after experiencing a terrifying event. It's often identified with members of the military who have seen combat, first responders who were involved in a deadly incident, and survivors of child abuse.

PTSD can last for years as memories of the trauma trigger an intense emotional—and sometimes physical—reaction. Symptoms can be

1. psychological (e.g., depression, fear, severe anxiety);
2. behavioral (agitation, hostility, hypervigilance, social isolation, self-destructive conduct); and
3. physical (headaches, dizziness).

Nightmares and insomnia are common.

Some of these symptoms are the same as the symptoms experienced by a person who has suffered a concussion. But in the case of PTSD, the cause is psychological, not physical.

PTSD is treated with trauma-focused psychotherapy that is sometimes supplemented by medication to manage symptoms.

It's not unreasonable to suggest that fighters, by virtue of the circumstances of their profession, are candidates for post-traumatic stress disorder.

Fighters suffer brutal beatings. Jersey Joe Walcott, who was brutally knocked out by Rocky Marciano, later said, "It goes down on tape. And you play it back at funny times, when you're dreaming or just walking down the street."

But most fighters who have been beaten up are told simply to "shake it off" or "get over it."

A fighter who kills or inflicts serious brain damage on an opponent is also vulnerable.

There's a school of thought that boxing can help a person deal with post-traumatic stress caused by other trauma. But that's more anecdotal than scientific.

Major sports leagues offer counseling to players with emotional problems. There's no such organized support system in boxing. State athletic commission medical advisory boards have neurologists, orthopedists, ophthalmologists, and other specialists, but not psychiatrists. Most commissions treat psychiatric problems as disciplinary issues or not at all.

Some fighters (such as Mike Tyson and Tyson Fury) have suffered from psychiatric issues and been able to get help because of their celebrity status and moneymaking potential. But the great majority of fighters are on their own.

Jim Lampley, who studied fighters for decades, opines, "I don't have empirical data on this. But my instinct tells me that post-traumatic stress disorder is very real and overwhelming for some fighters who live with it every day of their lives, and that it's an underobserved, underreported, and understudied phenomenon."

Dr. Margaret Goodman (former chief ringside physician for the Nevada State Athletic Commission and one of the foremost advocates for fighter safety in the United States) concurs and says, "I don't know that the issue has ever been seriously studied. And it should be."

Let's open up the discussion. There are fighters in need who might be helped.

★ ★ ★

Once every year or two, a novelty song becomes a hit. And once every few years, a YouTube celebrity feud attracts attention. Thus it was that the November 9, 2019, encounter between KSI and Logan Paul at Staples Center in Los Angeles was the fourth-most-watched fight of 2019 on DAZN. Taking note, DAZN then streamed a January 30, 2020, matchup between Jake Paul (Logan's brother) and AnEsonGib (a.k.a. Ali Loui Al-Fakhri) on the undercard of Demetrius Andrade vs. Luke Keeler three days before the Super Bowl in Miami. For the uninitiated, the name "AnEsonGib" means that Al-Fakhri has an EsonGib—a "big nose" spelled backward.

Little Brother vs. Big Nose was a sophomorically packaged mess. That said, the success of KSI vs. Logan Paul speaks to the intrinsic appeal of boxing. Most likely, even more viewers would have watched two NBA stars or two big-name NFL players box. But KSI vs. Logan Paul and its progeny also show how far boxing has fallen.

Fans of most sports want to see excellence. Very few people would pay money to watch KSI and Logan Paul play tennis or one-on-one basketball against each other. Boxing, on the other hand, is now being presented as a trash sport. And other trash sports do it better than boxing.

If you want feuds and action, check out WWE.

"Oh! WWE is fake," you say. "We want the real thing."

Okay. Here's the real thing. More than 1.14 million viewers watched the July 4, 2019, Nathan's Hot Dog Eating Contest on ESPN. By contrast, the December 14, 2019, ESPN fight card headlined by Terence Crawford averaged 1.35 million viewers. That was the largest average for a Top Rank fight card on ESPN in 2019.

Now imagine what ESPN paid for Terence Crawford's services as opposed to what Joey Chestnut received for winning the Nathan's Fourth of July hot dog eating contest.

In sum, traditional boxing is failing to attract viewers on a basis that's cost efficient from the networks' point of view. DAZN, ESPN, FOX, and Showtime are all paying huge license fees pursuant to output deals with boxing promoters. They have to demand a better product from these promoters.

★ ★ ★

There's a tendency to ignore the issue of illegal performance-enhancing drugs where women boxers are concerned and to focus on men. The World Boxing Council Clean Boxing Program wasn't expanded to include women until September 2019. And because women fighters generate less revenue than their male counterparts, women boxers and their promoters are less likely to pay for serious PED testing on their own.

That's unfortunate because there are danger signs on the horizon.

Heather Hardy was tested by the Voluntary Anti-Doping Association as part of the WBC Clean Boxing Program after the weigh-in for her September 13, 2019, fight against Amanda Serrano at Madison Square Garden. The test came back positive for furosemide (Lasix), which is used as both a masking agent and a weight-loss diuretic. Hardy was fined $10,000 and suspended for six months by the New York State Athletic Commission.

On January 24, 2020, the WBC announced that an "A" sample taken from Alejandra Jiménez by VADA pursuant to the WBC Clean Boxing program on January 10, 2020 (one day before Jimenez's January 11 split-decision victory over Franchon Crews-Dezurn in a super-middleweight title bout) had tested positive for Stanozolol.

Victor Conte has an encyclopedic knowledge of performance-enhancing drugs and has worked with numerous boxers at his SNAC training facility in northern California.

"There's not a lot of hard data available on PEDs and women's boxing," Conte acknowledges. "But I believe that, not only do PEDs increase things like speed, endurance, and the damage caused by punches for women boxers, they have a much greater effect on the performance of women boxers than they do for men."

"I'll give you an example," Conte says. "The baseline level of circulating testosterone in a female is only ten percent of what it is for a male. And what we found in the past was that, if a male and female sprinter were given similar dosages, it had the effect of shortening a 100-meter race for the man by two meters so his time might drop from, say, 10.2 to 10 seconds. But for a woman on a similar dosage, the gains were proportionally greater. It had the effect of shortening a 100-meter race by four meters so her time might drop from 11.2 to 10.8 seconds. I believe there's a similar correlation when you're looking at speed, endurance, and explosive power in boxing."

Summarizing the situation, VADA CEO Dr. Margaret Goodman says ruefully, "The bottom line is that the women are using PEDs now just like the men."

★ ★ ★

Kudos to Matt Christie (editor of *Boxing News*). In a recent editorial, Christie spoke to those who complain when writers take off their rose-colored glasses and address boxing's problems honestly and in depth.

Christie wrote, "If the people in power are never challenged and get too used to talking to those they know they can control—those who try a little too hard to please their subjects and fire questions but don't come armed with evidence to challenge the answers—it will become increasingly difficult for the rulebreakers to be held accountable for their crimes. To produce an in-depth investigation or feature, one that is balanced and fair and factually correct, one that uncovers the truth for the benefit of boxing and its fighters and holds decision makers accountable, can take several weeks or even months. The process of researching and securing the right interviews, conducting them and transcribing them and then crafting the story, is a long and arduous one if done correctly. Though I accept that we now play a numbers game—views, likes, comments—the real purpose of the story should always be considered while telling it. The job of the boxing journalist isn't to try and trip up anyone. Very often, those at the heart of the sport deserve tremendous praise. But ultimately the job of the boxing journalist is to serve boxing's interests: the fighters, the fans and its future by shining a light on both the good and the bad."

★ ★ ★

Only a few boxing gyms have names that resonate, and most of them exist only in memory. Gleason's Gym is alive and thriving.

Gleason's was founded in 1937 by a fighter named Peter Robert Gagliardi, who changed his name to Bobby Gleason for marketing purposes and opened a gym on Westchester Avenue in the Bronx. Dues were two dollars a month. In 1974, he moved the gym to Eighth Avenue and 30th Street in Manhattan, several blocks from Madison Square Garden.

In 1981, Gleason's was sold to Ira Becker. Two years later, Becker brought Bruce Silverglade in as his partner. In 1986, they relocated the gym to the second floor of a shabby industrial building in the shadow of the Brooklyn Bridge. When Becker died in 1994, Silverglade took control of the business. Three years ago, Gleason's moved yet again, this time to its current location at 130 Water Street in Brooklyn.

The ghosts travel with the name.

Phil Terranova, who won the world featherweight title in 1943, was the first champion to come out of Gleason's. Jake LaMotta was the second. Since then, the gym has hosted well over a hundred world champions, including fifteen claimants to the heavyweight throne. Some made Gleason's their home. Others were just passing through.

Legendary champions who have laced up their gloves in Gleason's over the decades include Muhammad Ali, Joe Frazier, Sonny Liston, George Foreman, Larry Holmes, Mike Tyson, Riddick Bowe, Floyd Patterson, Ingemar Johansson, Marvin Hagler, Ray Leonard, Thomas Hearns, Roberto Duran, Michael Spinks, Roy Jones, Emile Griffith, Carmen Basilio, Dick

Tiger, Carlos Monzon, Pernell Whitaker, Aaron Pryor, Carlos Ortiz, Sandy Saddler, Alexis Argüello, Wilfredo Gómez, Julio César Chávez, and Barry McGuigan. That's quite a list.

Gleason's opens on weekdays at 5:00 a.m. and stays open until ten o'clock at night. The hours on Saturday and Sunday are 8:00 a.m. to 6:00 p.m. Silverglade, now seventy-three, opens the gym himself on weekdays and stays until early evening. It's not uncommon for a fighter to be sitting on the stoop when Bruce arrives at five o'clock in the morning. An hour later, a dozen or more people are on the floor. Silverglade is also on site for much of the weekend. "I love running the gym," he says. "Every day is different here."

Boxing is in Silverglade's blood. His father, a New York City cop, was one of the founders of the National Police Athletic League and served as team manager for the 1980 and 1984 US Olympic teams. Bruce is universally respected within the boxing community. He's a well-liked "boxing guy."

Gleason's has about 1,200 members who come from all parts of the New York metropolitan area. The monthly membership fee is $99 ($149 if the member wants a permanent locker). There's a $20 discount for registered amateurs. Those who are so inclined can sign up on a weekly basis ($50) or for one day ($20).

The concrete floor covers 13,600 square feet (including locker rooms and several small office cubicles). There are four boxing rings and one more that's suited for wrestling. Also, heavy bags, speed bags, double-end bags, treadmills, stationary bikes, and elliptical machines. The red walls are covered with posters and photographs.

Ninety-two trainers are allowed to ply their trade in the gym.

The roster of current members includes seventy professional boxers (fifty-five men and fifteen women).

Overall, a third of Gleason's clientele are women.

"A few MMA fighters come here to work on their punching, but we're really not an MMA gym," Silverglade says. "I had a cage at the old location for six or seven months, but it didn't attract much business so I got rid of it."

As a small business owner in a unique small business, Silverglade relies on various income streams to make ends meet. The gym has been home to weddings and bar mitzvahs. There are instructional clinics and occasional amateur fight cards. Tourists pay a ten-dollar spectator fee.

Film crews love the location. More than a few big-name actors have prepped for roles at Gleason's. Robert De Niro (*Raging Bull*) and Hilary Swank (*Million Dollar Baby*) won Academy Awards after training there. Wesley Snipes *(Streets of Gold)*, Jennifer Lopez *(Money Train)*, John Leguizamo *(Undefeated)*, and Craig Bierko *(Cinderella Man)* also learned the rudiments of boxing at Gleason's.

About half of the gym's members are businessmen. Silverglade is candid in acknowledging, "The gym survives because of white collar boxing."

Then he makes a point that means a lot to him.

"Gleason's is a true melting pot," he says. "The mix of people here is staggering. Professional boxers, raw amateurs, street kids, scared women, white collar boxers. There's a niche for everyone at Gleason's."

Visitors to the previous incarnation of Gleason's were greeted by a huge sign inscribed with a quote from the *Aeneid* that read, "Now, whoever has courage and a strong and collected spirit in his breast, let him come forward, lace on the gloves, and put up his hands."

That sign now hangs in today's Gleason's Gym in front of a mirrored wall.

Reece Chapman is eleven years old and in fifth grade at Kessler Elementary School in Helena, Montana. He watches fights on television with his father and says "they're fun to watch," but adds, "Boxing against someone who hits hard probably isn't much fun."

Recently, Reece visited Gleason's Gym with ring announcer David Diamante. Reece thinks that Diamante is "definitely cool." He was captivated by David's dreadlocks and loved his greeting when they met: "Hey, Reece! What's up, dude?" He also likes the fact that David rides around on a motorcycle.

The sounds of boxing filled the air when Reece arrived. Gloves thudding into heavy bags; the grunting that accompanies punches thrown; a buzzer at regular intervals simulating three-minute rounds and the one-minute rest period in between.

Reece moved around the gym, stopping at the edge of a ring to watch two heavyweights who were sparring. His eyes opened wide.

Hector Roca, Joan Guzmán, and Heather Hardy passed by and said hello.

Sonya Lamonakis, who won four New York metropolitan area Golden Gloves championships while teaching sixth grade at a public school in Harlem, asked, "Do you like school?"

"Yes," Reece told her.

"Good answer," Lamonakis countered.

Like most people, Reece had never been in a boxing ring. Silverglade asked if he'd like get in one to see what it's like and handed him a pair of gloves for a photo op.

Reece put the gloves on and got in the ring. The next thing he knew, P. J. Lawson (a former amateur standout and now a certified USA Boxing trainer) was showing him the rudiments of how to bob, weave, and punch.

Reece was all smiles when he left the gym.

"What did you learn?" he was asked.

"I learned some things about boxing and the way people treat each other in the gym."

"People are here because they want to be here," Silverglade had told him. "And everyone treats everyone with respect. A boxing gym brings out the best in people."

★ ★ ★

Sean Connery, who rose to international stardom as James Bond, died on October 31, 2020, at age ninety.

Connery starred in myriad films and won an Academy Award for Best Supporting Actor for his role in *The Untouchables*. At the end of his long and distinguished film career, he was honored with knighthood. But the enduring image of Connery is as Agent 007 ("Bond, James Bond") who saved the world from villains like Auric Goldfinger and liked his martinis "shaken, not stirred."

Connery played Agent 007 in the first five Bond movies: *Dr. No* (1962), *From Russia with Love* (1963), *Goldfinger* (1964), *Thunderball* (1965), and *You Only Live Twice* (1967). He left the franchise over a monetary dispute but returned later for two more Bond films—*Diamonds Are Forever* (1971) and *Never Say Never Again* (1983).

The early James Bond films were innovative and cutting edge for their time, although they reflected an age in which it was acceptable to stereotype beautiful women as playthings.

Connery was succeeded in the role by George Lazenby, Roger Moore, Timothy Dalton, Pierce Brosnan, and Daniel Craig. David Niven also tried his hand in a more satirical interpretation of 007. But for millions of moviegoers, Connery will always be Bond. The others are imposters.

Agent 007 dominated Connery's public persona more than he would have liked. "There are a lot of things I did before Bond—like playing the classics on stage—that don't seem to get publicized," he said in a 1965 interview. "This Bond image is a problem in a way and a bit of a bore, but one has just got to live with it."

So what does this have to do with boxing?

Boxing was a foundation stone for Connery's success as an actor.

Requiem for a Heavyweight (1962) is justifiably celebrated as one of the greatest boxing movies of all time. The 1962 film starred Anthony Quinn as an over-the-hill fighter named Luis "Mountain" Rivera with a conniving manager (played by Jackie Gleason) and compliant trainer (Mickey Rooney). A young heavyweight prospect named Cassius Clay had a bit part in the film.

But before *Requiem for a Heavyweight* was a feature film, it was staged as a play on live television. Rod Serling wrote and produced it in 1956 for a popular American show called *Playhouse 90* with Jack Palance in the lead role (the fighter was then named Harlan "Mountain" McClintock). One year later, *Blood Money* (as the English production was titled) was televised by the BBC live in the United Kingdom.

Palance was slated for the lead role in the English production but pulled out at the last minute. Desperate for a replacement, the producers turned to an unknown actor named Sean Connery. After the show aired, a review in *The Times (of London)* praised Connery for his "shambling and inarticulate charm." Film offers for the young Scottish actor were soon pouring in.

★ ★ ★

For decades, it has been common for photographers and video crews to visit fighters' training camps before a big fight and shoot the action on fight night. Canelo Álvarez has made an unprecedented investment in creating a video record of his ring career. Ryan Birtcher is the point person in this effort.

Birtcher came out of the music industry and is the founder and president of Media Stranger, a highly regarded digital-content strategy and production company. He began working with Álvarez prior to Canelo's 2015 fight against Miguel Cotto and, by his own admission, "had no idea what I was walking into."

The core team that Birtcher has assembled for Canelo's fights includes John Kim (a fulltime editor at Media Stranger), Brendan Calder (a freelance cinematographer), and Andrew Jorgensen (a still photographer). Alternates fill in as needed from time to time.

Birtcher and his team visit Canelo's training camp several times before each fight. They're also on site for press tours, throughout fight week, and on fight night. They've amassed thousands of hours of video content and tens of thousands of photographs. Canelo owns the copyright on the material.

"You don't just show up and shoot a video," Birtcher says of his team's work. "You have to be creative and plan. We're there for hours before and after each event; planning, shooting, editing, and distributing content, all on the same day."

Some of the content is posted on Canelo's Instagram, Facebook, and Twitter accounts. Is there a documentary in the works?

"We're working on a special project," Birtcher says.

Asked for his insights on Canelo, Birtcher is effusive in his praise.

"I've been blessed to be around some special people in my life," Ryan notes. "But Saul is unique. His approach to training is unlike any other athlete, musician, anyone I've known. The hard work, the dedication, his poise and total focus; they're incredible. Saul doesn't run his mouth in public. He says what he needs to say with as little controversy and drama as possible. He's one of the smartest people I've met. He has good instincts when it comes to business and knows where to go for help.

"Saul sets the standard for professionalism for everyone on the team," Birtcher says in closing. "There's Chepo and Eddy and so many others behind the scenes who the world doesn't see. Each person on the team knows his role. Canelo values every one of them and makes them feel valued. He's generous and respectful toward everyone on the team. They're a family with intense loyalty between them. It's so special for me to be part of this."

★ ★ ★

Certain punches have a treasured place in boxing lore: the right hand that crashed against Jersey Joe Walcott's jaw and made Rocky Marciano heavyweight champion of the world; Sugar Ray Robinson's picture-perfect left-hook knockout of Gene Fullmer to reclaim the middleweight throne; and the left hook from hell that Joe Frazier visited on Muhammad Ali's jaw, driving The Greatest to the canvas in Ali-Frazier I.

But remember: Ali got up.

And speaking of another great fighter who got up. . . . On September 28, 1979, with 50 seconds left in round seven, Earnie Shavers landed what he later said was the hardest punch he ever threw flush on the jaw of Larry Holmes. Shavers wasn't just another puncher. With 68 knockouts on his final ring ledger, he was on the short list—the very short list—of "hardest punchers of all time."

Holmes went down like he'd been shot. Somehow, he managed to stagger to his feet at the count of seven and survive the final 40 seconds of the round. In round ten, he knocked Shavers out. "First, you get up," Larry said later. "Then you worry about whether or not you're all right."

There has been talk lately about whether Deontay Wilder is the hardest-punching heavyweight ever. Punching power is impossible to quantify with precision. That said, this writer recently asked Holmes to compare Shavers and Wilder in terms of punching power.

"I don't know," Holmes responded. "I've never been hit by Wilder. I've only seen him on television. But can't imagine anyone hitting harder than Earnie Shavers."

And what about those who say that Tyson Fury compares with Muhammad Ali in terms of boxing skills?

"They're crazy, man," Holmes answers.

★ ★ ★

In recent months, I've exchanged emails regularly with a reader known to me only as John. He expresses himself well and his comments are thought provoking. A few worth sharing are:

★ "The boxing fan is treated like yesterday's garbage. They call us 'The Gate' as if we are just a number, a digit, a less then important piece of the fight game. It hits me every so often. It gets at me."

★ "I never liked dancers other than the woman on the floor. Defense is fine, but don't forget to fight. Give me a guy who walks like he is hungry, like the world is a big lie and I am going to hurt someone tonight. Nothing wrong with a little nasty from time to time. Got to keep the street in your blood."

★ "I had a thought of writing about what it means to have a favorite fighter. What that is like, how that happens, how it turns into something good. Stats; throw them out. Wins and losses; I do not care. Height, reach advantage; stick it buddy. He is my fighter."

★ "If boxing wasn't a sport, someone would invent it today. Hell, fighting is all that's happening now."

★ ★ ★

A note on Sugar Ray Leonard, whose photograph by Wojtek Urbanek graces the cover of this book.

Leonard is boxing royalty. He burst upon the scene as a twenty-year-old gold medalist at the 1976 Montreal Olympics. The only loss in the first thirty-six fights of his pro career was a one-point defeat at the hands of Roberto Duran. He rebounded from that defeat to beat Duran twice.

Leonard was a complete fighter. He could box. He could punch. He had handspeed. He could take a punch. He had heart.

"And he was smart," trainer Don Turner noted. "Bill Russell smart. Ray did whatever he had to do to win. He won fights in so many different ways."

"People don't realize how tough Leonard was and how hard he hit," Duran said after their ring wars had come to an end. "I do because I fought him."

Leonard was a combatant in seven of the twelve fights contested among Marvin Hagler, Thomas Hearns, Roberto Duran, Wilfred Benítez, and himself. These fights have a special place in boxing lore. His record in them was 5 wins, 1 loss, and 1 draw.

Leonard–Hearns I was a time-capsule fight. Ray dug deep, fought through adversity, showed every quality that a fighter needs to be great, and stopped Hearns in the fourteenth round. That night, he entered the ranks of boxing immortals.

"Ray Leonard was somebody I always dreamed about photographing," Wojtek Urbanek says. "All photographers have lists like that in our mind. But the bar is so high that you don't think it will happen. This photograph was taken at a boxing writers dinner in 2019. I didn't even know that Ray would be there. I had just set up my equipment in a corridor off the main ballroom. Then I saw him coming toward me.

"Ray sat down in front of my camera," Urbanek remembers. "I took some photos. He was polite, and I didn't want to take up too much of his time. So after a while, I said thank you and that was that. Then he looked at some of the photos in my portfolio and said let's do some more. Before that, I was photographing the celebrity Ray Leonard and he was presenting himself in a certain way. Now he was trusting me and my camera, and everything came together perfectly.

"There's something special about boxers," Urbanek continues. "The history of human combat is in their eyes. This photograph is multilayered and can be interpreted in so many different ways. The cross accentuates the spiritual side of Ray. The fist is the fighter in him. Without the fist, it's devotional portrait. Without the cross, it's the moments before battle. There was magic at work that night. The classical triangular composition of Ray's eye, his fist, and the cross was a fortunate accident. Faith. Hope. Struggle. Reflection. They're all in this portrait. And it's Sugar Ray Leonard. What a privilege and honor it was for me that night."

This was a foreword that I wrote for Sporting Blood, *a collection of essays written by Carlos Acevedo.*

Sporting Blood

The internet has changed sportswriting, particularly when it comes to writing about boxing. Very few newspapers or magazines now have a writer on staff who understands the sport and business of boxing. Meanwhile, the number of websites devoted to the sweet science keeps growing. Some of these websites are quite good. Others are awful. Reprinting a press release with a new lead is not journalism. Simply voicing an opinion without more is not journalism.

As Carlos Acevedo—the author of *Sporting Blood*—wrote in another forum, "Boxing is immune to critical consensus because of the number of fanboys who pretend to be journalists. No other sport has such an unsophisticated mediascape covering it."

Acevedo was born in the Bronx in 1972 and now lives in Brooklyn. He was drawn to boxing as a boy, grew up reading *The Ring,* and recalls being captivated by Larry Holmes, Marvelous Marvin Hagler, and Marvin Johnson. Decades later, when the internet gave a platform to anyone with a computer and modem, he decided to write about the sweet science.

Acevedo's journey as a boxing writer began in 2007. Two years later, he founded a website called The Cruelest Sport. Since then, he has written for numerous print publications and websites including Hannibal Boxing (his current primary outlet), MaxBoxing, Undisputed Champion Network, Boxing Digest, Boxing World, Remezcla, and Esquina Boxeo.

"I love the fights and the narrative that comes with them," Carlos says. "Each fight is a story unto itself; a drama that exposes character and offers the ideal of self-determination."

I'm not sure when I first became aware of Acevedo's writing. I do remember laughing out loud years ago while reading his description of promoter Gary Shaw, who Carlos opined "deserves credit for tenacity, like certain insects that become immune over time to Raid and Black Flag." I first quoted him in my own writing in 2011 in conjunction with less-than-stellar refereeing by Russell Mora and Joe Cortez.

"Incompetence is usually the answer for most of the riddles in boxing," Acevedo wrote of Mora's overseeing Abner Mares vs. Joseph Agbeko. "But Mora was a quantum leap removed from mere ineptitude. He was clearly biased in favor of Mares and, worse than that, seemed to enter the ring with a predetermined notion of what he was going to do. Mares had carte blanche to whack Agbeko below the belt as often as he wanted."

As for Cortez's refereeing in Floyd Mayweather vs. Victor Ortiz, Acevedo proclaimed, "Cortez, whose incompetence has been steadily growing, is now one of the perpetual black clouds of boxing. Why let Cortez, whose reverse Midas touch has marred more than one big fight recently, in the building at all on Saturday night?"

Acevedo doesn't have a big platform. He doesn't have a wealth of contacts in the boxing industry or one-on-one access to big names. In part, that's because he has never compromised his writing to curry favor or ingratiate himself to the powers that be in an effort to gain access or ensure that he receives press credentials for a fight.

But Carlos has several very important things going for him: (1) He appreciates and understands boxing history; (2) he has an intuitive feel for the sport and business of boxing; and (3) he's a provocative thinker and a good writer who puts thoughts together clearly and logically.

Look at the Contents page of *Sporting Blood* and you'll see essays (in order) on Carlos Negrón, Jack Johnson, Roberto Duran, Esteban De Jesús, Aaron Pryor, Don Jordan, Joe Frazier, Johnny Saxton, Wilfredo Gómez, Lupe Pintor, Davey Moore, Johnny Tapia, Mike Tyson, Evander Holyfield, Bert Cooper, Sonny Liston, Jake LaMotta, Ad Wolgast, Tony Ayala Jr., Al Singer, Michael Dokes, Eddie Machon, Mike Quarry, and Muhammad Ali.

That's an eclectic mix. But each essay goes beyond the name of the fighter attached to it to underscore a fundamental truth about, and capture the essence of, boxing.

Acevedo calls boxing "a dark art." Phrases like "the hard logic of the ring" characterize the gritty realism of his writing. Some of the thoughts in *Sporting Blood* that captured my attention include:

* "Sadism, whether one admits it or not, is an essential part of boxing. So is masochism."

* "Nothing can take away from the terrible symmetry boxing gives its practitioners: a hardscrabble life, followed by a hardscrabble profession, followed by a hardscrabble retirement."
* "Disillusion is as much a part of boxing as the jab is."
* "In boxing, the enemies of promise are numerous: entourages, managers, promoters, injuries, other fighters. But self-destruction ranks up there with the best of the worst."
* "There is very little afterlife for a fighter who has failed to succeed."

Acevedo has an economical writing style that leads readers to the intended destination without unnecessary verbiage or digressions. Consider his description of Aaron Pryor's origins, a fighter who Carlos describes as "one of the most exciting fighters during an era when action was a prerequisite for fame."

After noting that Pryor "matched his unbridled style in the ring with an apocalyptic personal life that kept him in boldface for over a decade," Acevedo explains, "Aaron Pryor was an at-risk youth before the term came into vogue. Dysfunction was in his DNA. He was born out of wedlock in 1955 to an alcoholic mother whose moodiness could lead to impromptu gunplay. Sarah Pryor, who gave birth to seven children from five different fathers, occasionally whipped out the nickel-plated hardware when some of her brood became unruly. Years later, she wound up shooting her husband five times in the kind of supercharged domestic dispute in which the Pryor clan excelled.

"Pryor," Acevedo continues, "had a family tree whose branches were gnarled by tragedy. Its roots were blood-soaked. One of his brothers, Lorenzo, was a career criminal who once escaped from Cincinnati County Jail. Lorenzo eventually wound up doing hard time for an armed robbery conviction in Ohio. Another brother, David, became a transsexual hooker. His half-brother was shot and paralyzed by his father. His sister, Catherine, stabbed her lover to death. As if to solidify the epigenetics involved in the Pryor family—and to concretize the symbolism of the phrase 'vicious cycle'—Sarah Pryor had seen her own mother shot and murdered by a boyfriend when Sarah was a child."

Want more?

"As an eight-year-old already at sea in chaotic surroundings," Acevedo notes, "Pryor was molested by a minister."

There—in a little more than two hundred words, Acevedo has painted a portrait. Do you still wonder why Aaron Pryor had trouble conforming to the norms that society expected of him?

In a chilling profile of Tony Ayala Jr., Acevedo writes, "In the ring, he was hemmed in by the ropes. For more than half his life, he was trapped behind bars. The rest of the time? He was locked inside himself."

Ayala spent two decades in prison in conjunction with multiple convictions for brutal sexual assaults against women. Acevedo sets up the parallel between Ayala's misogynist conduct and his ring savagery with a quote from the fighter himself about boxing.

"It's the closest thing to being like God—to control somebody else," Ayala declared. "I hit a guy and it's like, I can do anything I want to you. I own you. Your life is mine, and I will do with it what I please. It's a really sadistic mentality, but that's what goes on in my mind. It's really evil. There's no other way to put it. I step into that dark, most evil part of me and I physically destroy somebody else, and I will do with them what I want."

Acevedo also has a gift for dramatically recreating the action in classic ring battles. After recounting the carnage that Ad Wolgast and Battling Nelson visited upon each other on February 22, 1910, he observes, "What Wolgast and Nelson produced was not, in retrospect a sporting event, but a gruesome reminder of how often the line between a blood sport and bloodlust was crossed during an era when mercy was an underdeveloped concept in boxing."

A vivid description of the December 3, 1982, title bout between Wilfredo Gómez and Lupe Pintor is followed by the observation, "At the core of these apocalyptic fights, where two men take turns punishing each other from round to round, lies the question of motivation. Not in the sporting sense; that is, not in the careerist sense or anything so mundane as competition, but in an existential sense. And while boxing lends itself far too often to an intellectual clam chowder (common ingredients: social Darwinism, atavism, gladiatorial analogies, talk of warriors), the fact remains that what Gomez and Pintor did to each other, under the socially sanctioned auspices of entertainment, bordered on madness."

This is powerful writing. Enjoy it.

Boxing, more than any other sport, pits its present against its past.

The Night the Referee Hit Back

The Night the Referee Hit Back (Rowman & Littlefield) is a collection of twenty-three essays about boxing written by Mike Silver and augmented by the transcripts of interviews that Silver conducted with five fighters.

Silver is a reliable historian and an ardent spokesperson for boxing's past. He looks back fondly on the time when the sweet science was "a relevant part of the social fabric" of America and had "the capacity to address issues involving history, ideology, violence, politics, gender, and race" (as evidenced by Jack Johnson, Joe Louis, and Muhammad Ali). "No other sport," Silver states, "can make that claim."

But Silver is a harsh critic of contemporary boxing. The essays in his current book return again and again to the theme voiced in *The Arc of Boxing* (his first book about the sport).

Simply put, Silver believes that boxing is a lost art and today's fighters are vastly inferior to those who plied their trade during "The Golden Age of Boxing" (which he identifies as the 1920s through the 1950s with a nod to a handful of fighters in the 1960s and '70s). He states—correctly, I believe—that too few fighters at the top of the food chain today are willing to go in tough and thus don't learn the lessons that come from fighting the best. He also has a low regard for contemporary trainers and writes, "If 95 percent of today's trainers showed up at Stillman's, they would be laughed out of the gym or assigned as bucket carriers since that low-level job would result in them doing the least damage."

"Boxing technique has fallen to its lowest level in over one hundred years," Silver laments. "The art of boxing as I knew it is dead and unlikely to be revived anytime soon."

There are two components to writing history: (1) getting the facts right, and (2) interpreting the facts. Silver is a reliable reporter of fact. But there are times when I take issue with his interpretation.

When I read *The Arc of Boxing* twelve years ago, I felt that Silver and the "panel of experts" he quoted approvingly went overboard in glamorizing the past and denigrating contemporary fighters. I simply didn't agree that Tami Mauriello at 190 pounds would have knocked out Lennox Lewis or that Tommy Loughran at 185 pounds would have outpointed Mike Tyson. Nor did I think that Bernard Hopkins in the 1950s would have been nothing more than a "good journeyman" or a "main event fighter in the small clubs."

These differences of opinion are rekindled by *The Night the Referee Hit Back.* The essays fall primarily into one of two categories—either an appreciative look at boxing's past or a not-so-appreciative look at the way things are now.

The first essay—"Boxing in Olde New York: Unforgettable Stillman's Gym"—is the best in the book. But there are too many instances where Silver idealizes the past.

For example, Silver notes the similarity in height and weight between Wladimir Klitschko and Jess Willard (who Jack Dempsey obliterated in three rounds) and concludes, "I have no doubt that Dempsey's superior speed and punching power would be the deciding factor in achieving the same result against Klitschko."

With regard to Klitschko vs. Tyson Fury, Silver writes, "The overall incompetence, amateurishness, and lack of fighting spirit of both contestants was astounding. I could not believe what I was seeing. That was the last straw for me. I figuratively threw in the towel on my once favorite sport. I really don't care if I never see another contemporary boxing match again."

I agree that Klitschko–Fury was a dreadful fight. But it was no worse than Jack Sharkey against Primo Carnera, Max Baer against James Braddock, and many other heavyweight championship fights from "the golden age of boxing."

Similarly, Silver proclaims, "If a prime Ted Lowry were fighting today, I have no doubt he could easily whip the current cruiserweight, light-heavyweight, and heavyweight champions on consecutive weeks."

Lowry is best known for having lost a dubious ten-round decision to Rocky Marciano in 1949. He never fought above 184 pounds and compiled a career record of 70 wins, 68 losses, and 10 draws.

Silver is on solid ground when he writes, "Once upon a time, winning a world championship was a rare and venerated achievement. It really meant something. Today every boxer, it seems, is wearing some kind of goofy title belt." But there are times when Silver says things that I think are just plain wrong and, in any event, impossible to verify (e.g., his contention that the 1977 fight between Muhammad Ali and Earnie Shavers "caused more head trauma [to Ali] than all three Frazier bouts put together").

Also, in comparing contemporary fighters with the past, let's remember that another reason there are fewer great fighters today is that there are fewer fighters. In the 1920s and 1930s, there were ten to twelve thousand boxers licensed at any given time in the United States. Now the total is closer to 2,500. So multiply today's numbers by four. Suppose you had four Terence Crawfords, four Errol Spences, four Vasyl Lomachenkos, four Canelo Álvarezes, four Naoya Inoues, and so on down the line in each of their respective weight divisions. All of a sudden, 2020 might look like a remarkable time for boxing.

The essay in *The Night the Referee Hit Back* that will cause the most controversy is entitled "The Myth of 'The Thrilla in Manila'."

Silver respects Muhammad Ali and Joe Frazier for the fighters they once were. And he acknowledges that Ali–Frazier I was a great fight. He begins to misfire when, writing of Ali–Frazier II, he states, "Ali was gifted with a twelve-round decision that many fans and sportswriters thought he lost." But the overwhelming majority of fans and sportswriters thought Ali won. There were times when the judges were overly kind to Muhammad. Ali–Frazier II wasn't one of them.

Silver then calls Ali–Frazier III "the most overrated boxing match in the history of the sport" and adds, "To accurately evaluate 'The Thrilla in Manila' based strictly on its merits as a prizefight is to come to the conclusion that it was no better or worse than a good tough club fight.

"There is a sloppy quality to the efforts of both men as they take their turns meting out punishment," Silver writes. "Many fans, still enthralled by the myth of 'The Thrilla in Manila,' love to refer to the 'ebb and flow' of a great fight. In this fight, the 'ebb and flow' becomes all too predictable. When a tiring Ali decides to 'ebb' against the ropes, he allows Frazier to 'flow' for up to a full minute without returning any meaningful counterpunch. When Ali is rested enough to come off the ropes, he will 'flow' back for ten or fifteen seconds with a few swift arm punches before returning to the relative safety of the rope-a-dope. By the middle rounds, with the pattern of the fight firmly established and the possibility of a sudden ending very remote, a fan who understood what was really going on could have walked out to the concession stand for a hot dog and beer, returned to his seat several minutes later, and be unconcerned about having missed anything important."

Silver concedes that, in Manila, Ali and Frazier "displayed the fighting spirit and never surrender attitude that is the inner core of every great champion." But he then remarks, "To say it was a great fight because of this battle of wills is to see only one aspect of a fight that, when viewed in its totality, was seriously flawed. What if the fighters involved were not named Ali and Frazier but instead were two heavyweight contenders named 'Smith' and 'Jones'? Same fight, just different names. Would 'The Thrilla' still be remembered today as a great fight?"

My answer to that question is "yes." Arturo Gatti and Micky Ward weren't elite fighters. But their first encounter was—and will always be remembered as—a great fight. And the fact that it was Ali and Frazier in Manila instead of Smith and Jones does matter, just as it matters that it was Joe Louis and Max Schmeling at Yankee Stadium on June 22, 1938.

Ali–Frazier III showcased many of the qualities that make boxing and boxers great. To say that it wasn't a great fight because neither man was as good as he'd once been is like saying there has never been a great college football game because an ordinary NFL squad would have beaten either college team.

Silver's critique begs the question, "If The Thrilla in Manila is over-rated, what does he think qualifies as a 'truly great prizefight'?" The first fight he lists in that regard is Rocky Marciano's 1952 knockout of Jersey Joe Walcott to claim the heavyweight throne—a fight that Silver calls "perhaps the best heavyweight championship bout of all time." The second is Archie Moore heroically fighting back from the brink of defeat to knock out Yvon Durelle in 1958.

I agree that both of these fights were great fights. But let's not forget that Walcott was a faded thirty-eight years old when he fought Marciano. And Durelle (a Canadian fisherman) had 19 losses on his ring ledger when he fought the forty-two-year-old Moore.

On February 14, 1951, thirty million people—one-fifth the popula-tion of the United States—watched the sixth and final fight between Sugar Ray Robinson and Jake LaMotta on television. That would be equivalent to sixty-four million viewers today. One thing Mike Silver and I can agree on is that it's sad those times are long gone.

There are very few one-name phenomena in sports. Bundini was one of them.

Bundini

If Drew Brown Jr. (better known as "Bundini") had never done anything else, his place in history would be assured by his origination and choreography of the phrase: "Float like a butterfly, sting like a bee . . . Rumble, young man, rumble . . . Aaaaahhh!"

Those words and the exclamation that followed captured the essence of Cassius Clay—and later, Muhammad Ali—both in the ring and out of it. They shaped the perception of one of the most important athletes of all time. *Bundini* by Todd D. Snyder (Hamilcar Publications) is the story of this complex, enigmatic man who spent the most noteworthy years of his life in Ali's orbit.

Bundini was born on March 21, 1928. His father was a violent, uneducated man, poor in the rural South. Unable to stand the abuse, Bundini's mother left the marital home when Bundini was seven, taking his younger brother with her. Bundini was left alone with his father. He quit school in the third grade and was functionally illiterate throughout his life.

Many of the details of Bundini's life are shrouded in mystery. He joined the US Navy (he said) at age thirteen. His duties were those of a ship's porter. The moniker "Bundini" (he said) was bestowed on him after some girls called out "Bundini! Bundini! Bundini" (which he said meant "lover") as his ship pulled out of a port in India. He was discharged from the Navy at age fifteen after throwing a white officer overboard for slapping him and calling him a "nigger" or (alternative version) threatening the officer with a meat cleaver. He spent the next twelve years with the Merchant Marines (civilian mariners overseen by a combination of US government and private-sector interests).

In 1952, Bundini married Rhoda Palestine, an unorthodox woman who had grown up in a white Orthodox Jewish family in the Brighton Beach section of Brooklyn. To get by, Bundini told her, they'd have to hustle.

"When Drew said we had to hustle," Rhoda later elaborated, "I took it on as a role, and really as a learning experience. I didn't care to make that much money. Just enough. And I was young, twenty-two, so I believed that nothing could get in our way."

Snyder elaborates on what that meant, writing, "For Rhoda, the hustle could be likened to that of a marriage counselor or psychiatrist. In the Harlem streets, hotels, and nightclubs where such activity frequently took place, Rhoda learned how to spot an easy target. As she gained confidence in her new trade, Rhoda became adept at getting men to pay her for conversation, as opposed to sexual pleasure. Fully immersed in Harlem street culture, the couple survived day to day."

Rhoda later claimed that, for Bundini's thirtieth birthday, she "paid for a gal to be with him."

Drew Timothy Brown III, their son, was born on January 20, 1955. Three years later, the couple divorced. There were later attempts at reconciliation and cohabitation, but those efforts always ended in acrimony.

Bundini joined Sugar Ray Robinson's entourage as an "odd-job man" in 1957 and worked for Robinson for close to seven years. The night before Cassius Clay's March 13, 1963, fight at Madison Square Garden against Doug Jones, Robinson offered some advice to the young fighter.

"I told him he needed somebody to watch over him, somebody to keep him happy and relaxed," Sugar Ray later recounted. "I had just the guy for him."

Clay hired Bundini in late 1963 after signing to fight Sonny Liston for the heavyweight title and brought him to the 5th Street Gym in Miami. He also invited Bundini to work his corner for the February 25, 1964, Liston fight, the first time Bundini had ever worked in a professional fighter's corner.

Bundini was a motivator. He was more spiritual than religious. He was also a heavy drinker and recreational drug user who rejected many of the core principles of Elijah Muhammad's teachings, including the doctrine that white people were "devils." He was exiled from Ali's camp after the May 25, 1965, Liston rematch, primarily because of friction with the Nation of Islam hierarchy, and was absent from Muhammad's next seven fights.

It was an ugly separation. Bundini was at ringside rooting for

Floyd Patterson when Ali faced the former champion in Las Vegas on November 22, 1965. But he was back in the fold when Ali fought Zora Folley at Madison Square Garden on March 22, 1967 (Muhammad's last fight before being exiled from boxing).

One of the appeals that Bundini had for Ali was that neither man was grounded in the same reality that most people know and experience. There was an aura of fantasy about them that led to wonderful flights of imagination. He lifted Ali's spirits and was in his corner for forty-four of Muhammad's sixty-one professional bouts.

After Ali retired from boxing, Bundini worked with a few other fighters. But he never reached the heights again. He hustled. He drank heavily. At age fifty-nine, while drunk, he fell down a flight of stairs in the Los Angeles motel where he lived. He lay at the foot of the stairs for ten hours before being discovered. The fall rendered him a quadriplegic. He died three weeks later on September 28, 1987.

Snyder is drawn to writing about fathers and sons. His first book—*12 Rounds in Lo's Gym*—was in significant part about his relationship with his father. *Bundini* is a book about Bundini's son—Drew Timothy Brown III—as well as Bundini.

Drew revered his father and reveled in his access to the Ali circus. But the relationship between father and son was sometimes difficult to maintain. Once, when Bundini was physically abusing Rhoda during an attempt at reconciliation, Drew threw his father to the ground and threatened to kill him. Drew also faced the challenge of growing up in two vastly different worlds. His father represented one set of values while his mother and her family represented another. He was bar mitzvahed and, at one point, lived as an exchange student on a kibbutz in Israel.

Drew went to college at New Mexico State University in Las Cruces but flunked out after two semesters. Then he attended Southern University in New Orleans and graduated in 1977. After a series of unsatisfying jobs, he entered the officer candidate school at the Naval Air Station in Pensacola, Florida, completed the program in 1981, and was commissioned in the United States Navy. After serving in the armed forces, he worked for three decades as a cargo pilot for FedEx. His daughter is an attorney with a law firm in New York. His son is an orthopedic surgeon in Tampa. That's quite a journey for the Brown and Palestine families.

But there were problems. Alcoholism had plagued Drew's father and grandfather. It plagued Drew as well.

The parallels between father and son were obvious. In 1968 (while Ali was in exile from boxing), Bundini's World—a bar on Second Avenue in Manhattan—opened for business. Two years later, it closed. Decades later, Drew's résumé included ownership of a New Orleans nightclub that also failed.

"We both made the same mistake," Drew acknowledged to Snyder. "We were our own best customers. My life started changing when I started falling down, drunk. My wife took a picture of me on the ground one time. That was my rock bottom. The disease of alcoholism was a major part in the reason for Laurie [Drew's wife and the mother of his two children] leaving."

In early 1998, driven by the fear that he would one day find himself at the bottom of a staircase, Drew entered treatment for the disease that had ravaged his family. He and Laurie are on good terms today. He has remarried. Were Bundini and Rhoda still alive, they would be proud of their son and his accomplishments.

Snyder's book contains a wealth of information about Bundini and captures his spirit. He also writes eloquently about Ali, calling him a "warrior whose self-belief knew no boundaries."

"Ali's second reign was made possible," Snyder observes, "not by blinding speed or fast-twitch reflexes, but rather by his supreme level of mental toughness, a legendary ability to endure. It wasn't that Ali was unwilling to make the sacrifices necessary to be great. The tragedy lies in the fact that he did."

"To be heralded as great," Snyder adds with regard to Ali, "to be recognized as not only great but perhaps the greatest of all the greats, is a feeling that hardly any human being will ever get the chance to experience."

But there are some nagging issues with regard to Snyder's work.

In his Introduction to *Bundini,* Snyder writes, "The book you are about to read does not aim to hide behind the illusion of neutrality. I want you, the reader, to see Bundini through the eyes of his son. I do not think of this text as a biography, not in the traditional sense. I don't consider myself an investigative journalist. I am a storyteller and these are the stories Drew Brown III and his family are ready to share with the world. I don't confuse oral history with irrefutable evidence. I present this collection of family stories, corroborated by a variety of Bundini insiders, as evidence of an oral tradition that keeps Bundini alive in the hearts and minds of those who loved him most."

That's an honest statement. But it's also a red flag.

Snyder is an associate professor at Siena College. He understands the importance of accuracy in scholarship. In writing *Bundini*, he undertook a great deal of archival research and interviewed a wide range of people. Full disclosure requires me to note that I was one of the interviewees. Much of the narrative comes from more than fifty interviews that Snyder conducted with Bundini's son over the course of fourteen months. In many instances, there's no contemporaneous documentation to support the narrative. That's significant because there are places where one wonders how reliable the narrative is.

Snyder sometimes fails to differentiate between fact and "storytelling." The more I read, the more I had the uncomfortable feeling that there were times when he was bending the narrative to glorify Bundini and highlight the role that one or more of his interviewees played to the detriment of others.

For example, talking about Ali vs. George Foreman, Drew Brown III is quoted as saying, "That fight is what really started Don King. My daddy got him the fight. There may never have been a Don King without my father."

But Bundini didn't get King the fight. Ten million dollars from Zaire's President Mobutu Sese Seko (five million for each fighter) got King and the people he was fronting for the fight.

Jeremiah Shabazz, who was instrumental in converting Ali to Islam and remained a presence throughout Muhammad's ring career, isn't mentioned in the book. Nor are entourage members like Pat Patterson, Lana Shabazz, Ralph Thornton, and Booker Johnson. More significantly, Howard Bingham's role as possibly the most important constant in Ali's life for decades is trivialized while others are elevated beyond what their true standing was.

Snyder glosses over the end of Ali's ill-conceived challenge to Larry Holmes, writing, "After the completion of nine humiliating rounds, trainer Angelo Dundee stopped the bout, screaming to referee Richard Greene, 'I'm the chief second and I say the fight is over!' Bundini, his face contorted in disappointment, begged Dundee for 'one more round.'"

Viewing that sequence on YouTube, one can see and hear Dundee telling Greene, "That's all." Bundini then grabbed onto Dundee's sweater and pleaded, "One more round." Dundee shouted, "Fuck you! No!" Then he turned back to Greene and said, "The ballgame's over. I'm the chief second. I stop the fight."

The question that begs exploration is how Bundini could have been so thoughtless and cruel as to advocate for allowing the slaughter to continue.

There are also instances in *Bundini* where statements presented as fact are clearly wrong.

All authors make mistakes no matter how hard we try to avoid them. In *Muhammad Ali: His Life and Times*, I wrote that Bundini died soon after he "suffered a stroke and was found by a maid in a motel room." Snyder writes that Bundini was found "at the bottom of the staircase" leading to his motel room. Also, Bundini's son told Snyder, "My father was drunk when he fell down those steps." I accept Snyder's work on this issue as a correction of my own.

There are places where Snyder's work invites correction.

Snyder writes that the New York State Athletic Commission chose to license Ali after Muhammad's comeback fight against Jerry Quarry in Atlanta for financial reasons. More specifically, he states, "In a surprise turn of events, the New York State Athletic Commission followed Atlanta's lead and reissued Ali's boxing license. Now that the ice had been broken, New York boxing's movers and shakers were not going to sit back and simply allow Ali to make money fighting in other states."

But that's not what happened. The New York State Athletic Commission was forced to license Ali by a federal judge named Walter Mansfield, who ruled that the denial of a license was a clear violation of Ali's constitutional rights.

Snyder recounts an incident that supposedly happened prior to Ali–Frazier I when Bundini, followed by fifty fans he'd just met, arrived at Madison Square Garden and refused to bring Ali's gloves into the arena unless the cops at a side entrance allowed the fans into the Garden with him. The cops relented. In Snyder's retelling, "Leaping over the barricade and scurrying into the Garden like children on Christmas morning, the boys showered Bundini with high fives, handshakes, and hugs."

But that doesn't ring true. Rather, it seems based on an incident that occurred six years later when Ali fought Earnie Shavers at Madison Square Garden. On that occasion, Ali arrived at the employees' entrance with fifty to sixty fans he'd collected along the way and demanded that they be allowed in. Harry Markson (president of MSG Boxing) was called to the scene and agreed to let twenty of the fans in.

But Markson, unlike cops on the street, had the authority to do that. Unlike Ali–Shavers, Ali–Frazier I had the tightest security of any fight in the history of Madison Square Garden. And most significantly, Ali (by virtue of being Ali) had the stature to impose his will in situations like this. Bundini didn't.

In Snyder's defense, his recitation of the gate-crashing scene at Ali-Frazier I comes directly from Bundini's son (who says he was there). Still, reading *Bundini*, there are times when it's hard to know where factual history ends and the "storytelling" begins.

A key example of this is Snyder's explanation of what happened to the *Ring Magazine* championship belt that was presented to Cassius Clay after he dethroned Sonny Liston in 1964. Snyder calls the matter of the belt "a dark cloud that looms over all that Bundini accomplished in the sport." The most common belief is that Bundini sold the belt. But there have been particularly unflattering versions of the sale, including the claim in the sometimes unreliable 2001 biopic *Ali* starring Will Smith that Bundini stole the belt and sold it for drug money.

Snyder disposes of questions regarding the fate of the belt with an explanation from Bundini's son who, he says, "discussed the incident multiple times with his father."

"My father didn't sell the belt," Drew Brown III told Snyder. "He took a hammer and knocked out some of the precious stones. He did that because the Black Muslims withheld his pay [after Ali–Liston II when Bundini was exiled from Ali's camp]."

But there's a problem with that explanation.

Craig Hamilton is the foremost boxing memorabilia dealer in the United States. Over the years, he has been retained by almost every major auction house in the United States to authenticate Ali memorabilia.

"There were no precious stones in the *Ring* belts of that era," Hamilton says. "There was no gold in them either. They were made of base metal and had a cloth sash. There were no stones of any kind in them at all. If the author had taken the time to find a photo of the belt, he would have known that.

"After he beat George Foreman in Zaire," Hamilton continues, "Ali won the Hickock Belt. That belt did have some gold and precious stones in it, and no one I know has a clue where that is either. But that was almost ten years after the time you're talking about, and Bundini was back in Ali's camp by then. Stories like this make me so mad. Nat Fleischer [editor of *The Ring*] was a cheap guy and *The Ring* was a small magazine. Precious stones? Are you kidding me? If Bundini had the belt, which his son seems to think he did, then the odds are that he sold it. He certainly didn't take out the precious stones and sell them because there weren't any."

So where does that leave us?

Bundini was important. He was at ground zero with Muhammad Ali for a long time. Snyder's book, despite its flaws, adds to the understanding of both Bundini and Ali.

"Float like a butterfly, sting like a bee . . . Rumble, young man, rumble . . . Aaaaahhh!"

As Snyder reminds us, after those words were spoken, "the theatrics of professional sports would never be the same."

The parade of new books about Muhammad Ali continued throughout 2020.

Cassius X

Music was the lifeblood of cultural change in the 1950s and 1960s. *Cassius X: The Transformation of Muhammad Ali* by Stuart Cosgrove (published by Lawrence Hill Books, an imprint of Chicago Review Press) focuses on Cassius Clay's involvement with the Nation of Islam in the years leading up to his 1964 triumph over Sonny Liston and the expanding reach of what Cosgrove calls "Black music" during that time.

Cassius X is divided into six chapters with a coda titled "Requiem." Each chapter is set in a particular city—Miami, Detroit, Philadelphia, New York, London, and Miami again—that was the site for one or more pivotal events in Clay's life. In each instance, Cosgrove describes Clay's life and the music scene in that city in depth.

For example, the first chapter ("Miami") includes a graphic portrayal of racial injustice in the segregated American South as well as Clay's early involvement with the Nation of Islam and the origins of his friendship with Sam Cooke (a pioneering singer and songwriter of that era). The second chapter ("Detroit") details the origins of Motown Records and contains an interesting recounting of a 1962 journey that Cassius, his brother, and Sam Saxon (who introduced Clay to the Nation of Islam) took to Detroit to attend a Nation of Islam rally overseen by Elijah Muhammad and Malcolm X. In "Philadelphia" (where Sonny Liston and his mob overlords lived), the racist underpinnings of Dick Clark's enormously influential *American Bandstand* television show are explored.

Cosgrove is a Scottish author, journalist, television executive, and TV host with a scholarly interest in music. He's passionate about his subject and puts words together well. His writing is infused with interesting nuggets of information such as the fact that three records recorded by Sonji Roi (Ali's first wife) were released after their marriage fell apart. But there are problems with his work.

The biggest problem is that *Cassius X* is riddled with factual inaccuracies. The red flags begin to appear in the first chapter when Cosgrove writes that Tony Esperti (Clay's third professional opponent) was "assassinated in a mob hit" in 1967 by a member of the Gambino crime family and adds, "The coroner described it as the perfect execution—a single lethal bullet to the brain."

"That's interesting," I said to myself. I made a note to praise Cosgrove in this review for that bit of information. Then something in the back of my mind cautioned, "Wait a minute!"

Muhammad Ali fought 50 different opponents in his 61 professional fights. I keep a list of which opponents are still alive and the date of death for those who are no longer with us. Tony Esperti died in 2002. I have photographs of him that were taken in 1979. Yet *Cassius X* dramatically recounts his 1967 "execution" in a Miami steakhouse. In reality, Esperti was the perpetrator of the crime in question.

Unfortunately, there's more.

Cosgrove writes that "more myths have congregated around Sonny Liston than any boxer before or since."

I take issue with that. Let's start with Joe Louis who (among other myths) inspired the allegorical tale of a Black prisoner in the moments before his execution crying out "Save me, Joe Louis!" No one is said to have cried out, "Save me, Sonny Liston!"

Cosgrove also writes, "Liston won twenty-six consecutive bouts over five years, and his title-winning victory on September 25, 1962 [over Floyd Patterson] broke the record for consecutive heavyweight victories."

But Rocky Marciano won 49 fights in a row and retired from boxing with an unblemished record. Joe Louis won 34 fights in a row after his 1936 loss to Max Schmeling. The last time I looked, 49 and 34 were more than 26.

Cosgrove writes that Angelo Dundee "panicked" after Henry Cooper dropped Cassius Clay with a left hook in round four of their 1963 fight. That's not true. To the contrary, Dundee saw Clay through the crisis.

Similarly, the fatal 1962 encounter between Emile Griffith and Benny Paret is mistold. After writing that Griffith was "the reigning welterweight champion" at the time (he wasn't), Cosgrove states that Griffith "lost control" during the final sequence of punches and informs readers, "Referee Ruby Goldstein was tugging at Griffith from behind, pulling him off. As Emile, berserk, struggling passionately in Goldstein's embrace, was dragged away, Paret, now obviously senseless, crumpled slowly and collapsed."

That's inaccurate. All Cosgrove had to do was go to YouTube and watch a video of the fatal round. If he had, he would have seen that Griffith stopped throwing punches and stepped back the moment that Goldstein intervened. Is simple fact-checking too much to ask of a seasoned professional like Cosgrove?

Errors like these make it difficult to know how much of Cosgrove's factual recitation in other areas (such as music) can be trusted.

Here I might add that Cosgrove writes of a week that the writer Tom Wolfe spent with Clay in 1963 and states, "Wolfe sensed that his simplistic poetry and superficial boasting disguised a deep understanding of business and finance."

I don't know what Wolfe "sensed." I do know that it's ludicrous to suggest that Clay (or Muhammad Ali) had "a deep understanding of business and finance."

That brings us to Cassius Clay and the world of music.

Cosgrove equates Muhammad Ali's ultimate success with the rise of rhythm and blues and (ultimately) hip-hop to become "the preeminent form of popular music in the world."

Reinterpretations of history are always welcome when solidly grounded. And there's a lot of interesting information in *Cassius X* about Clay's transformation to Muhammad Ali, the Nation of Islam, and the music of that era. But there are times when Cosgrove's methodology of viewing Clay through the prism of music comes across as forced.

I'm not a scholar with regard to popular music from the 1950s and 1960s. But I know it pretty well, having been young and an ardent listener during that time. Lloyd Price and Chubby Checker (acknowledged by Cosgrove to have been important figures in that era) have been guests for dinner in my home. My first real bond with Ali when I began spending time with him while researching *Muhammad Ali: His Life and Times* (published in 1991) was music.

Muhammad was four years older than I was, but we'd grown up with many of the same songs. We'd drive from the airport to his home in Berrien Springs or be in his car on the way to a restaurant. We'd pop a tape of songs sung by Black recording artists into the cassette player and sing along.

"I can't believe you know all the words," Muhammad said to me one evening. "I never would have thought it."

Cosgrove has an impressive resume. Among his many credits, he's the

author of a three-book study of soul music. That said, there are places where
he falls victim to hyperbole in advancing his thesis. "Twist and Shout," first
recorded by the Top Notes and made famous by the Isley Brothers (two
Black vocal groups) was not "the song the Beatles had become synonymous
with" when they came to the United States in 1964. *A Christmas Gift for
You* featuring Darlene Love and the Ronettes was not "one of the greatest
pop albums of the era." It was a celebration of a certain style of music but a
repetitive and formulaic compilation. *Sam Cooke Live at the Harlem Square
Club, 1963* is an excellent recording but not "universally acclaimed as one
of the greatest live albums of all time."

Cosgrove writes that sports columnist Jimmy Cannon "erupted when
he learned about the Beatles meeting Cassius in Miami" in 1964 and that
Cannon wrote, "Clay is part of the Beatle movement. He fits in with the
famous singers no one can hear and the punks riding motorcycles with iron
crosses pinned to their leather jackets and Batman and the boys with their
long dirty hair and the girls with the unwashed look and the college kids
dancing naked at secret proms held in apartments and the revolt of students
who get a check from dad every first of the month and the painters who
copy the labels off soup cans and the surf bums who refuse to work and the
whole pampered style-making cult of the bored young."

That's a dramatic quote. But Cosgrove puts it in a misleading context.
Cannon wrote those words in 1966 after Ali was reclassified 1-A by his draft
board and uttered the words, "I ain't got no quarrel with them Vietcong."
That was more than two years after Clay met the Beatles.

And Cosgrove writes about Clay's dalliance with singer Dee Dee Sharp
as a serious relationship before characterizing it more accurately as a "brief
affair" and then exaggerating its gravitas again.

There's also some sloppy copyediting. By way of example, *Cassius X*
states that Sonny Liston refused to allow Liston–Clay I to be shown on
closed circuit in theaters in New Orleans "if the seating in New Orleans
was not segregated." I assume that Cosgrove meant "integrated."

These flaws are disappointing because Cosgrove has a lot to say that's
of interest. At its best, *Cassius X* contains some very good—even enlight-
ening—material on the evolution of music in the 1950s and 1960s and
Cassius Clay's sojourn through that time.

The young Muhammad Ali, Gerald Early wrote, "radiated happiness, a joy in being alive."

Gordon Parks X Muhammad Ali

Gordon Parks X Muhammad Ali, published by the Nelson-Atkins Museum of Art in collaboration with the Gordon Parks Foundation, celebrates the convergence of two iconic figures in the ongoing struggle for racial equality and carries with it the gravitas of two giants.

Gordon Parks was born into rural poverty in Kansas in 1912. He was the youngest of fifteen children. His father was a farmer. Parks taught himself the art of photography and, in the 1950s, was the first Black staff photographer hired by *Life* (then the most popular and influential magazine in the United States).

In 1956, *Life* sent Parks to photograph the mores of the segregated American South. In 1960, he left his fulltime position with the magazine but continued to work for *Life* on an annual contract basis. A cascade of images chronicling key moments and participants (famous and anonymous) in the Civil Rights Movement followed. Over time, Parks became one of the most acclaimed photojournalists in the world.

"I don't have time to just make pretty pictures," Parks said years later. "I would think that the stories that I did that touched people, touched lives, and helped lives would be the ones that I would most want to be remembered by."

And speaking of the people who were captured in his photographs, Parks declared, "It's not important at that particular moment that I express my feelings. It's important that I let the world know what they are thinking and what they're going through. So I become an instrument for them. That's what the camera does."

A true Renaissance man, Parks was also a successful author, screenwriter, composer, and film director. Among his many film credits, he directed the first (1971) film version of *Shaft* starring Richard Roundtree. He died in 2006 at age 93.

Parks and Ali met in 1966 when Parks was assigned to photograph Muhammad for *Life*. They represented very different generations in the struggle for Black equality. Parks was fifty-three years old. He had grown up in an era when the Black athlete on a pedestal was Joe Louis, followed in time by Jackie Robinson, both of whom were critical of Ali's stand on racial issues and the military draft.

Ali was twenty-four.

Parks had grave reservations about the road that Ali was taking. And he was familiar with the issues involved, having provided the photographs and text for a 1963 feature in *Life* on the Nation of Islam and a 1965 piece about Malcolm X that ran in the aftermath of Malcolm's assassination.

"I met Muhammad Ali in Miami when he started training for [his second fight against Henry] Cooper," Parks later recalled. "His public image was in tatters. He stood accused in the press of sins ranging from talking too much to outright anti-white bigotry. There had been rumblings of dislike for him ever since he became a Muslim after the first Clay–Liston fight in February 1964. Then late last winter when he declared, 'I don't have no quarrel with them Vietcongs,' he became in the public eye not just a loudmouthed kid but 'a shameless traitor,' as one paper put it. At that point, I began to feel a certain sympathy for him. There was a side to this brash poetry-spouting kid that I admired. I was not proud of him, as I had been proud of Joe Louis. Muhammad was a gifted Black champion and I wanted him to be a hero but he wasn't making it. I also felt, however, that he could not possibly be quite so bad as he was made out to be in the press."

Parks spent several weeks with Ali in Miami and London in May and June of 1966. At their introductory meeting, the photographer later recounted, "I felt free to tell him quite directly that I had come to Miami to see whether he was really as obnoxious as people were making him out to be." Parks also confessed to Muhammad that he'd been rooting for Floyd Patterson one year earlier when the two men fought.

But Ali won Parks over. And the fruits of their time together appeared in a photo essay titled "The Redemption of a Champion" published in the September 9, 1966, issue of *Life*. Parks also wrote the text, which read in part, "I never witnessed the hate he [Ali] is assumed to have for whites. But I did see him stand in the burning sun for an hour signing autographs for southern white children."

Four years later, Parks photographed Ali in Miami again; this time for the October 23, 1970, issue of *Life*—a cover story that hit newsstands just prior to Ali's comeback fight against Jerry Quarry in Atlanta.

All together, Parks shot roughly one thousand images of Ali, most of them in black and white. Twenty-nine were in color—a prerequisite for the 1970 cover.

Gordon Parks X Muhammad Ali has superb production values. It's 218 pages long and printed on 10- by 11½-inch hard, glossy stock. The photographs are divided into three sections: Miami 1966, London 1966, and Miami 1970.

The work also includes essays by Kareem Abdul-Jabbar, April M. Watson (a project co-editor), historian Gerald Early, Julián Zugazagoitia (CEO of the Nelson-Atkins Museum of Art), and Peter W. Kunhardt Jr. (executive director of the Gordon Parks Foundation).

Abdul-Jabbar highlights the genius of Parks's photography, writing, "His work revealed the richness as well as the harshness of the lives of Black Americans. His images captured the vast depth and abundance of the Black experience, the giddy elation and debilitating agonies." Abdul-Jabbar also recounts Parks's reservations regarding Ali's fitness to be a leader for Black America when the two men first met in 1966. "It's not only white people," Parks told Ali. "A lot of Negroes don't like the way you act."

Watson, in a lengthy and excellent essay, gives Parks his due as a trailblazing craftsman who "worked both within and against a racially inscribed system" and places the Ali–Parks photos in the context of their time.

"Despite considerable differences in age, upbringing, and political and religious views," Watson writes, "Parks implicitly understood that he and Ali shared a similar struggle as they carved discrete spaces for themselves within a racially inscribed, media-manipulated, social and political landscape. Parks leveraged his own hard-won influence and power, and his access to *Life*'s vast platform, to symbolically extend Ali a helping hand at this critical point in his career as the young fighter was struggling to forge an identity that would ultimately defy the media's preconceptions and proposed narratives."

And Watson concludes, "Parks and Ali were linked by more than those two times they worked together. While they had very different stances and ideologies, both men were pioneers in a uniquely American fight for justice."

The original *Life* photo essays are also reproduced in *Gordon Parks X Muhammad Ali* so readers can see how Parks's images were used in the articles and the text that ran with them. In a sign of the times, seven advertisements with thirteen models accompanied the photo essays. Not one of the ads had a person of color in it.

Literary Notes

The University of Illinois Press has published some excellent biographies of boxers in its Sport and Society series. Books about Rocky Marciano (by Russell Sullivan), Billy Conn (Andrew O'Toole), and John L. Sullivan (Michael Isenberg) come quickly to mind. *I Fight for a Living* by Louis Moore is an offering of a different kind.

In Moore's words, "*I Fight for a Living* uses the stories of Black fighters' lives from 1880 to 1915 to explore how working-class Black men used prizefighting and the sporting culture to assert their manhood in a country that denied their equality and to examine the reactions of the Black middle class and white middle class toward these Black fighters. While other works on Black fighters have explored Black boxers as individuals, this book seeks to study these men as a collective group."

Moore then makes what he calls "three interrelated arguments":

1. Prizefighting and the sporting culture provided Black men a surrogate to the racist job market that had forced them into drudge labor."
2. "Black fighters publicly performed their manhood in a myriad of ways that were understood as manly in the sporting culture and, if they chose, simultaneously conformed to acceptable hegemonic middle-class manhood."
3. "The Black pugilistic success on a national and local level shattered the myth of Black inferiority."

Moore has put an enormous amount of time and effort into meticulously researching his subject. That said, many readers will find *I Fight for a Living* too academically oriented and dry for their liking. There's no dramatic writing about the fights themselves. And while it's hard to argue with points #2 and #3 above, there are times when Moore goes too far in treating boxing as just another job. Boxers aren't like other laborers. There's something intrinsically different about them. There's something in fighters that very few people have.

Still, one quote from *I Fight for a Living* stands out in my mind.

Prior to fighting James Jeffries in 1910, Jack Johnson was asked about the claim that he had a "yellow streak" that Jeffries was going to lay bare for all the world to see.

"Remember what I am going to tell you now," Johnson responded. "Men with the yellow streak in them do not work themselves up until they reach a world's championship. They stumble and fall, and the yellow splashes all over them long before they get within reaching distance of a title."

★ ★ ★

Championship Rounds—a collection of columns by Bernard Fernandez, the much-decorated former boxing writer for the *Philadelphia Daily News*—is characterized by the insight and professionalism that have marked his writing for decades.

The first piece—a profile of referee Mills Lane who was horribly incapacitated by a stroke in 2002 at age sixty-four—signals to the reader that there will be interesting nuggets ahead.

"The patrician scion of a Southern dynasty in Savannah, Georgia," Fernandez writes, "young Mills hailed from a banking family. How wealthy were the Lanes? Well, the Mills B. Lane House in historic downtown Savannah, completed in 1907, was hailed as a jewel of the antebellum South when it was placed on the market in 2007 with an asking price of $7.6 million. It seems a safe bet that no other referee was raised in a mansion that boasted a marble entrance, Corinthian columns, parquet floors, 29 handcrafted canvas murals, nine fireplaces, five bedrooms, eight full baths, three half-baths, and a large in-ground pool."

Looking back on James "Buster" Douglas's journey to Tokyo to fight Mike Tyson, Fernandez recalls, "The skinny-dipping girl swimmer in the opening scenes of *Jaws* stood a better chance against the Great White Shark than poor Buster did against Tyson." But Buster, in Bernard's words, became "the greatest conqueror named Douglas to set foot on Japanese soil since General MacArthur."

Fernandez also has an ear for good quotes. Some of my favorites in *Championship Rounds* are:

* Seamus McDonagh (on his knockout defeat at the hands of a vastly superior Evander Holyfield in 1990): "Your whole sense of self-worth can be completely smashed."
* Former junior-middleweight contender Tony Ayala (while serving fifteen years in prison after being convicted on multiple criminal charges relating to a particularly brutal rape): "Tonight, I'll go to sleep in a prison cell. Tomorrow morning, I'll wake up in a prison cell. That is my present situation, and all I can do is make the most of it. At some point, I'll be free and have a job. And I'll deal with that too."
* George Foreman: "I went into the Job Corps because the last job I had paid me minimum wage, $1.25 an hour. But I never saw that extra quarter. They were only paying me a dollar an hour. I was hoping that, if I got some training at the Job Corps, I could get up to $2.50, maybe even three dollars an hour."
* Emanuel Steward (on Wladimir Klitschko): "I've trained many fighters. And Wladimir is one of the few who can turn out the lights without using the dimmer switch first."
* Roberto Duran (dismissing the obvious signs that age had robbed him of his skill as a fighter): "I will fight and I will win for as long as I care to because I am Duran."

★ ★ ★

Mark Kriegel recently wrote an appreciation of Pete Hamill, one of his mentors, who died earlier this year. Kriegel, an acclaimed wordsmith in his own right who now works for ESPN, talked about the influence that Hamill had on his career and referenced a novel that Hamill encouraged him to write. *Bless Me, Father* was published by Doubleday in 1995.

"Looking back," Kriegel wrote self-disparagingly in his tribute to Hamill, "I take solace in what a friend from our short-story group said: 'Some of us got to write the bad ones.' I wince when I look at those pages. But it's nothing compared to the shame I'd have felt if I never wrote it at all."

That piqued my interest. Kriegel has written excellent biographies of

Joe Namath, Pete Maravich, and Ray Mancini. I was curious to see what he'd done in fiction. So I went to AbeBooks.com (the best used-book site on the internet) and bought a hardcover copy of *Bless Me, Father.*

Kriegel wrote about cops and courts as a reporter for the *New York Daily News* prior to moving to the *New York Post* as a sports columnist in 1991. He started writing *Bless Me, Father* in 1992 at age twenty-nine and finished the first draft around his thirty-first birthday.

Chapter 1 introduces the reader to Frank Battaglia, a street thug who has run his record as a pro to 13–0 and wants to fight at Madison Square Garden. Through mob connections, he gets an undercard slot against a journeyman loser at the old (1965) MSG. Without a setup opponent or his friends and a baseball bat to back him up, Battaglia (a bully and coward at heart) quits in the first round.

Fast-forward to 1986. Battaglia has become a force in the mob hierarchy. The oldest of his two sons (Buddy) has committed suicide by jumping off a roof. Frank forces his surviving son (Nicky, age sixteen) into the gym to train for the Golden Gloves. The last thing Nicky wants to do is box and get hit.

Bless Me, Father is fast-paced pulp fiction that moves nicely from scene to scene with boxing as a recurring theme.

Nicky trains at Costello's Gym, "where broken old men ride piggyback on the vain dreams of young men." His trainer—Toodie Gleason—is evocative of Teddy Atlas with an Atlas-like scar on his cheek. Toodie was trained as a young man by Paddy Blood (based on Cus D'Amato) who was in Battaglia's corner at Madison Square Garden on the night that Frank quit.

As Toodie wraps Nicky's hands on his first day in the gym, he tells Nicky, "I know why you're here. You're here same as me. Your old man asked us to be here. But we both know your old man don't really ask, does he? . . . Here you can't cheat. This ring is the most honest place in the world. You can't hit no one with a bat. Can't get your boys. Can't talk your way out of it. In the ring, you can't call your old man . . . You gotta trust me. I'm gonna trust you. Otherwise someone gets hurt. And I ain't someone . . . Guys will punch you in the face. They will lay you right the fuck out. This shit is for real, pally."

After Nicky receives some perfunctory instruction on the first day,

Kriegel writes, "Already, Toodie knows enough to tell that the kid is natu-rally graceful, a good athlete. But not a fighter."

I liked the first two-thirds of *Bless Me, Father*. Then the book fell apart for me. The rest seemed contrived and unrealistic. When I shared this thought with Kriegel, he told me that he felt the exact opposite.

"The only part I'm happy with is the last part," Mark said. "The first part is too talky and too much like all the gangster movies I ever saw. The last third is more original."

Will Kriegel write another novel someday?

"I don't know," he answered. "I hadn't thought about it for a long time but I'm thinking about it now. Making it up is hard. But I might try again."

And despite his reservations about *Bless Me, Father*, Mark is glad he wrote it.

"The best thing about the book for me," Kriegel said, "is that it intro-duced me to themes I would use well later in my career. It was a North Star that illuminated the direction in which I was supposed to go."

★ ★ ★

James Patterson is one of the world's bestselling authors and a brand unto himself. He has written or co-authored more than 150 books, 67 of which have risen to the #1 slot on the *New York Times* bestseller list. Patterson's website lists 28 titles that he has authored or co-authored in 2020 alone, with four more due before the end of the holiday season. In recent years, he has been credited with authoring 6 percent of all hardcover fiction sold in the United States. These are staggering numbers.

There's an issue as to how much of the output credited to Patterson is his own work. As noted above, many of his books are co-authored. And publishing is a strange business. By way of example, Robert Ludlum died in 2001. Thirty books have been written and published under his name since then.

That said, one can assume that, when Patterson co-authored *The President Is Missing* with Bill Clinton, Patterson rather than the former president did most of the writing.

Patterson has also launched a line of books aimed at young readers under the imprint Jimmy Patterson Books. *Becoming Muhammad Ali*, co-authored with Kwame Alexander (a writer and poet whose most celebrated work has been in the field of children's literature) is his latest offering in that genre.

Becoming Muhammad Ali is a novel. For the uninitiated, that means it's classified as fiction. The story is told in the first person by a narrator named Lucky who informs readers that, when he was growing up in Louisville, Cassius Clay was his best friend. Lucky's prose is intertwined with poetry, some of which was written in theory by young Cassius Clay and the rest by Lucky.

The storyline traces Clay's growing up in Louisville through his first Golden Gloves National Championship with brief references to some of Ali's professional fights. The book is likely to become a bestseller because of Patterson's name and the marketing apparatus behind it. That said, the methodology chosen by the authors raises several issues.

The novelization of a famous person's life works best when it's placed within a historically accurate framework. I have no problem with the authors creating Lucky, inserting him into the narrative, and imagining a history between him and Cassius. Changing the known historical record is another matter. And there are times when Patterson and Alexander do that. It's hard to know where reality ends and fantasy begins in their recounting of young Cassius Clay's life. Fact and fiction blur, which can be confusing for a young reader. I know it was confusing for this old one.

To take one small example; *Becoming Muhammad Ali* identifies a neighborhood bully named Corky Butler (presumably based on Corky Baker, a real-life contemporary of Clay's) as the person who stole twelve-year-old Cassius Clay's bike. That theft led Cassius into boxing. But in reality, Clay never learned who stole his bike, and much of his interaction with Corky as recounted in the book is fantasy.

Also, there are more than a few unintended factual errors.

One poem declares that Sugar Ray Robinson "wipes the mat with his opponents 173 times, almost half of them before the first round ends." But BoxRec.com credits Robinson with 20 first-round knockouts in his 199-fight career (which is a far cry from "almost half" of 173).

Another poem talks of Joe Louis "battering each of his 51 opponents in knockouts as heavyweight champion until he met the Brockton Bomber."

That's just wrong. Louis had 26 fights as champion and won 23 of them by knockout. Then he retired, lost a comeback fight against Ezzard Charles, and after that had 8 non-title fights (winning 5 by decision and 3 by KO) before being knocked out by Rocky Marciano.

Similarly, the book says that, after Ali–Frazier III, Muhammad lost his next two bouts and that they were the last fights of his ring career. But Ali won six consecutive fights after Manila before losing three of his final four bouts.

Also, Willie Pastrano (who interacted briefly with young Cassius Clay) did not have "one of the most powerful left hands anybody had ever seen." To the contrary, he was a notoriously light puncher with only 14 knockouts to his credit in 83 professional fights.

Some of the poems in *Becoming Muhammad Ali* are moving; others are funny. They would have been just as good if the facts had been accurate.

At its best, *Becoming Muhammad Ali* is an entertaining impressionistic journey through Ali's youth as Cassius Clay. Given the talent of its co-authors, it could have been better.

★ ★ ★

My Brother, Muhammad Ali by Rahaman Ali with Fiaz Rafiq (Rowman & Littlefield) styles itself as the "definitive" Ali biography. It isn't. That becomes clear early in the book when Rahaman repeats the long-discredited claim that Cassius Clay threw his Olympic gold medal in the Ohio River after being denied service at a Louisville restaurant.

The gold medal tale had its origins in Ali's 1976 "autobiography"—*The Greatest: My Own Story*—published by Random House and ghostwritten by Richard Durham (an editor for the Nation of Islam newspaper, *Muhammad Speaks*). Before any material was submitted to Random House, each page had to be approved and initialed by Herbert Muhammad (Ali's manager and the son of Nation of Islam founder Elijah Muhammad).

"I'm not sure the book is the true story of Ali's life," Random House editor-in-chief James Silberman, who helped edit the manuscript, later acknowledged. "Where corroborative sources were available for events such as fights, it was accurate. But there were stretches where there was no source other than Herbert or Ali himself."

As recounted in *The Greatest*, Cassius and a friend named Ronnie King
were refused service in a "whites only" restaurant after Clay returned home
to Louisville following the Olympics. That led to a confrontation with a
motorcycle gang, whereupon Cassius threw his gold medal off the Jefferson
County Bridge into the river.

The tale—to put it politely—was allegorical. Ali later acknowledged
that either the medal was stolen or he lost it. Now Rahaman is reviving
the myth. Only in Rahaman's version, Ronnie King and the motorcycle
gang have been airbrushed out. Rahaman was the one with Cassius on the
bridge. And the incident was precipitated by Cassius ordering a cheese-
burger in the restaurant; the waitress saying, "We don't serve Negroes," and
Cassius responding, "I don't eat them either."

That punchline, by the way, was the creation of Dick Gregory, the
trailblazing comedian and social activist who began performing in the late
1950s. Years later in public speaking engagements, Ali appropriated it.

So much for the "definitive" Ali biography.

It's a tricky business, deciding who should be called great.

Which Active Fighters Deserve to Be Called Great?

During the economic shutdown, boxing fans have been watching videos of great fighters from the past. It brings home the point that "great" has become the most overused term in boxing.

We lose sight sometimes of what athletic greatness means at the professional level. Too many people—including people who write about sports—don't understand what it takes to be a world-class athlete. Yes, there's training, the work ethic, the teachers and coaches. But to be a world-class athlete, a man or woman must be endowed with genetic gifts that only a minuscule portion of the world's population has.

Imagine the best basketball player in a given high school. He, or she, is pretty good. Okay. Let's elevate that to the best high school basketball player in the county. Take that one step further to the best basketball player in each state. Now you have fifty elite high school basketball players. Given the fact some states produce more elite athletes than others, the odds are that fewer than half of these high school stars (the #1 player in each state) will be chosen in the NBA draft. Now look at the NBA. Only a handful of players active today will be remembered as "great."

Today's athletes are better than their counterparts were decades ago. In most sports, technique has evolved in remarkable ways. And athletes are better conditioned now than their predecessors were as a consequence of advances in conditioning and nutrition. The men who won gold medals in swimming at the 1932 Olympics wouldn't have qualified for the *women's* finals at the past three Olympic games.

Boxing has evolved differently from other sports in that today's fighters are arguably not as technically sound as their predecessors. But they're far better conditioned. Today's pound-for-pound elite would have been competitive in any era. They might not have beaten the best, but they would have been competitive against them.

Was Benny Leonard a great fighter for his time? Absolutely. But put Benny Leonard in his prime (the 1920s) in the ring against Vasyl Lomachenko, and I'm betting on Lomachenko. That's not to say that Lomachenko is as great in his era as Leonard was in his. It's to say that times change.

That said, very few of today's fighters have earned the right to be called great.

Greatness has to be earned. The business of boxing today is as much about publicity and hype as it is about merit.

"Great." . . . "Legendary." . . .

Too many people don't have a clue what these words mean. Why prove you're the best in the ring when it's so much easier and less risky to stand behind a marketing machine that heralds you as an all-time great?

A fighter isn't great simply because someone tells us he is.

Greatness is forged in adversity. When boxing was boxing (as the saying goes), fighters had to go in tough and beat other, equally talented fighters to be considered great.

Larry Holmes (who deserves to be called "great") gets it right when he says, "What makes a fighter great is the opponents he beats."

One fight doesn't make a fighter great. It takes a body of work.

A fighter doesn't have to be unbeaten to be great. Sugar Ray Robinson, Joe Louis, Muhammad Ali, and Ray Leonard proved that.

"It's what a fighter does after he loses that makes him great," Angelo Dundee said.

Being immensely talented is different from greatness. There's a difference between being exceptionally good and great.

Rating a fighter before his career is over is a perilous exercise in quantifying greatness. After Mike Tyson's annihilation of Michael Spinks, many people were calling him the greatest heavyweight of all time. The young Mike Tyson is still considered by many to have been great. But later fights showed deficits in his emotional makeup as a fighter.

Not every fighter who has been inducted into the International Boxing Hall of Fame was great. But Canastota is often where the discussion crystalizes.

Floyd Mayweather, Roy Jones, Andre Ward, Miguel Cotto, and Wladimir Klitschko top the list of fighters who have retired within the past three years and are certain to be inducted. One can argue that Klitschko was dominant in his era but not great. He fell apart several times during fights and lacked the inquisitors that are necessary to prove greatness.

Among active fighters, Manny Pacquiao clearly meets the standard for greatness. In many ways, he's a throwback fighter. Pacquiao has boxed almost five hundred rounds over the course of 71 professional bouts. He has fought eighteen times against ten fighters who are either in or will be in the Hall of Fame: Marco Antonio Barrera, Juan Manuel Márquez, Erik Morales, Oscar De La Hoya, Ricky Hatton, Miguel Cotto, Shane Mosley, Floyd Mayweather, Tim Bradley, and Keith Thurman. His record against these ten fighters is 13 wins, 4 losses, and 1 draw.

As for today's other elite fighters, a look at the current pound-for-pound rankings begs the question: "Who have these guys beaten?" Put aside the hype and look at their records. They might be great but they haven't proven it yet.

Don King and Bob Arum despised each other. But they promoted in an era when the revenue in boxing had to be generated by fights. It didn't come from poorly tutored television executives or foolish investors. So King and Arum put aside their differences and promoted genuine super-fights.

Boxing's current business model deprives elite fighters of the opportunity to prove and improve upon their skills by fighting other elite fighters. Except on rare occasions, the best no longer fight the best. We don't know what most of today's top pound-for-pound fighters would do if faced with an abundantly skilled opponent who asks questions of them that they haven't been asked before. Instead, we're left to speculate as to which fighters might someday be great or might have been great if only they'd fought the best.

Imagine Terence Crawford or Errol Spence against Floyd Mayweather in his prime. Those would have been fascinating fights. Who would have won? We'll never know. But it would be nice to know who wins a fight between Crawford and Spence. The winner would take a significant step toward being legitimately classified as great. Right now, all we can do is speculate. Neither of them has been tested like Ray Leonard was against Thomas Hearns, Roberto Duran, Marvin Hagler, and Wilfred Benítez. Crawford's signature victory is against Julius Indongo. Spence won a split decision over Shawn Porter (who lost previously to Keith Thurman and Kell Brook) and beat an undersized Mikey Garcia. Crawford and Spence might have greatness in them, but they haven't proven it.

Vasyl Lomachenko has the requisite talent, work ethic, and mindset for greatness. But he has had only fifteen pro fights and his most formidable opponent was Gary Russell Jr. (who Lomachenko beat by majority decision). There are inquisitors Lomachenko can face. Teofimo Lopez (not an easy out) would be a building block in constructing a legacy. It would be nice to see Vasyl in the ring against Gervonta Davis, Devin Haney, and (at 135 pounds) Mikey Garcia. But the sand is running through the hourglass for Lomachenko. Like the young Muhammad Ali, he relies to a great degree on exceptionally fast reflexes and fights with his legs. When his reflexes and legs forsake him, Vasyl will have a problem.

Mikey Garcia is a very good fighter without a signature win on his resume. He fought Errol Spence for a bank full of money. But once the bell rang, Mikey didn't "dare to be great."

Gennady Golovkin looked great until he was tested. Then he began to look exceptionally good.

Oleksandr Usyk acquitted himself well in the World Boxing Super-Series cruiserweight tournament but looked mediocre in his heavyweight debut against Chazz Witherspoon.

Naoya Inoue and Roman "Chocolatito" Gonzalez are in the conversation for greatness. But Inoue struggled against an over-the-hill Nonito Donaire in his most visible fight. And Gonzalez had problems after moving up in weight.

Tyson Fury has been mentioned as a candidate for greatness but hasn't come close to earning it yet. His two wins of note—a lackluster decision over a faded Wladimir Klitschko and a good performance against Deontay Wilder the second time around—are a platform to build on. But there's no way to know what direction Fury will go in.

So who's left?

Canelo Álvarez, more than any other active fighter, is on the cusp of greatness.

Canelo's critics will say he was outboxed by Floyd Mayweather and that two of the "names" on his resume—Shane Mosley and Miguel Cotto—were past their prime when he beat them. But Canelo was only 23 years old when he fought Mayweather at a catchweight of Floyd's choosing. He has beaten Austin Trout, Erislandy Lara, Gennady Golovkin, Danny Jacobs, and Sergey Kovalev. He has continued to improve while going up in weight and succeeded at every level.

And let's not forget; Joe Louis came back from a knockout defeat at the hands of Max Schmeling to return the favor. Muhammad Ali was out-pointed by Joe Frazier and then beat Frazier twice. Ray Leonard lost by decision to Roberto Duran but prevailed over "Manos de Piedra" in two later encounters. Canelo was denied the opportunity to even the score against Mayweather.

When asked prior to his fight against Sergey Kovalev where he thought he stood on the list of great Mexican fighters, Canelo answered, "The day that I retire is the day that we can judge my place in history."

On that day, Canelo Álvarez will be judged great.

Legendary promoter Mickey Duff used to say, "Some fighters are three-smart for their own good."

What If Deontay Wilder Had Accepted DAZN's $100 Million Offer?

On December 1, 2018, Deontay Wilder and Tyson Fury fought to a twelve-round draw in Los Angeles. The fight generated a modest live gate of $3,515,122 with an estimated 315,000 buys on Showtime Pay-Per-View in the United States and 420,000 more with BT Sport in the United Kingdom. But their anticipated rematch was expected to put up stronger numbers. Team Fury was offered a fifty-fifty split to fight Wilder at Barclays Center on May 18, 2019, with Showtime PPV and BT Sport reprising their roles. Then things got complicated.

On February 18, 2019, ESPN, Top Rank, and Queensberry Promotions (Fury's promoter) announced a multiyear agreement that called for Fury to fight at least twice annually in the United States. All of his fights were to be televised in the US on an ESPN platform. Wilder was then offered a multi-fight deal that would have seen him fight in spring 2019 on ESPN or ESPN+ against a relatively easy opponent for a purse of $12.5 million before moving to a Fury rematch for a minimum guarantee of $20 million. However, Wilder's management team (guided by Al Haymon and Shelly Finkel with input from Jay Deas) preferred that Deontay remain with Showtime. And Haymon didn't want to work with Top Rank CEO Bob Arum. The ESPN offer was turned down. But by then, DAZN had entered the fray.

On March 12, 2019, Wilder, Haymon, and Finkel met with DAZN executive chairman John Skipper in New York and were offered two alternative packages. The first offer was $100 million for three fights on DAZN to be divided as follows: $20 million to fight Dominic Breazeale in May 2019, $40 million to fight Anthony Joshua in autumn 2019, and $40 million for an immediate rematch with Joshua in early 2020. Alternatively, Wilder could opt for the same package with a $20 million fight against a non-threatening opponent thrown in between the two Joshua outings. The first fight with Joshua would have been in the United States and the second in the United Kingdom.

Wilder turned down DAZN's offer in favor of a one-bout deal to fight Breazeale on Showtime. Explaining his decision in terms of self-empowerment, he declared, "I move as I please. Those guys [Joshua and Fury], they have to do as they're told. I make commands and demands. They take them. I move where I want. ESPN and DAZN, they wanted a long term on me. I like to dictate my own career. I don't like people to have too much control over me and my career because I know what it is and I know where it's going."

A year and a half later, it's time to ask, "How would boxing be different today if Wilder had accepted DAZN's offer?"

First, let's note that, even if Team Wilder had agreed in principle to the offer, there's no guarantee that a deal would have been consummated. Skipper set forth the basic concept and numbers that DAZN was offering, and Team Wilder shot them down. The dialogue never got to the point of discussing details, such as what would happen if Wilder or Joshua lost before they fought each other.

But let's assume that the details were ironed out and a Wilder–DAZN contract was signed.

History tells us that many of the deals DAZN has made during the past two years didn't work out as planned. It's possible that Team Joshua would have balked at the terms DAZN offered to their side for two Joshua–Wilder fights.

There were other contingencies as well.

DAZN envisioned being able to opt out of the contract or reduce the money it paid to Wilder if Deontay lost to Dominic Breazeale. Wilder took care of business on May 18, 2019, when he knocked out Breazeale in the first round. By then, Jarrell Miller (who was slated to fight Joshua at Madison Square Garden on June 1) had tested positive for banned per-formance-enhancing drugs and been replaced as A.J.'s opponent by Andy Ruiz. If Wilder had fought Breazeale on DAZN, it's possible that Joshua would have gone straight to the Wilder fight once Miller tested positive. But more likely, the lure of a big payday for an "easy" fight against Ruiz would have been too enticing for Team Joshua to pass up.

What would Joshua's loss to Ruiz have done to the proposed Joshua–Wilder matchup?

Under the contract terms contemplated by DAZN, if Joshua lost or was otherwise unavailable to fight Wilder, Deontay would have received a $40 million purse from DAZN to fight the best (in terms of marketability and skill) available opponent in each of his next two fights. It would have been DAZN's responsibility to deliver Joshua or another opponent.

Had Wilder signed with DAZN, most likely his bank account would be larger than it is today.

In elaborating on his rationale for rejecting DAZN's offer, Deontay proclaimed, "Soon, I will be the highest paid athlete in the world. You'll see. I'm betting on myself. I look at the bigger picture. You sell me a number, and I know there's going to be a bigger number than that. They saw a guy they thought they could throw some money at and that would be it. But they found out the hard way. I'm not no fool. I know the cards that I hold in this division. I bet on myself because I know that I hold all the keys and I possess the power. I'm a living walking icon. I am the best heavyweight in the world. I am the most dangerous and exciting heavyweight in the game, period. Everyone is going to want somebody like me. So why would I give that all away when I can bet in on myself."

So Wilder bet on himself. After turning down the DAZN offer, he fought Breazeale and then rematches against Luis Ortiz (on November 23, 2019) and Tyson Fury (on February 22, 2020).

Wilder's purse for fighting Breazeale was reported to the New York State Athletic Commission as being $4 million. The real number is speculative with industry estimates ranging from $12.5 million to $18 million. Showtime Sports president Stephen Espinoza told BoxingScene.com that Deontay's purse for fighting Breazeale was less than $20 million but that the path he had chosen left him "generally in the same neighborhood with the financial opportunities." It's believed that Premier Boxing Champions (the promotional-management company controlled by Al Haymon) contributed millions of dollars to Wilder's purse to keep Deontay away from DAZN.

Wilder's official purse for the Ortiz rematch was reported to the Nevada State Athletic Commission as being $3 million. It's thought that he was guaranteed roughly $20 million for the bout, which was distributed on pay-per-view by FOX and engendered a disappointing 225,000 to 275,000 buys. Since FOX is believed to have needed 500,000 buys to break even, that translated into a lot of red ink for the network.

ESPN.com reported that Wilder and Fury were each guaranteed $25 million for their February 2020 rematch.

So let's assume for the moment that Wilder's purses before deductions were $15 million for Breazeale, $20 million for Ortiz II, and $25 million for Fury II. That comes to $60 million, which is a lot of money. But it's less than Deontay would have earned had he signed with DAZN.

What fights would boxing fans have seen pursuant to a Wilder–DAZN contract?

As noted above, when Jarrell Miller tested positive for PEDs, Matchroom and DAZN might have pulled down the Madison Square Garden card and gone straight to Joshua–Wilder. Based on what we now know about Joshua's chin, it's not unreasonable to suggest that Deontay would have fared better against A.J. than he did against Fury the second time around.

Once Joshua lost to Ruiz, substituting Fury as an opponent for Wilder on DAZN would have been problematic since, by then, Fury was locked into a deal with Top Rank and ESPN. And the loss to Ruiz would have devalued Wilder–Joshua when it finally happened.

Would DAZN USA be in a significantly different place than it is now had the Wilder deal gone through? Probably not.

Joshua–Wilder was the fight that boxing fans wanted to see at that time, and the bout would have been a strong subscription driver for DAZN. But play out the scenarios. First, Joshua lost to Ruiz, which would have devalued Joshua–Wilder when it finally happened. Now suppose that, when Jarrell Miller tested positive for PEDs, Matchroom and DAZN pulled down the Madison Square Garden card and went straight to Joshua–Wilder. It would have been big. But it wouldn't have had the ESPN and FOX platforms to promote it the way Wilder–Fury II did. And even with those platforms, Wilder–Fury II generated only 750,000 buys.

Also, quite possibly, DAZN would have lost Wilder when the contract expired.

What can be said with certainty is that, if Wilder had taken DAZN's offer, Top Rank, Queensberry, and Fury would have been on the outside looking in instead of Fury being the dominant figure on the heavyweight landscape that he is today.

As for Wilder's future, Deontay has said that he'll enforce his contractual right to a third fight against Fury before either man fights another opponent. We know that there will be a sixty-forty revenue split in favor of Team Fury when that happens. What we don't know is how big the pie will be and what the guarantees will be for each fighter.

Contractual details have been kept close to the vest by the parties involved. But it's known that Top Rank will be responsible for Fury's guarantee while PBC (and possibly FOX) will be responsible for Wilder's. There's likely to be less money to divide up this time than there was for Wilder–Fury II.

ESPN and FOX (which jointly handled the pay-per-view for Wilder–Fury II) went all in on that promotion. There's a widespread belief that FOX needed between 1.1 and 1.2 million buys to break even on the fight. And Top Rank is believed to have gone deep into loss territory to pay Fury. FOX/PBC and ESPN/Top Rank have no intention of losing more money on Fury–Wilder III. But neither fighter wants to take less than he was guaranteed for their second bout. Certainly, Fury doesn't.

Also, one area where Wilder–Fury II met financial expectations was the live gate. According to the Nevada State Athletic Commission, the fight generated $16,916,440 from 15,210 tickets sold. But the coronavirus is expected to gut the live gate for Fury–Wilder III.

"All sorts of places have been mentioned as possible sites," Frank Warren (who heads Queensberry Promotions) told Boxing Scene recently. "Macau, Australia, the Middle East. But if you ask me what we know with certainty about Fury–Wilder III, the answer is 'nothing.' There's no date. There's no venue. We are where we are, and no one knows where we are."

Underground Fight Clubs and the New York State Athletic Commission

Kids gather in the schoolyard to watch when other kids fight. And some kids like to fight. Put these phenomena together in an adult world, add in a profit motive for fight organizers in an atmosphere of disrespect for the law, and underground fight clubs are the result.

For most people, familiarity with underground fight clubs begins and ends with the 1999 movie *Fight Club* starring Edward Norton and Brad Pitt. But that was fiction. Underground fight clubs exist in the real world too.

The fighters have varying mindsets and motivations. Some of them are trying to find themselves. Some want attention. Others like beating people up and are willing to take punches in exchange for the opportunity to do it. Sometimes both fighters are paid. Often only the winner is. Many of the fighters get nothing more than what one of them calls "my Rocky moment."

The organizers like to say that the fights offer a healthy release for anti-social tendencies. That two men who have a gripe between them settle it in the fight club rather than with guns or knives on the street. But the truth is that most of the fighters have no idea who they'll be fighting until they arrive at the club on fight night.

For the organizers, there's a profit motive. Spectators pay for admission. In some instances, there's gambling with the house taking a piece of the action.

The fights are for real. There are no formal weight limits. Some of the fights are competitive. Others are brutal one-sided beatdowns. Fighters are allowed to take far more punishment than would be the case in a sanctioned amateur bout. Generally, those in attendance feel as though they've gotten their money's worth. If a fighter is seriously hurt and has to be taken to the hospital, doctors are told that he was assaulted on the street.

Four decades ago, Cus D'Amato developed young Mike Tyson's ring skills in "smokers." Years later, several incidents in which Tyson devastated opponents in these encounters were widely recounted. Teddy Atlas worked with D'Amato at the time and was responsible for bringing Cus's young fighters from Catskill to the Bronx for fights between 1977 and 1982.

"Tyson got his start at those smokers," Atlas recalls. "But the smokers I took fighters to in those days were different from what you're talking about going on now. Right now, there are a lot of opportunities for amateurs to fight and the amateur shows are pretty well run. Kids can put what they're learning in the gym into practice to become better fighters. Back then, there weren't enough sanctioned amateur shows, and a lot of the shows they had were badly run. There just weren't enough opportunities to develop young fighters, and the smokers filled that void. We weren't doing it to make money. We were doing it to help make kids better fighters.

"I'm not saying everything at the smokers was perfect," Atlas continues. "Were there abuses? Absolutely. But for the most part, the smokers were well run. A lot of them were run better than what you had then as authorized amateur fights. The amateurs were pretty bad then. You'd have a kid come in with a passport that said he'd had four or five amateur fights, and the truth was that he'd had twenty or thirty. The officiating was poor. And like I said; there weren't enough opportunities to fight. The coaches who brought kids to the smokers took their responsibilities seriously. The matchups were fair. We knew when to stop a fight. We were looking out for the best interests of the young men we were working with, not playing to the blood lust of the crowd. What you're talking about happening underground today takes boxing—if you want to call it boxing—to a different place from what I just described."

Joe Higgins has been involved with amateur and professional boxing for decades. While several of his fighters have risen in the professional ranks, his most notable contributions have been at the amateur level. He was president of USA Boxing Metro New York from 2003 through 2008 and has taught countless young men how to box and also the life lessons that come with the learning process.

"I lost a wonderful young man who was also a tremendously gifted fighter when Patrick Day died last year," Higgins says. "The hurt of that will stay with me as long as I'm alive. So believe me; I know how dangerous boxing is when it's done right. And anything that's not properly sanctioned and regulated is more dangerous. I understand the concept of taking a guy off the street and giving him the satisfaction of boxing. But you have to do it the right way. These underground show aren't legit. I tried for a long time to get guys who were fighting in them to become legit. You try to dialogue with them. You show them that there's a way to do this right. Some of them listen; some of them don't. And you also tell them, 'You think you're tough? The real tough guys are the ones who are fighting in sanctioned fights.'"

In the past, underground fights were largely hidden from public view. As Brad Pitt told a room full of fight club hopefuls, "The first rule of fight club is: you do not talk about fight club. The second rule of fight club is: you do not talk about fight club."

Now, however, some clubs brazenly post videos on social media and YouTube.

The Bronx and Brooklyn are the most fertile areas for underground fights in New York. In November 2015, Vice Sports ran two segments on a club then called the BX Fight Club. The segments have amassed more than 1.465 million views on YouTube.

Early BX Fight Club fights were conducted on asphalt in the park. Later ones were contested in a quasi-regulation indoor boxing ring. One of the "creators" (promoters) of BX Fight Club told Vice Sports, "It's a good way to relieve frustration, stress. We don't got no real problem. I don't know you. You don't know me. We're gonna go in there and punch for a few minutes, and that's it."

The VICE Sports video shows celebrities like Shaquille O'Neal and Fat Joe at the fights and 50 Cent in the ring extolling the virtues of the club. The grand prize at the end of "season one" was a Rolex watch. For season two, it was a 14-karat gold Cuban-link necklace. "I was very desperate for money," a competitor explained on camera. "I hear that they're handing out Rolexes and gold chains." In season three, a Mercedes-Benz S550 and Nissan Ultima were dangled in front of participants.

In one BX Fight Club encounter, the crowd started chanting "one more round" after a scheduled three-round fight ended. One of the fighters wanted to continue. The other didn't. Then the crowd chant changed to "Are you pussy?" and the reluctant combatant was shamed into a fourth round with the added incentive of a hundred-dollar bill thrust in his face by one of the promoters.

The promoter could afford it. BX Fight Club is listed on YouTube as having 136,000 subscribers. Some BX Fight Club videos have been viewed close to a million times.

Lines of succession are murky to outsiders. But subsequent to the Vice Sports segments, BX Fight Club morphed into Rumble in the Bronx. YouTube viewers are now asked to subscribe to the Rumble in the Bronx channel, which at present claims 42,300 subscribers. Whatever income there is from these subscriptions is supplemented by YouTube's automated ad placement.

One recent participant in a Rumble in the Bronx fight recounted for this writer through an intermediary how he was recruited after being seen by an organizer at a local recreational center. There was a telephone call explaining what Rumble in the Bronx was about and the question: "Are you interested?" He said he was. Later, he got another telephone call telling him when and where to go. He had no idea who he'd be fighting until he arrived on site on fight night.

Rumble in the Bronx fights are contested on thin gym mats with metal crowd-control barricades instead of ring ropes. They're akin to sophisticated barroom brawls contested at a Golden Gloves novice level. The fights are three rounds long, two minutes a round, with some rounds running a bit over.

Tournaments are part of the Rumble in the Bronx format. A typical tournament has eight combatants with each round taking place two or three weeks apart. On March 23, 2020, Rumble in the Bronx posted the video of a first-round fight that took place on March 7. The second round of the tournament was supposed to be contested on March 28, but organizers canceled the event because of the coronavirus crisis.

Let's cut to the chase. The underground fights—at least, in New York—are illegal.

Under the New York State Penal Code, a person cannot consent to being assaulted. Striking and injuring another person is an assault whether or not the participants agree to fight. It's not a defense that a person consented to be assaulted by participating in a fight any more than consent allows a person to be shot to death without criminal consequences. The assault is legal only when it takes place with the approval, and under the oversight of, a combat sports regulator empowered by the state.

The New York General Business Law gives the New York State Athletic

Commission "the sole direction, management, control and jurisdiction over all authorized combative sports" and "all determinations regarding the authorization of amateur and professional sanctioning entities." It further states, "The conduct of combative sports outside the supervision of the commission or an authorized sanctioning entity is prohibited."

Under this law, anyone other than a spectator who "advances a prohibited combative sport" is guilty of a Class A misdemeanor punishable by up to one year in prison. In addition to promoters, this prohibition applies, among others, to anyone who participates as a "referee, judge, matchmaker, timekeeper, professional, manager, trainer, or second." If the person has been convicted of a similar crime within the previous five years, he (or she) is guilty of a Class E felony punishable by up to four years in prison. Prosecution for criminal acts falls within the domain of the district attorney's office.

Alternatively, the New York State Attorney General can institute a civil proceeding seeking a penalty of up to $10,000 (or twice the profit from the illegal venture, whichever is greater) for a first violation of the law and up to $25,000 (or twice the profit from the illegal operation, whichever is greater) for subsequent violations.

These provisions of the law apply to both professional and amateur combat sports. And they're supplemented by the Rules and Regulations of the New York State Athletic Commission.

The NYSAC cedes control over some amateur events to "authorized sanctioning entities." But these entities must be licensed by the commission.

Also, while many underground fight clubs style themselves as holding "amateur" events, the combatants are paid under the table or are fighting for prizes that classify them as "professionals." Under New York law, a fighter is a professional if he competes for "any purse, money, prize, pecuniary gain, or other thing exceeding seventy-five dollars in value."

Underground fight clubs routinely flout the NYSAC Rules and Regulations. Promoters, managers, trainers, matchmakers, referees, judges, and timekeepers must all be licensed by the commission. And they aren't. But the most significant violations by these underground clubs concern medical issues.

The NYSAC Rules and Regulations as they relate to professional fights require:

1. Pre-fight medical examinations for all combatants.
2. At least one commission-designated doctor and at least one ambulance with medical personnel consisting of at least one paramedic with appropriate resuscitation equipment to be continuously present at ringside.
3. A post-fight medical evaluation of each combatant by an on-site commission-designated physician immediately following each match.

Additionally, promoters are required to provide medical insurance for both amateur and professional combat sports events. And boxing rings must conform to clearly defined safety criteria. Fighting on a one-inch-thick gym mat set over a concrete floor with metal crowd-control barriers in lieu of ring ropes falls far short of the legal standard.

So . . . what is the New York State Athletic Commission doing about underground fight clubs?

The commission could (a) send a cease-and-desist letter to the promoters of these underground fights; (b) refer the matter to the attorney general's office for civil sanctions; or (c) refer the matter to the district attorney's office for criminal prosecution.

However, the NYSAC has opted for a fourth course of action. It acts as though the issue doesn't exist and has done nothing.

In recent years, the New York State Athletic Commission has retreated into an increasingly insular world. The executive director lives in Canada and spends relatively little time in New York. The commissioners are completely out of touch with the nuts and bolts operation of boxing and day-to-day occurrences. There was a time when NYSAC representatives visited gyms to see if conditions were safe and ensure that proper medical equipment was on hand. They don't do that any more. There was a time when the commission sent a list of fighters who were on medical suspension to gyms so that a fighter who had been knocked out a week earlier wouldn't be allowed to spar. These notifications are no longer sent.

Do the people who run the New York State Athletic Commission even know that these illegal fight clubs exist within their jurisdiction? With more than a million views on YouTube, they should. But when asked about the situation, an NYSAC spokesperson refused comment. And one NYSAC employee says, "This commission is leaderless. And the people who should be leading don't have a clue about what goes on."

Underground fight clubs aren't exclusive to New York. But New York is where they operate most brazenly today. An entity can't hold itself out as a government regulator of combat sports and ignore that this is happening.

There will be a lot of desperate people in the year ahead. People who are desperate for money, and people who are desperate for something to feel good about in their lives. But getting beaten up in underground fight clubs won't improve the quality of their lives. The fighters are entitled to respect for getting in the ring and fighting. But that doesn't make it right.

The ritual ten-count was heard again in 2020.

In Memoriam

I've been thinking recently about Richard Penniman (better known as Little Richard) who died on May 9 at age eighty-seven.

Little Richard was born in Macon, Georgia, in 1932 and was one of the founding fathers of rock and roll. Like Muhammad Ali, he grew up Black in the segregated American South. Both men were electrifying, brash, dynamic, instinctive showmen, and a lot of fun.

Unlike Ali, Little Richard wore thick pancake makeup onstage and glitter on his eyelids. His pompadour was as recognizable in his heyday as Don King's electric hairstyle was decades later. He was flamboyant, uninhibited, and outrageous with what was sometimes described as a "gender-bending" persona. Elvis Presley seemed tame by comparison.

There were no Black entertainment icons in America in the 1950s when rock and roll was changing the culture and Little Richard made his mark. He recorded his breakout hit, "Tutti Frutti," in 1955. "Good Golly, Miss Molly," "Long Tall Sally," "Rip It Up," and "Lucille" followed.

After his death, Jon Pareles of the *New York Times* wrote, "Little Richard hit American pop like a fireball, a hopped-up emissary from cultures that mainstream America barely knew. He had a spectacular presence in every public appearance: eye-popping outfits, hip-shaking bawdiness, sly banter and a wild-eyed unpredictability that was fully under his control. He had an androgynous, exultant falsetto scream. He plowed across the piano with a titanic gospel-and-boogie left hand and a right hand that hammered giant chords and then gleefully splintered them. He invented a larger-than-life role for himself. He was a challenge to 1950s proprieties: to segregation, to musical decorum, to chastity, to straightness. And his genius, beyond the music that made everybody pay attention, was to embody that challenge not as an openly angry threat or a reactive counterattack, but as pure pleasure within reach, as the joy of sheer freedom."

In 1992, an entertainment special was taped in Los Angeles to celebrate Muhammad Ali's fiftieth birthday. Ella Fitzgerald, Whitney Houston, Dustin Hoffman, Billy Crystal, and many more A-list celebrities performed with Ali sitting in the front row.

Go to YouTube. Type in "Little Richard Muhammad Ali." You're in for a treat.

Little Richard was introduced and walked onstage. Ali rose. Muhammad loved 1950s rock and roll. It was the music of his youth. The two men embraced. Then, as Little Richard moved to the piano just in front of Ali's seat, Muhammad pointed toward him and shouted, "The King!"

"You didn't say that loud enough," Little Richard countered. "Say it again, honey."

Microphone in hand, he walked back toward Muhammad, who dutifully said it louder.

Little Richard then sat at the piano, looked back at Ali, and proclaimed, "You know, I'm for real about this thing. And I love you. Happy birthday, baby. I'm in my fifties too. I know how it feels." That was followed by an exaggerated falsetto laugh. The audience laughed with him, and Little Richard responded with a comically timed, "Shut up!" Then he returned his attention to Ali; declared, "I could hardly wait to get out here and play this song for you;" and segued into "Good Golly, Miss Molly."

The day after the concert, Muhammad told me, "The best part about last night was Little Richard."

I don't know where Richard Penniman is right now. But wherever he is, I'd like to think that he's not resting in peace. I imagine him rocking and rolling at a piano with Muhammad Ali sitting in the front row.

★ ★ ★

Jimmy Glenn—one of the most beloved people in boxing and a fixture on the New York boxing scene for decades—died on May 7 at age eighty-nine after a monthlong battle with coronavirus.

In the past, I've written at length about Jimmy's life. For now, I'll say simply that he was a thoroughly decent man and one of the kindest people

I've ever met. When Jimmy looked you in the eye and said, "You know, I really like you," he meant it.

Dick Gregory once said of Muhammad Ali, "Being in his presence was like entering a warm room on a bitter-cold winter night."

That's how I felt about Jimmy Glenn.

★ ★ ★

Bill Gildea, a superbly talented writer, died on June 14, 2020, at age eighty-one from pneumonia and complications of Parkinson's disease.

Gildea worked for the *Washington Post* from 1965 until his retirement in 2005. During that time, he covered virtually every major sports spectacle including more than fifty fights. In 2015, the Boxing Writers Association of America honored him with the Nat Fleischer Award for Career Excellence in Boxing Journalism.

Gildea's most important boxing writing came after his retirement as a journalist. In 2012, Farrar, Straus & Giroux published his meticulously researched work, *The Longest Fight*.

The book was keyed to the historic first fight between Joe Gans and Battling Nelson in Goldfield, Nevada, on September 3, 1906. There had been "mixed race" fights in America before Gans–Nelson, but never one of this magnitude. The bout attracted national attention. Arrangements were made for round-by-round summaries to be disseminated by telegraph throughout the United States. The fight lasted two hours, forty-eight minutes, making it the longest championship bout of the twentieth century. It began in the Nevada desert at 3:23 p.m., under a broiling sun with temperatures in excess of one hundred degrees, and ended at 6:11 p.m. Gans dominated for most of contest. The granite-jawed Nelson fouled repeatedly while being beaten to a bloody pulp and was disqualified for flagrant low blows in the forty-second round.

The Longest Fight recreated a sense of time and place and crafted a moving personal portrait of Gans. It also put Gans–Nelson in context in a way that rings particularly true today.

"Gans," Gildea wrote, "was the first African American boxing champion. But his achievements in the ring are not foremost in this story. They frame the story. The heart of it is this: what it was like a century ago to be Black in America, to be a Black boxer, to be the first Black athlete to successfully cross the nation's gaping racial divide, to give early-twentieth-century African Americans hope. Gans was the first African American, after horse racing's early Black jockeys and the cyclist Major Taylor, whose athletic ability even hinted at the possibility that sports could be a springboard for racial justice in American life."

Writing about boxers, Gildea once observed, "We everyday people say quit while you're ahead. We may miss them, but we are spared watching their diminishment."

Bill had a difficult last few years. Those who loved him bore witness to his physical diminishment. But he was a wonderful writer and a terrific guy.

★ ★ ★

The sad news spread like a black fog through the boxing community today (July 24, 2020). Naazim Richardson, who overcome a stroke in 2007 and returned to training fighters, has died.

Brother Naazim, as he liked to be called, came from hard origins that included a stint in prison when he was young. He was best known for training Bernard Hopkins late in The Executioner's ring career. He was also the man who discovered illegal inserts in Antonio Margarito's knuckle pads before Margarito fought Shane Mosley in 2009. The inserts were removed. Mosley knocked Margarito out in the ninth round.

Richardson was a philosopher and storyteller. "Verbally, I can dance with you," he said. Among the thoughts he shared over the years were:

* "Fights between elite fighters aren't won in training camp. Fights at the highest level are won on lifestyle. People make a joke out of Ricky Hatton blowing up, gaining forty, fifty pounds between fights. And then they say, 'Look how hard he works when he's training.' But think about how much better he'd be if he stayed in shape all year long. Bernard fought Félix Trinidad on a Saturday night. He was back in the gym on Tuesday."
* "Things are at a point now where, when you fight Manny Pacquiao, you're fighting the man and you're also fighting the perception of how great he is. People are so busy watching Pacquiao that they don't see

what the other guy does. It's like Joe Frazier said about fighting Ali. When Joe hit Ali, they talked about how great Ali's jaw was. When Ali hit Joe, it was, 'Look how fast Ali's hands are.'"

* "Continuity is one of the keys to training a fighter. Sometimes you see a kid who has gone from foster home to foster home, and he doesn't know what it's like to have a parent. It's the same thing with a fighter who moves from trainer to trainer."

* "There are times when being a trainer is like being a parent. A lot of trainers spend years building a kid. And then a celebrity trainer steals him. It's like raising a child. Imagine if you raise a child, change his diapers, teach him to walk and talk. And then, after years of parenting, if he turns out to be the kind of person you hoped he'd be, someone comes along and tells you that he's not your kid anymore."

* "A fighter takes two things from every fight—punishment and experience."

Naazim Richardson brought out the best in the people. There was a quiet strength and dignity about him.

★ ★ ★

Ricardo Jimenez died on October 11, 2020, at the much-too-young age of sixty-four in the wake of a stroke that he suffered several days earlier.

Ricardo was one of the nicest people in boxing. A soft-spoken man with a round face and neatly groomed walrus mustache, he served for years as a publicist for Top Rank and was the promoter's interface between the English- and-Spanish-speaking worlds in boxing.

Jimenez treated everyone with respect. That included all members of the media whether we worked for a large television network, a major metropolitan daily, or a small internet site. He was unfailingly courteous, always returned telephone calls, and whenever possible facilitated the fulfillment of requests for information and access. He understood what writers need and walked the extra mile to get it for us. Everyone—fighters, writers, trainers, managers, promoters, even rival publicists—liked him.

This one really hurts.

Boxing and the Coronavirus

In March 2020, COVID-19 became a factor in everyday life.

From 9/11 to COVID-19

Félix Trinidad and Bernard Hopkins were supposed to fight at Madison Square Garden on September 15, 2001. Then 9/11 intervened. After Trinidad–Hopkins was postponed, I visited an empty Madison Square Garden on the night that would have been.

"Tonight was a perfect mid-September evening," I wrote. "Clear skies, temperature in the low sixties, a hint of autumn in the air. No events were listed on the Garden marquee; just the digital image of an American flag at half-mast. This was to have been 'ground zero' tonight. Bernard Hopkins versus Félix Trinidad for the undisputed middleweight championship of the world. Screaming partisans had been expected to turn Madison Square Garden into a sea of red, white, and blue flags. Puerto Rican flags. A half-dozen uniformed New York City cops stood outside the employees' entrance at the corner of Eighth Avenue and 33rd Street. Other cops were sprinkled in and around Penn Station which lies beneath the Garden. The main arena was dimly lit, its floor still covered with ice put in place for New York Rangers practices earlier this week. Eventually, things will return to normal in America, although the definition of 'normal' will change."

I thought about that night this week. Fight cards were scheduled to be promoted by Top Rank at Madison Square Garden on March 14 and March 17. The first of these was to have featured US Olympian Shakur Stevenson. The second—a St. Patrick's Day special—would have been headlined by Irish Olympian Michael Conlan. Then COVID-19 (an acronym for "coronavirus disease 2019") intervened.

The 1918 influenza pandemic, commonly referred to as the Spanish flu, infected an estimated 500 million people (roughly 25 percent of the world population at that time). No firm numbers are available, but it's estimated that the illness was responsible for 50 million deaths.

The population of the United States in 1918 was 106 million. An estimated 670,000 Americans died as a consequence of contracting the

Spanish flu. That's equivalent to 2.1 million deaths in the United States today.

Most fatalities from influenza occur in infants under the age of two and adults over age seventy. The Spanish flu was unique in that almost half of the 670,000 deaths in the United States were of men and women between the ages of twenty and forty.

Most viruses abate during the warm summer months. The 1918 Spanish flu came in two waves. The second wave, which swept over America in October, was deadlier than the first.

The first cases of COVID-19 were traced to China in November 2019. On March 11, 2020, the World Health Organization formally classified the spread of the disease as a "pandemic." As of this writing (March 14, 2020), more than 145,000 cases in 130 countries resulting in 5,400 deaths have been confirmed. That's a death rate of 3.7 percent as compared to one-tenth of one percent for more common forms of influenza.

There have been more than 2,600 confirmed cases of COVID-19 resulting in 56 deaths in the United States.

All of these numbers will rise.

Efforts to combat the spread of COVID-19 have resulted in travel restrictions, the quarantine of geographic regions, event cancellations, and the shutdown of businesses. Schools and other institutions have closed their doors. Religious services have been canceled. Millions upon millions of people have changed their habits. Many are now working from home.

This is the new normal.

The sports world has ground to a halt.

Team rosters in baseball and other sports were depleted during World War II, but the games went on. Champions like Joe Louis reported for military duty, but professional boxing continued.

This is different.

On March 11, the National Basketball Association announced that it was canceling all games until further notice. That same day, the NCAA announced that the men's and women's basketball championship tournaments would be played with no one other than essential personnel allowed in the arenas. One day later, the NCAA announced that March Madness and all other NCAA winter and spring championship events had been canceled in their entirety.

On March 12, Major League Baseball announced that it was canceling all remaining spring training games and delaying the start of the regular season (scheduled for March 26).

On March 13, officials at Augusta National Golf Club announced that the Masters, scheduled for April 9 through April 12, had been postponed.

When the NBA, March Madness, Major League Baseball, and the Masters shut down, people pay attention.

Boxing matches in the United States and around the world have been canceled.

On March 11, governor Gavin Newsom announced that California public health officials had advised him that, until at least the end of March, gatherings of more than 250 people should be postponed. One day later, the California State Athletic Commission announced that all combat sports events in the state through the end of March had been canceled.

In New York, the Metropolitan Museum of Art, Metropolitan Opera, Carnegie Hall, and New York Philharmonic Orchestra announced temporary closures. Broadway shows were suspended through at least April 12. For the first time since its inception 258 years ago, the St. Patrick's Day Parade was postponed.

As for the Shakur Stevenson and Michael Conlan fight cards, on March 12, Top Rank issued a press release that read, "Due to the coronavirus pandemic and to ensure the health and safety of boxing fans and the fight participants, the March 14 and March 17 events at Hulu Theater at Madison Square Garden will proceed without spectators. The only individuals granted access to the events will be essential production and support staff in addition to fighters and necessary team members and credentialed media. Both events will still be shown live on their respective ESPN platforms."

Fighters risk their lives every time they step into the ring. State athletic commission inspectors and others who work in close proximity with fighters and their camps on fight night shouldn't. Moreover, COVID-19 has been taking a toll on hospital emergency rooms, which would make treatment for a fighter who is seriously injured during a fight even more problematic.

Thus, on the night of March 12, Top Rank announced, "After close consultation with the New York State Athletic Commission, it has been determined that Saturday's and Tuesday's events cannot proceed in light of the ongoing Coronavirus crisis."

Dozens of future fight cards have been canceled. Others are in limbo.

Sports will recover. There was no World Series in 1994 due to a rift between management and the Major League Baseball Players Association. Baseball survived and came back strong. More recently, NBA and NFL seasons have been shortened by labor unrest with no long-term damage to either league.

As for now, the immediate message is, "This is serious. This is not a time for games."

September 11 was a blow to most Americans. But after the initial attacks, it didn't directly threaten their lives. COVID-19 does. It's not a Democratic or Republican virus. It's not a Christian, Jewish, or Muslim virus. It's a not a straight, gay, or transgender virus.

Medicine is far more advanced now that it was in 1918. But medicine can't cure every malady (think cancer). And even under the best of circumstances, medical treatments take time to develop. As famed scientist Wernher von Braun noted, "Crash programs fail because they are based on the theory that, with nine women pregnant, you can get a baby a month."

It's likely that, no matter how devastating COVID-19 becomes, someday it will be looked upon as little more than a blip in the timeline of history. That's how the 1918 pandemic appears to us now. But for those who live (and die) through the present crisis, the immediate consequences are very real. The 1918 pandemic seems less distant and more real in our minds now than it did a month ago.

Boxing Grinds to a Halt:
The Past, the Present, and the Future

Boxing, like all live spectator sports, relies on the here and now for revenue. If fights don't happen, people don't get paid.

In recent weeks, boxing has ground to a halt. Fighters, trainers, managers, promoters, arena personnel, and others down the line are out of work. Even the sanctioning bodies (which are accustomed to win-win propositions) are losing money. Their sanctioning-fee spigot has been turned off and their 2020 conventions (if they occur at all) are unlikely to turn a profit.

The coronavirus pandemic has been compared to the 1918 "Spanish flu." For society at large, that's an apt comparison. But sports in 1918 were nothing close to the national obsession and moneymaking machine that they would become in the Roaring Twenties and are today. Some high school and college football games were canceled in 1918. The Stanley Cup finals ended midway through the series after a contingent of players on the Montreal Canadiens roster fell ill. But boxing was largely unaffected.

October, November, and December were the worst months of the 1918 pandemic. The sweet science was somewhat curtailed during that time. BoxRec.com reports that Harry Greb fought twenty-two times between January 4 and September 21, 1918, but not at all during the rest of the year. Benny Leonard fought twelve times between between April 8 and September 23, but not again until 1919. Jack Dempsey, who fought twenty-one times in 1918, took an eight-week hiatus from the ring toward the end of the year. But club fights carried on.

World War II also had an impact on boxing. More than four thousand active professional fighters served in the United States military during the conflict. Many of them were forever denied their chance for ring glory. They came out of the war with their bodies broken or didn't come home at all.

Joe Louis enlisted in the US Army in 1942. Rather than assign him to active combat, the Army placed him in Special Services, a role in which he participated in close to one hundred boxing exhibitions. There were no "champions in recess" or "champions emeritus" in those days. The Brown Bomber's championship was frozen for the duration of the war. He defended his title on March 27, 1942, and not again until June 9, 1946.

Active fighters who served in the military during World War II included Ezzard Charles, Joey Maxim, Billy Conn, Gus Lesnevich, Fred Apostoli, Freddie Cochrane, Lew Jenkins, Bob Montgomery, Beau Jack, Marty Servo, and Tony Zale. Each of them was a world champion at one time or another during his ring career.

Meanwhile, boxing went on. Fight cards were filled by fighters who were too old or too young to serve in the military, had physical conditions that disqualified them from military service, or were otherwise ineligible to serve. Madison Square Garden (the Mecca of Boxing) was often reduced to featuring club-level fighters in main events.

It's too early to predict with certainty how boxing will come back from the current crisis. We don't know how severe the pandemic will be or how long it will last. But the sweet science will face strong headwinds when it returns.

Baseball was boxing's only competition as a national sport after the 1918 pandemic and World War II. Now boxing is a niche sport. When arenas reopen, the sweet science will be competing with other sports for dates. Teams with season ticketholders will have first dibs on arenas. Concert tours will be rebooked.

In recent years, the live gate has diminished in importance as a factor in the economics of boxing in the United States. But it's still a significant revenue stream.

What will happen to live attendance for sports in general when our games resume? Will people want to sit in close proximity to 5,000 or 20,000 or 50,000 other fans to watch a game? How will they feel about standing on long lines before putting their smartphones in dirty plastic bins and walking through metal detectors? Will they feel comfortable lining up at concession stands? Will the average fan have enough discretionary income to buy tickets? Will corporations still pay big dollars for luxury suites?

There has been talk of fights without spectators. But that would still

put the fighters' camps, state athletic commission employees, TV personnel, and others at risk. And unique to boxing—suppose a fighter is seriously
hurt. Transporting him to an emergency room would be complicated by
coronavirus precautions. And what would happen once the fighter is there?
Emergency rooms are already overcrowded and not functioning as they
should.

After 9/11, the norms changed. For example, airport security was never
the same again. There will be new protocols for sports. We just don't know
yet what they will be.

Boxing will have a more difficult row to hoe than many sports. There
are no season-ticket packages in boxing. Each fight has to be sold on its
own merits.

How long will it be before people feel comfortable getting on a plane,
flying to Las Vegas, hanging out in a casino, and going into an arena with
16,000 other fans to watch a fight? When the reboot comes, will insurance
companies deny coverage for certain coronavirus-related eventualities that
previously have been covered?

It's unlikely that arenas will be full again until there's an effective vaccine to combat COVID-19. This means that the live gate for fights will be
adversely affected for the foreseeable future.

Also, major sports have an institutional framework that will help them
recover once the crisis has passed. Weaker teams will be helped by their
affiliation with stronger ones. But not in boxing.

People in the boxing community might say, "We're all in this together."
But some boxing people who are mired in quicksand will climb onto the
backs of others and trample them down to save themselves.

By and large, the major promoters in boxing don't cooperate with each
other. The television networks and streaming video services don't help each
other out. Adam Silver can guide the NBA as a unified entity. Who will
guide boxing in this time of crisis?

Right now, the money to underwrite boxing in the United States comes
primarily from ESPN, FOX, DAZN, and Showtime. Boxing on television
and streaming video will rebound before live gates do. But as part of this
process, network–promoter contracts will be reinterpreted and adjusted.

Most contracts have a "force majeure" clause that relieves the parties of
certain obligations in the event that unforeseeable circumstances intervene

on a grand scale. Without knowing more about how the various network–promoter contracts for boxing are written, it's impossible to know with certainty how they'll be affected by the coronavirus. In all likelihood, most of them already have been temporarily suspended and will be extended by the duration of the suspension.

Will the advertisers come back? Viewers will still be buying beer. But chances are that they'll buy fewer automobiles in the near future.

Meanwhile, just as ESPN, FOX, DAZN, and Showtime have contractual obligations to promoters (and vice versa), promoters have contractual obligations to their fighters. Many promoter–fighter contracts will also be affected by force majeure clauses.

Right now, the fighters are in a bad place. It's hard to train when gyms are closed. And in many areas of the country—especially cities—they're closed. Fights have to be planned in advance, but that's impossible today because no one knows when circumstances will allow for fights. Moreover, the bubble in license fees and purses occasioned by DAZN's entry into the marketplace is about to burst. For the foreseeable future, there will be fewer fights and, most likely, smaller purses.

There's a school of thought that pay-per-view fights might benefit from the coronavirus crisis because they're safe stay-at-home entertainment. But many Americans will be hurting financially. The Hispanic market—the most reliable component of boxing's pay-per-view base—has been particularly hard hit.

People will be struggling to pay for essentials like food, rent, and medical care. For many, paying $79.95 for a fight won't make sense. Promoters will wax eloquent about "giving a gift to the fans" and cutting the price of a pay-per-view card to $44.95. But that's not likely to convince people who have lost their jobs and seen their savings dwindle to pay up. They'll have more important things to worry about than fistfights.

The balance of power at the promotional level in boxing is likely to tilt further in favor of the haves over the have-nots in the year ahead. Many small and mid-level promoters who are already being squeezed might not survive. Most of them don't have TV contracts for their shows and are almost wholly dependent upon the live gate.

Also, large promoters have libraries that they can monetize to cushion the coronavirus blow. Top Rank already has a deal in place to exploit its library on ESPN platforms. Don King Productions and Main Events (both of which have seen their clout in the boxing industry fade) can offer similar content. The Golden Boy and Premier Boxing Champions libraries have value. Small promoters don't have that asset.

Boxing fans hope that the country is going through what will be a relatively short period of economic and social disruption and that sports will soon return. An optimist might even say that this is an opportunity for the sweet science to reinvent itself. But a successful reset for boxing will require forceful, knowledgeable executives at the television networks and DAZN.

When fight programming resumes, what level of quality control will the networks enforce? Will matchups be better, worse, or the same as before? Will elite fighters be willing to go in tough? Will fighters and promoters take greater risks for the big score (which, with a few exceptions, won't be as big as it would have been before)?

It's a pipe dream to think that boxing or anything else will return to "normal" soon. The restoration of normalcy will be a long, slow process. No one knows how long it will take or what the new normal will be. Boxing could start up again and then have to shut down once more. All of us will be in danger until an effective vaccine for COVID-19 is developed. And then we'll wonder when the next pandemic might come.

Meanwhile, let's get our priorities in order. Health is #1. Restoration of the economy is #2. The fate of boxing is far down the ladder.

Unarmed combat is still, in some respects, an outlaw sport.

UFC's Coronavirus Gambit

Saturday night, April 18, 2020, was supposed to be a big night for UFC. In the midst of the nationwide sports shutdown occasioned by the coronavirus pandemic, UFC 249 was scheduled to be televised as a pay-per-view event in conjunction with ESPN.

The price tag was $64.99. The promotion would have had America's live sports spotlight all to itself. Then reality intervened, dealing a harsh blow to UFC and its parent company, Endeavor.

Endeavor is a global entertainment corporation whose holdings include WME (a talent agency), WME IMG (an entertainment, sports, and fashion subsidiary specializing in event planning and marketing), and On Location Experiences (event hospitality packages). In 2016, it purchased UFC in a highly leveraged transaction for an amount reported to be slightly more than $4 billion.

As of August 2019, Endeavor had a long-term debt of $4.6 billion. It planned to raise money through a public stock offering the following month but canceled the offering because of insufficient interest in the marketplace. The recent industry-wide halt in film production and postponement of live sports and entertainment events as a consequence of the coronavirus wreaked further havoc with its balance sheet. On April 13, S&P Global lowered Endeavor's credit rating from B to CCC+ with a "negative" future outlook. It's unclear how Endeavor will pay the interest on its debt, let alone repay the principal.

In 2018, ESPN contracted to pay $1.5 billion for the right to televise thirty UFC fight cards a year for five years on its cable TV platform and streaming service. The deal was subsequently extended by two years as part of an agreement that gives ESPN the exclusive right to distribute UFC pay-per-view events in the United States.

The income from these events is crucial to Endeavor's financial well-being. But UFC events scheduled for March 21, March 28, and April 11 of this year were canceled because of the coronavirus pandemic. Within this framework, UFC 249 loomed large on the balance sheet.

UFC 249 was originally scheduled for Barclays Center in Brooklyn on April 18. But public safety dictated a halt to competitive sports events, as was recognized by most leagues and states. UFC president Dana White bridled at the restriction and sought a way around it.

On April 7, the *New York Times* reported that UFC was planning to stage fights at the Tachi Palace Casino Resort in Lemoore, California, starting with UFC 249 on April 18. The casino had announced on March 24 that it was suspending all gaming operations to "prioritize the health and wellness of guests and staff amid concerns about the spread of the coronavirus [and to] assist public efforts to reduce exposure to the virus." However, the casino is on Tachi-Yokut tribal land. Because of this, it was debatable whether the State of California had the authority to enforce its statewide shelter-in-place order and preclude UFC 249 from happening.

UFC produces its own events and would have provided television production personnel for UFC 249. Because the Tachi-Yokut tribe doesn't have its own athletic commission, UFC would have also overseen regulation of the fight card. No members of the general public were to be allowed on site as spectators.

"I locked up this venue for two months," White told ESPN. "I'm going to continue to pump fights out. Anyone who shows up to this event and who is a part of it will be safer than anyone who is sitting at home in their house. They're going to have access to the best medical attention, the best doctors, the best treatment that they can possibly get. You're safer being at this event with me than actually being at home or going to the grocery store."

White also told ESPN that he had secured a private island where he would soon be able to promote UFC shows for athletes who were barred from entering the United States.

"I've got an island," he explained. "The infrastructure is being built right now. We're going to do all of our international fights on this island. If I keep putting up fights in the US with US fighters, I'm gonna run out my talent very soon. This is a global sport. We had a lot of fights scheduled internationally. Those will continue. I have an island where, hopefully, we can fly everyone into by mid-May."

On April 8, Endeavor president Mark Shapiro told the *New York Times,* "Dana knows that he can pull this off in a very safe and controlled way that will keep his fighters and the crew safe."

A source says that there had also been discussions about Donald Trump "giving a shout out" to UFC during one of his press briefings: "It would have fit with the president's message about reopening the country and sure as hell driven pay-per-view buys."

Initially, ESPN was supportive of the plan to stage UFC 249 at Tachi Palace. It wasn't lost on senior management that the undercard would draw huge ratings because of the dearth of live sports on television and that there was a likelihood of substantial pay-per-view buys.

White played into this theme when, just prior to Tachi Palace being confirmed as the site, he was asked by Mike Greenberg on the ESPN morning show *Get Up* where the fights would be contested.

"We're gonna be live on ESPN," White answered. "It doesn't matter where the fight is going to happen. First of all, no fans can come to the fight. The only place that you can watch the fight in the United States is ESPN. I know several news sources are putting out places where they think it is. ESPN is where it is."

But the venture became more controversial than UFC thought it would be.

On April 6, the Association of Ringside Physicians released a "Letter from the Board" that declared, "The Association of Ringside Physicians has been actively following the recommendations of the CDC as well as other professional medical societies concerned with the spread of COVID-19. Sporting events across the world have been canceled in response to the increased risk of infection and transmission by participants, fans, officials, and support staff. It is our recommendation that all combat sporting events be postponed until further notice. This includes any and all events, regardless of the number of people involved. Any combat sport taking place during this global pandemic places the athletes, officials, and anyone else involved in the event under unnecessary risk of infection and transmission of Covid-19. In addition, combat sports athletes often require medical attention after a bout, and we do not wish to see any additional strain on an already overwhelmed medical system."

Dr. Nitin Sethi is widely respected within the boxing community for his service on a part-time basis as chief medical officer for the New York State Athletic Commission. In recent weeks, he has put aside much of his regular practice as a neurologist to serve on the front lines in the battle against COVID-19. Responding to UFC's plan, Dr. Sethi wrote to his colleagues, "Even if an event is held behind closed doors and all those present (not just the athletes) are tested for the coronavirus, the risk of transmission from person to person remains. Controlling the spread of the COVID-19 pandemic is far bigger than any boxing or MMA event. It is a matter of social responsibility and an obligation to act for the benefit of the society at large."

The Association of Boxing Commissions was in uncharted waters when it came to UFC 249. Unfortunately, those in charge steered the ship on a zigzag course until it landed on jagged rocks.

An April 7 statement issued in the name of the ABC (and riddled with typographical errors) read, "The Association of Boxing Commission and Combative Sports (ABC) Board of Directors are very concern with an event being on tribal land without the regulation by a tribal/state athletic commission. The ABC concurs with the Association of Ringside Physicians that it's a very trying time for the entire world. Fighter safety is paramount. If the fight occurs, it will be considered a non-sanctioned event since a state/tribal commission will not be present. All officials that decide to participate in the event, they may be sanctioned on a tribal/state level."

The following day, ABC President Brian Dunn issued a statement to ESPN and several other news outlets backing away from this position: "I have discussed the matter with the ABC Board of Directors and officials from the UFC. They agreed to increase medical presence and regulate the event by international standards. The official ABC position is neutral on the matter, as we do not have jurisdiction."

Then, on April 9, Dunn turned 180 degrees away from the ABC's April 7 statement and announced, "After speaking with UFC officials, the ABC board of directors determined this event could be listed as sanctioned. When the UFC does international events, they regulate themselves using Nevada Athletic Commission inspectors, and this event on sovereign land is no different. There will be no sanctions imposed by the ABC for any athletes or officials involved in the event. If the UFC continues to properly regulate future events, which I am sure they will, future events will be treated the same. We would treat events held on mystery islands the same as well."

Here, it's worth noting that the ABC Medical Committee was not consulted before any of these three statements were issued. Nor was the ABC Legal Committee.

After the third statement was issued, Greg Sirb (executive director of the Pennsylvania State Athletic Commission) told this writer, "The ABC needs to meet a few more times [via videoconferencing] so we can fully grasp what was before us. And we should do that sooner rather than later."

Pat English (a member of the ABC legal committee) was more direct, adding, "I think that holding this event is sickening when you consider the number of people necessary to stage the event and the strain on medical resources that exists today, particularly in California."

The California State Athletic Commission took a dim view of the proceedings. California at the time had more reported cases of coronavirus than all but four other states.

In the past, the CSAC has regulated events at Tachi Palace. But on April 7, the commission issued a press release that read, "First and foremost, the Commission's priority is the health and safety of fighters and the public. With that in mind, the Commission canceled all events through May 31 based on guidance issued by California Governor Gavin Newsom and the California Department of Public Health to help flatten the curve against the spread of COVID-19. The Commission will not participate in the UFC event on April 18, regardless of the event location."

Attention then turned to the Nevada State Athletic Commission, which was said to be willing to provide ring physicians, inspectors, and other regulatory personnel to oversee the event. NSAC executive director Bob Bennett spoke to this point in an interview with this writer.

"Let me clarify the role of Nevada in this because there have been a number of misstatements about it," Bennett said. "UFC contacted a number of Nevada officials—referees, judges, inspectors, doctors—and asked them to work the show. To the best of my knowledge, none of them agreed to work the show. Some of them were considering it. But I want to make this very clear. The fact that UFC might have used Nevada officials would not have meant that the event was sanctioned by the Nevada commission. Under Nevada law, our officials are independent contractors. California law is different. [California State Athletic Commission executive director] Andy Foster can tell commission employees not to work a show and refuse to use them again in California if they do. Under Nevada law, our commission can't do that. We can't tell our officials what they can and can't do out of state. We had a problem last year with Julio César Chávez Jr. He wouldn't take a PED test so we refused to license him in Nevada and the promoter took the fight to Arizona. Several of our officials worked the undercard for that fight. They had a right to do so."

As for whether or not UFC 249 should proceed as planned, Bennett declared, "You're asking me about this fight card, so I'll tell you what I think. We've always had a productive professional relationship with UFC but we couldn't accommodate them on this. It ran counter to the guidelines that have been established for public safety in the State of Nevada. They were going to test everyone involved with the show, but there aren't enough tests to go around where they're really needed. They were going to have special equipment to sanitize the arena. But we need that equipment in hospitals and essential businesses. People should follow the science. They should listen to Dr. Fauci and Dr. Birx and do what the science dictates. The guidelines are there for a reason and everyone should try to work within them. The science should dictate where we go next."

On April 9, United States senator Dianne Feinstein (D-CA) issued a statement that read, "I'm concerned by reports that Ultimate Fighting Championship plans to hold a pay-per-view event in California in defiance of the state's shelter-in-place order. This event would involve dozens of individuals flying to California and driving to a casino for a purpose no one can honestly claim is essential. I understand this event is scheduled to take place on tribal land and therefore is not subject to state law. However, at best, this event ties up medical resources and sends a message that shelter-in-place orders can be flouted. At worst, participants and support staff could carry the virus back to their home communities and increase its spread. I call on Ultimate Fighting Championship and the Tachi-Yokut Tribe to reconsider this event and delay it until a later date. We have to be responsible and mindful of all local, state and federal public health guidelines. Going ahead with this event is not the right move."

Then the other shoe dropped. California governor Gavin Newsom spoke directly with high-ranking Disney officials and asked that the fight be canceled.

The Walt Disney Company (which owns 80 percent of ESPN) ordered ESPN not to be involved. Endeavor (which, as previously noted, owns UFC) didn't want a war with Disney.

Thus, on April 9, Dana White told Brett Okamoto of ESPN, "Today, we got a call from the highest level you can go at Disney and the highest level at ESPN. And the powers that be there asked me to stand down and not do this event on Saturday."

White also told Okamoto that all other UFC events had been postponed indefinitely but added that UFC would go ahead with plans to conduct fights with international fighters on a private island at some time in the not-too-distant future.

Later that day, ESPN issued a statement that read, "ESPN has been in constant contact with the U.F.C. regarding U.F.C. 249. Nobody wants to see sports return more than we do, but we didn't feel this was the right time for a variety of reasons. ESPN expressed its concerns to the U.F.C. and they understood."

So . . . what happens next?

On April 9, Dana White told Brett Okamoto, "Fight Island is real. It's a real thing. The infrastructure is being built right now. That thing is going to happen."

Former UFC heavyweight champion Randy Couture had his say on that when he appeared on *Weighing In.* After telling hosts Josh Thomson and John McCarthy that he had "mixed feelings" about the matter, Couture declared, "Everybody else is on lockdown. Why do you think it's okay to go out and try and put on a show and put athletes in harm's way, potentially, with so many unknowns? I felt like there was some selfishness going on in pushing this as far as they did. Now, we're still hearing talk about 'Fighter Island' and all of this other crazy stuff. 'Pandemic Island' is what we should call it."

But the likelihood is that fight fans will see UFC on television before Fight Island is open for business. White is now targeting May 9 for UFC's next telecast at a site to be determined.

If UFC had slated UFC 249 for a Native American reservation in Oklahoma or Mississippi (whose governors have resisted calls for a shutdown), there wouldn't have been an appeal from the states' capitals to Disney to shut down the fights and the event probably would have proceeded as planned on April 18.

Will Disney now support a UFC card held in another state?

Florida governor Ron DeSantis is taking a position that's very different from the position that Gavin Newsom took. DeSantis has stubbornly resisted social distancing. He refused to close Florida's beaches during spring break in the face of the burgeoning coronavirus crisis and has touted hydroxychloroquine (an unproven drug) as an effective treatment for COVID-19.

On April 9, Florida amended its list of "essential services" to add "employees at a professional sports and media production with a national audience including any athletes, entertainers, production team, executive team, media team, and any others necessary to facilitate including services supporting such production—only if the location is closed to the general public." On April 13, DeSantis declared that WWE (which is a theatrical production, not a sport) is an "essential business."

DeSantis might even go so far as to lobby Disney (which has extensive holdings in Florida including the Walt Disney World Resort) to televise future UFC events that occur in his state.

As of this date, Florida ranks in the top ten nationally in both confirmed coronavirus cases and deaths as a consequence of the coronavirus.

It's also worth noting that, if UFC's contract had been with FOX rather than ESPN, it's likely that UFC 249 would have been held as planned. Given its political leanings, FOX probably wouldn't have pulled the plug.

How should one evaluate the propriety of what UFC tried to do in California and intends to do in another state?

There will be a lot of talk in the weeks ahead about how UFC is "doing this for the fans" and to "provide entertainment for people who are confined to their homes." That's nonsense. Everyone knows why UFC is doing this. For the money. That's not a bad thing, but let's be honest about it. We're not talking about a noble effort to provide entertainment for sports fans who are starved from the lack of watching people beat each other up. We're not even talking about free television. We're talking about taking money from the pockets of "little people" (pay-per-view buyers) and putting it into the coffers of ESPN (Disney) and UFC (Endeavor).

All sports are looking for ways to reboot. But in pursuit of this goal, UFC tried—and is continuing to try—to circumvent protocols that have been put in place for the public good.

It's a given that, despite precautions, some people who are working on site at future UFC events will contract the coronavirus. As a statistical matter, some of the people who are on site would have contracted the coronavirus in the course of their daily lives had they stayed close to home.

But each person who contracts COVID-19 as a consequence of being at a UFC event and returns home risks spreading the virus and putting more people at risk.

Also, each UFC event will divert medical resources that are urgently needed elsewhere.

Dana White has sought to allay fears regarding the danger to individuals who participate in future UFC events with the promise, "They're going to have access to the best medical attention, the best doctors, the best treatment that they can possibly get."

But let's look at what that means.

Which of the people involved with UFC promotions will be tested for COVID-19? Fighters? Their cornermen? Fight night officials? Hotel workers like food handlers, housekeepers, and security personnel? TV production crews?

It's a matter of record that test kits are in short supply. Too many people who are dying can't get tested. Police officers, postal carriers, bus drivers, and other truly essential personnel can't get tested. And UFC is planning to commandeer hundreds of test kits to promote fights.

Having doctors administer pre-fight medical examinations and be on site with paramedics and ambulance drivers for UFC events will divert medical personnel from emergency situations.

Also, fighters inflict damage on each other. Suppose a fighter is hurt and has to be taken to an emergency room?

People in combat sports like to talk about the health and safety of the fighter. Here, the health and safety of everyone involved with the promotion and, by extension, an exponentially greater number of people will be at risk. This risk might be worth the reward for UFC. But not for society at large.

The coronavirus crisis won't end quickly. People won't suddenly wake up on a warm, sunny morning and go out to mix and mingle and hold hands. Recovery will be a long, slow, incremental process.

Meanwhile, not having sports right now might be one of the best things this country has going for it because it impresses upon people just how serious the coronavirus pandemic is. When Adam Silver suspended the NBA season indefinitely on March 11, it got everyone's attention and sent a powerful message.

Learning to live without sports is better than dying with them.

What would happen next? All we knew with certainty in May 2020 is that something would.

What Will Fans See
When Boxing Comes Back?

Boxing, like the rest of the world, is in chaos. There have been no major fights for two months and no boxing cards are scheduled at present in the United States. This article isn't about the propriety of holding fights. It's about what the state of boxing will be when it returns.

Boxing lends itself to the resumption of competition more easily than most sports. It's event driven as opposed to relying on a full schedule. Fewer people are involved in putting each fight card together than are required for other sports. When and where boxing returns will depend to a great degree on what the governors in various states allow. There will be boxing in some states. Florida has made that clear. Texas and other jurisdictions are sure to follow.

For the foreseeable future, fight cards will be held without spectators in attendance. As promoter Frank Warren noted, "Fans will have to settle for the armchair over the ringside seat. We are going to be a television product for a period of time, and we have got to make the best of it. No sport wants to be operating behind closed doors. But that is how it is going to be, so we have to face up to the reality."

Without spectators on site, small promoters who rely on the live gate to make ends meet won't be able to promote.

Other revenue streams (such as sponsorships) will also be diminished. And there will be significant additional costs for COVID-19 testing and other medical precautions. These medical expenses—incurred in conjunction with fighters, their camps, arena employees, TV production personnel, and others involved with each promotion—will be borne by the promoter.

The course of boxing in the United States over the next year will be determined primarily by four alliances: (1) ESPN and Top Rank, (2) FOX and Premier Boxing Champions, (3) Showtime and Premier Boxing Champions, and (4) DAZN in conjunction with Matchroom and Golden Boy.

The first few fights back will get a ratings bump on television. But it's unclear what the budget for these fights will be. Each network and promoter has a contract that lays out guidelines for license fees. But any party to these contracts can seek relief claiming "force majeure" (a legal concept that frees the party from performing certain contractual obligations in the event that unforeseeable circumstances beyond that party's control interfere with performance). Should negotiations with regard to force majeure occur, the networks will have the upper hand. The promoters need the networks more than the networks need the promoters.

If Major League Baseball falls off the map and football (college and pro) finds it impossible to proceed this autumn, it will increase the demand for boxing, and network budgets for the sweet science might increase. On the other hand, even if boxing gets good ratings as one of the few games in town, it won't necessarily attract advertisers. When the economy was booming, boxing wasn't attracting advertisers the way the powers that be hoped it would. With the economy in shambles, overall spending for advertising is likely to decline.

Top Rank hopes to return in early June with fight cards in Las Vegas televised on ESPN and ESPN+. On May 11, Bob Arum told Sirius XM Radio, "We plan to launch in a safe, secure way. We're making arrangements with a hotel. We can get everybody tested, put them in a bubble, and get these fights on. Unfortunately, because a lot of it requires so much extra work and care and testing, we're going to limit our fight shows to four fights a card. That's the bad side. The good side is, we hope, we're arranging with ESPN to do two or three events every week."

But a lot has to happen before Top Rank can move forward with fights in Nevada. Medical protocols have to be put in place. The arrangements have to be approved by the Nevada State Athletic Commission. There has to be a deal for a site, hotel rooms, meals, and the like. Also, Top Rank and ESPN have to agree on financial terms.

The loss of the live gate will hurt Top Rank more than its primary competitors in the United States because Top Rank has been more successful than its competitors in selling tickets. Industry sources say that Top Rank has told ESPN that it needs more money, not less, from the network to make up for the loss of the live gate plus increased medical costs and other expenses associated with the coronavirus. ESPN, which has its own financial issues, has been largely unsympathetic to that point of view.

When asked by this writer on May 11 whether Top Rank's existing promoter–network contract with ESPN will be renegotiated or reinterpreted, Top Rank president Todd duBoef said, "Everything is up in the air right now. We're all trying to figure this out. I'd rather not discuss the economics of it."

When all is said and done, Top Rank will have to deliver shows to ESPN. And it will have to deliver fights that don't require a live gate to be financially viable.

Premier Boxing Champions has alliances with FOX and Showtime. Al Haymon doesn't want PBC to be the first boxing promoter to come back in the United States. He's biding his time and waiting to see how things shake out.

Questions have been raised at FOX regarding whether the financial arrangements for the Wilder–Fury rematch earlier this year were in the network's best interests. And PBC's other offerings on FOX have moved the needle less than expected. That might lead to reinvigorating PBC's ties with Showtime.

PBC has an exclusive with regard to *Showtime Championship Boxing* dates. ShoBox is an open shop. Showtime Sports president Stephen Espinoza was less than enthralled with the content that his network received from PBC in 2019.

Showtime has a hard commitment for boxing from senior management for the next two years. The network doesn't rely on advertising revenue. It doesn't televise non-combat sports. It has a long tradition in boxing, knows the sport, and has the capacity to put together successful pay-per-view promotions. The current financial crisis could be an opportunity for Showtime to reassert itself on the boxing scene.

On May 4, Espinoza revealed, "I don't think we are going to be one of the first ones to come back. There is a feeling that the audience is desperate for sports, which is probably true. But we're not going to take advantage of that and throw a bunch of stuff out there to say we're back. We need to take our time and come back with the right fights at the right time to try and reduce the risk as much as possible while doing premium-level fights that are worthy of the audience."

Eight days later, Espinoza confirmed, "We're targeting sometime in July to return. And obviously, we're spending a tremendous amount of time right now trying to make the environment as safe as possible. That involves working with PBC as they set up protocols for the fighters and promoters. And it's also working with our parent company as we set up protocols for our employees and contractors."

Then there's DAZN.

On May 20, 2015, Richard Deitsch of *Sports Illustrated* moderated a forum in which he discussed the future of broadcast sports with NBC Sports Group chairman Mark Lazarus, CBS Sports president Sean McManus, FOX Sports president Eric Shank, and John Skipper (then president of ESPN). During the Q&A portion of the program, Richard Sandomir of the *New York Times* asked, "For those of you who do and those of you who don't associate with Al Haymon on the PBC, how do you think that strategy is going to play out in terms of building interest for boxing?"

Skipper's answer was direct and to the point: "Last time I checked my XY-axis quadrant, it's not in the right quadrant."

Skipper is now executive chairman of DAZN Group. And the last time anyone checked the XY-axis quadrant for DAZN USA, it wasn't in the right quadrant. DAZN gave boxing fans in the United States better fights in 2019 than any other network. But the content came with a high price tag for DAZN.

DAZN's subscriptions in the United States, which were already at a disappointing level, have dropped as a consequence of the economic shutdown. In today's environment, it will be hard to get these subscribers back. Last year, Bloomberg.com reported that, worldwide, DAZN lost $627 million in 2018 (the most recent year for which financials are publicly available). The value of DAZN USA keeps going down.

DAZN has been funded by Len Blavatnik, a Ukranian-born billionaire who has both UK and US citizenship. A source at DAZN says that Blavatnik has instructed DAZN USA to be "more cash conscious" moving forward.

DAZN USA struggled last year in a booming economy. It will be more difficult for it to succeed in a depression. Quite possibly, DAZN will ask that various contracts be renegotiated. This could run the gamut from its relationship with Matchroom to contracts with individual fighters.

The Saudi Arabian government might also become a factor in keeping DAZN USA afloat. Saudi Arabia hosted the rematch between Anthony Joshua and Andy Ruiz in 2019. The Saudi government now seems to be moving toward investing in entertainment businesses rather than events.

Meanwhile, fight fans can expect to see significant systemic changes when boxing returns.

First, purses will drop.

With DAZN spending money like a proverbial drunken sailor on leave, the balance of power with regard to fighter purses shifted toward fighters in recent years. By way of example, Demetrius Andrade is a very good fighter. But he has never beaten a top-echelon fighter. Nor has he been a magnet for ticket sales, TV ratings, or subscription buys. A source close to Andrade says that his purse for fighting Luke Keeler on DAZN on January 30, 2020, was $2.4 million. And just prior to that bout, Andrade signed a contract extension that calls for him to be paid a minimum of $11 million for four fights as long as he keeps winning.

DAZN's checkbook drove purses higher across the board as other networks were forced to compete with its offers. But because of COVID-19 and DAZN's current financial problems, high purses for fighters who don't generate equivalent revenue to the benefit of networks and promoters are about to shrink. Even fighters with guaranteed purses and multi-bout contracts could see their income drop. Force majeure doesn't end just because there are fights. It can—and will—be invoked in some instances by promoters in an attempt to get out from under excessive contractual minimum purses.

Earlier this month, Bob Arum declared, "Some fighters have different views, and after we talk with them, if those views make it impossible to use 'em, next man up. We have like ninety fighters that fight for us. There are a lot of fighters that fight under Lou DiBella's promotion or Kathy Duva's. Fighters, I envisage, will be fighting for a place on these cards. If a fighter said, 'No, I don't wanna fight without an audience; you have to pay me more or I just don't fight,' that's okay. I respect that. Next man up. Nobody is indispensable in this environment."

Adjustments will be made to what everyone earns. It's hard to imagine people in boxing at any level—promoters, fighters, TV networks—making as much money in 2020 as they did in 2019.

Also, despite the rhetoric, the quality of fights that boxing fans see in the months ahead is likely to be less attractive than before the layoff. Big fights will be difficult, if not impossible, to make because of the absence of a live gate. It would be nice if fans saw the best matchups possible at lower levels, but the odds are that we won't. We'll see stay-busy fights and showcase fights unless fighters are willing to go in tough for less. Networks and promoters might take issue with this prediction. The quality of the fights that viewers see will speak for itself.

With live gates removed from the equation, boxing in the foreseeable future is likely to have more pay-per-view fights than before. Pay-per-view is designed to effectuate a big score now, not build the sport.

The COVID-19 shutdown represents an opportunity for boxing to reset. The absence of other sports gives the sweet science a window to shine and expand its fan base. Part of the sales pitch for putting on fights sooner rather than later is that, because there are virtually no other sports at the moment, casual sports fans will be drawn to boxing. But if the fights that viewers see are disappointing, casual sports fans are likely to distance themselves even further from boxing, as happened after Mayweather–Pacquiao.

At present, everything is speculative. Safety protocols that look good on paper can fail in their implementation. The number of new COVID-19 cases in the United States will rise in some places as the economy reopens. Regardless of plans that might be made for big fights like Canelo–Golovkin III and Fury–Wilder III, a fight that promises a live gate can be shut down on a moment's notice. Even if spectators are allowed at fights, ticket sales will suffer. It will be a long time before fans feel comfortable in a crowded arena. It's unlikely that there will be boxing with a significant number of spectators on site until an effective vaccine is developed AND people are confident about it. That means 2021 at the earliest.

What will happen next? Your guess is as good as mine.

UFC president Dana White was firmly aligned with Donald Trump in America's culture war.

More on UFC and the Coronavirus

On May 9, 2020, UFC 249 was contested at the VyStar Veterans Memorial Arena in Jacksonville, Florida. Smaller UFC events were held at the same venue on May 13 and May 16. These cards were the first major sports events in the United States since the pandemic shutdown began in mid-March. And they were UFC's first promotions since an empty-arena show in Brazil on March 14.

UFC 249 was available to ESPN+ subscribers for $64.99. New sub-scribers could buy the event plus an annual subscription (which costs $49.99) for $84.98. The May 13 and May 16 UFC fight cards were available on ESPN and ESPN+

The fights took place with the blessing of Florida governor Ron DeSantis, who has declared professional sports an "essential business." A twenty-four-page plan prepared by UFC and labeled "proprietary and con-fidential" outlined the steps that UFC said it would take to guard against the spread of COVID-19 in conjunction with the shows.

On paper, the plan was credible. It said all the right things, begin-ning with an introduction that read, "Ultimate Fighting Championship ('UFC') acknowledges the impact that COVID-19 has had on the health and safety of people worldwide. We commend the forward-thinking plans implemented by federal, state, and local governments to combat the spread of COVID-19 and its impact on the community."

The plan then divided the health and safety procedures proposed by UFC into five categories: (1) social distancing, (2) advanced screening and testing procedures, (3) protective guidelines and self-reporting procedures, (4) cleaning procedures, and (5) medical procedures.

Fighters were to arrive in Jacksonville by plane or motor vehicle on Tuesday or Wednesday of fight week. At the hotel, each fighter and his or her camp would be subjected to medical screening including a diagnostic swab coronavirus test, antibody test, temperature check, and interview. They were to self-isolate "within reason" until their test results came back and even then not mingle in large groups. Further medical screening would take place throughout the week. Each fighter's team would be given its own workout room. There would be twenty-four-hour room service and a market on site. Protective equipment and products such as sanitizers would be readily available.

"If any UFC personnel do not comply with this plan," the document pledged, "they will not be permitted to remain on premises at the Arena or related host hotel accommodations for the Jacksonville events."

Spectators would be barred from the fights.

"I didn't want to stop putting on events at all," UFC president Dana White told Greg Bishop of *Sports Illustrated*. "I wanted to keep right on going. We'll figure this thing out. All the rules and all the plans, I actually found it fun. I like chaos, man. I like trying to figure things out. I'm into that shit. I'm a weirdo. We're trying to figure out how to make it as safe as possible. We're gonna go so overboard making sure everybody is healthy and safe that I just don't see how we can possibly fuck this up."

But White added a cautionary note: "Listen, there's no guarantee. There's no way I can say it's one hundred percent. Nothing is one hundred percent, especially when you're dealing with, like, a virus."

The Association of Ringside Physicians (ARP) approved of the UFC plan.

On April 6, the ARP had released a letter from its board of directors that declared, "It is our recommendation that all combat sporting events be postponed until further notice. This includes any and all events, regardless of the number of people involved. Any combat sport taking place during this global pandemic places the athletes, officials, and anyone else involved in the event under unnecessary risk of infection and transmission of Covid-19. In addition, combat sports athletes often require medical attention after a bout, and we do not wish to see any additional strain on an already overwhelmed medical system."

Then on April 25, as reported by Mark Raimondi of ESPN.com, ARP president Don Muzzi had a ninety-minute telephone conversation with UFC's chief physician, Jeff Davidson. After talking with Davidson, Muzzi (an anesthesiologist) strongly advocated that the ARP reverse its previous position.

There are twelve ARP board members. Eleven of them participated in a Zoom video-conference call to discuss the matter.

"There were strong feelings on both sides of the issue," one participant told this writer. "But a majority of board members, at Don's urging, accepted the view that somebody had to move forward and test the waters and that UFC was a good candidate to do that."

On May 2, the ARP reversed its call for an indefinite suspension of all combat sports and issued a statement that read, "The Association of Ringside Physicians recognizes that the circumstances regarding the COVID-19 pandemic are continually changing and evolving. As stay-at-home orders are relaxed, athletic commissions and combat sports governing bodies are looking to restart operations. Although it is impossible to eliminate all risk associated with COVID-19, precautions can be made to reduce the risk of viral transmission. Many athletic commissions, organizations and promoters are developing new guidelines to limit exposure to all involved at events, including athletes, their teams, commission personnel and support staff. Combat sports event procedures regarding COVID-19 precautions should be actively developed, regularly reviewed, and modified based on the evolving knowledge and scientific evidence put forth by public health authorities. These guidelines should also involve local and regional public health officials as well as infectious disease experts and epidemiologists."

Thereafter, speaking of the UFC plan, Muzzi declared, "In today's world, it's as safe as possible."

Some people praised Muzzi's leadership. Others took a contrary view. Several ARP board members were irked that Muzzi sent the statement out without showing the final wording to them for comment. One former ARP board member sent an email to a colleague complaining, "He [Muzzi] is an 'expert' for hire who molds his opinion to support whoever or whatever can boost his ego and or pocket book." Gareth A. Davies, the seasoned combat sports writer for *The Telegraph,* tweeted, "Unfortunate when physicians compromise beliefs for personal gain & to be cageside."

UFC 249 fit nicely into Donald Trump's call for the resumption of professional sports in America. Four years ago, Dana White addressed the Republican National Convention in Cleveland, praising Trump's business acumen and loyalty. Now Trump returned the favor, recording a congratulatory message that aired during UFC's May 9 preliminary fights on ESPN+.

Mike Tyson famously said, "Everyone has a plan until they get hit." In a similar vein, protocols are fine unless there are holes in them or they aren't followed. Not everything went well insofar as UFC's coronavirus protocols were concerned.

The first sign of trouble came when Ronaldo "Jacaré" Souza (who'd been scheduled to fight Uriah Hall at UFC 249) arrived in Jacksonville on Wednesday, May 6, and told UFC officials that several family members might have had the coronavirus. Souza was immediately tested and "isolated in his hotel." It took forty-eight hours for the test results to come back, at which time the results were positive, not only for Souza but also for two members of his team.

UFC then issued a statement saying, "As per UFC's health and safety protocols, all three men have left the host hotel and will be self-isolating off premises where UFC's medical team will monitor their conditions remotely and will provide assistance with any necessary treatment. The response to this development is indicative of the effectiveness of the health and safety measures UFC has put in place for this event."

But prior to the positive test results, UFC had allowed Souza to remain on the card. On Friday morning, wearing a facemask and gloves, he had weighed in and fist-bumped both Dana White and Uriah Hall. And one has to wonder how many people Souza and his team infected on the way to Jacksonville.

Thereafter, MMA Junkie posted some observations by Zachary Binney, an Atlanta-based epidemiologist on staff at Emory University. Among other things, Binney noted, "The UFC and Dana White were negligent. Tried to restart early, the predictable thing happened, and they mishandled it. If this was your system working as designed, your system is bogus.

"The timeline is important here," Binney continued. "Wed—Souza, training in Orlando and knowing he had a possible positive test in his family, travels to Jax. Bad move by him and his people. He arrives, informs UFC of family case, is tested and apparently isolated pending results. That's all good (though keep in mind, he shouldn't be in Jax in the first place). And then why is he at the staredown Friday, two days later? Reckless by UFC. Today his test comes back positive, fight is off. Hopefully he and all his contacts (including other fighters at the staredown!) will quarantine for two weeks and stop their particular transmission chain. No, I don't buy this is the system working as designed and proof UFC and Dana White are being responsible. Actually, the UFC's own statement indicts the hell out of them."

Moreover, there were instances when UFC personnel disregarded their own protocols. Dana White didn't wear a mask at the weigh-in for UFC 249. In addition to fist-bumping Souza, he had close contact at the weigh-in with other fighters and UFC personnel working the show. All of this and more led the *New York Times* to look back on UFC 249 in a May 13 article headlined "UFC's Coronavirus Plan Proves No Match for Reality" that declared, "UFC officials and fighters routinely deviated from the outlined procedures in the days leading up to UFC 249 and on the night of the pay-per-view event itself."

The *Times* then reported, "At UFC 249, [Justin] Gaethje [who defeated Tony Ferguson] and [commentator Joe] Rogan shouldn't have touched, let alone stood within six feet of each other. There were supposed to be no face-to-face in-Octagon post-fight or backstage interviews according to the plan. Instead, interviews were to be conducted via headset with UFC interviewers or commentators stationed in a separate arena zone. Wrapping up the televised event, the analyst Daniel Cormier explained how Rogan had received permission to do interviews that violated social distancing guidelines. That wasn't the only part of the operation's plan that went unheeded. The plan prohibits all contact-based greetings and said that all personnel would be required to wear face masks and gloves in connection with their job functions, an edict that Dana White, the UFC president, repeatedly ignored. On Friday after the official weigh-ins, the fighter Michelle Waterson hugged White before her staredown and embrace of her opponent, Carla Esparza."

Here, one might add that there's something inherently nonsensical in saying that it's too dangerous for fighters to touch each other at the weigh-in and then allow them to grapple with each other for three five-minute rounds.

Also, there were numerous holes in UFC's overall plan. For example, the protocols that UFC submitted to Florida authorities for UFC 249 anticipated that 199 fighters, fighter team members, production personnel, and other UFC employees would be on site. That didn't take into account arena personnel, hotel employees, Florida State Athletic Commission personnel, and others involved with the promotion, most of whom were subject to guidelines that were far more lax than the UFC protocols.

And let's get real. It's hard to believe that only three of the tests administered in conjunction with UFC 249 came back positive. Assuming that UFC tested 199 people for each of the three events, that would indicate a positive test result rate of well under 1 percent. The national average is multiples of this number. How many other positive tests were there? UFC should be open and tell people how many positive test results there were. Most likely, three is not the whole story.

To repeat: it's hard to believe that only three of the tests administered in conjunction with UFC 249 came back positive.

Also, what sort of follow-up has there been? Have there been subsequent tests for people who were on site for UFC 249? Suppose fifteen people who were on site for UFC 249 test positive afterward? Who will be notified?

As Trent Reinsmith wrote on *SB Nation*, "The risk of COVID-19 doesn't just magically disappear when a UFC event ends. The incubation period for COVID-19 is thought to extend to 14 days. We won't safely know if everyone—not just the fighters—who attended any of the three UFC Jacksonville events is healthy until May 31."

And remember, anyone who contracted the virus at one of the three UFC shows in Jacksonville became a carrier who could bring the virus home to his or her family and community. It's not just the fighters and others directly involved with the promotion who are at risk. MMA is dangerous. This extended the danger well beyond the combatants.

There are also nagging issues relating to the contracts that participants in the UFC events were required to sign.

UFC fighters are contractually precluded from fighting for any other promoter. That's par for the course. But if a fighter (many of whom are desperate for paychecks) wanted to fight on one of UFC's shows in Jacksonville, the fighter had to accept a draconian contract. Among other things, this contract provided that the fighter assumed all risk of contracting COVID-19 (including death) and absolved UFC of any and all liability regarding the same.

Mark Raimondi reported on ESPN.com that this waiver was required, not just of fighters but of "all participants—including media in attendance—involved in the fight card."

Here, the thoughts of Paul Edelstein are instructive. Edelstein is one of the foremost personal injury lawyers in the United States. Boxing fans know him as the lead attorney for the family of Magomed Abdusalamov and his work in securing $27.5 million in settlement payments from the State of New York and insurance companies representing New York State Athletic Commission physicians in conjunction with life-altering injuries suffered by Abdusalamov in a 2013 fight at Madison Square Garden.

Asked about the waiver of liability for COVID-19-related losses, Edelstein said that, most likely, the waiver is enforceable but that it would not survive a court challenge in the face of gross negligence or fraud by UFC. Also, if UFC didn't follow its own coronavirus protocols—and there's ample evidence that it didn't—the waiver of liability signed by participants might not hold up in court.

A second, more troubling contractual issue involves a non-disparagement clause that UFC participants were required to sign.

Non-disparagement clauses are common in contracts. A standard non-disparagement clause is similar to the following language that was included in the UFC contracts: "The Participant shall not, and shall cause its affiliates, agents and representatives not to, defame or disparage any of the Released Parties in any medium whatsoever in connection with the Activities."

But the UFC contracts went further and declared, "The Participant will not suggest or communicate to any person or entity that the Activities have been or will be held without appropriate health, safety or other precautions, whether relating to COVID-19 or otherwise. If the Participant is a Fighter, the Participant hereby acknowledges and agrees that, in the event that the Participant breaches this Paragraph 7, the Company may revoke all or any part of any prize monies or awards won by the Participant in connection with the Activities, including, but not limited to, purses, win bonuses, other fight-related bonuses and event-based merchandise royalties."

This clause first came to light on May 9 when an attorney named Erik Magraken tweeted, "Anyone know why you are not seeing any critical comments from fighters / corners / managers at UFC 249 about health and safety issues? Hint—it's not because everyone is 100% satisfied with the measures."

Showtime Sports president Stephen Espinoza quickly responded, "It's because they were required to sign a document which says that they can lose their whole purse and bonuses if they say anything negative about the COVID protocols."

UFC's "muzzle" clause ("gag order" if you prefer) would most likely not be enforceable in court. A traditional non-disparagement clause or confidentiality clause that protects proprietary information is one thing. But a contract clause runs counter to public policy when it cuts off the flow of information that could warn people of a serious danger to their health and thus increases the risk that people might contract COVID-19.

In that regard, Paul Edelstein states, "[That] part of the clause to me seems void. I do not believe you can silence someone from saying things were not properly provided by threatening to withhold payment. Public policy would outweigh confidentiality in my opinion."

Sheryl Wulkan, Margaret Goodman, and John Stiller (three of the most respected ring doctors in the United States) took issue with UFC's attempt to silence any deviation from its COVID-19 narrative. In a May 11 memorandum titled "Coronavirus, Combat Sports Policy, and UFC," they wrote, "If athletes must sign, as part of their contract, a waiver regarding non-disclosure of concerns surrounding COVID 19 safety protocols, it will be difficult to gather data necessary for epidemiologists, ringside physicians, lawmakers, and Commissions to improve their event planning for all contact sports and make them safer in the future."

The Florida State Athletic Commission accepted the UFC contracts, coronavirus gag order and all. It's unclear whether any of the doctors who worked UFC's shows in Jacksonville signed non-disclosure agreements with regard to UFC's medical protocols and the coronavirus.

Patrick Fargason (deputy communications director for the Florida State Boxing Commission) told this writer on May 21 that the FSBC provided a total of five physicians for the three UFC events, the UFC "brought in their own team as well," and that all of the doctors were paid by UFC. Asked whether any of these doctors had signed a contract that included a non-disparagement clause, Fargason stated, "The FSBC doesn't track information regarding any contracts signed by our physicians with the UFC or any other promoters."

Faced with questions about the COVID-19 gag order, Dana White denied that it applied to legitimate concerns regarding UFC's handing of coronavirus issues. "It's called an anti-disparagement clause," he told Yahoo

Sports. "And if I know what that is, that scumbag [Stephen Espinoza] is a lawyer and you would think he should know what that is. If a fighter says something that isn't true—if he says we didn't test anyone for this—that would [violate the agreement]. But if he said something that was true, his opinion, then that is different."

Further to that line of thought, White told Mark Raimondi, "[A problem] would be like if you came out and said, 'They never tested me. The UFC never tested me for the coronavirus.' But if you had something critical to say about the testing that was true, that wouldn't be disparagement."

But—and this is a huge "but"—that's not what the UFC contract says. The clause in question clearly gives UFC the right to take away a participant's entire purse and more for speaking out about UFC's coronavirus protocols even if what the participant says is true.

White has gone to great lengths over the years to cultivate a "tell it like it is" image. One reason for his enormous popularity is that his admirers see him as a stand-up guy who speaks the truth as he sees it. He's also very smart and a hands-on overseer. One has to assume that he knew what the UFC contract said. But faced with questions about the contract, he misled by misstating the facts. He feels free to voice his own opinion and call Stephen Espinoza "a creepy little fucker" (which he did after Espinoza's contract revelation). He has called Bob Arum "the biggest piece of shit in all of sports." But if a fighter expresses concern regarding UFC's handling of COVID-19 issues, the fighter can be fined his or her entire purse and fight night bonus.

If UFC can tell the world that its COVID-19 protocols are safe, UFC fighters and their teams (the people who are most at risk) should be allowed to warn others if they aren't. If White violated the COVID-19 protocols that he pledged to adhere to, people who he might have put at risk should know. We don't know how safe UFC 249 really was. And the contract clause that UFC put in place makes it clear that UFC doesn't want us to know.

UFC is owned by Endeavor—a global entertainment corporation that is struggling in the face of long-term debt in excess of $4.6 billion. As reported by the *Wall Street Journal* on May 11, Endeavor recently secured a $260 million loan arranged by JPMorgan Chase at an annual interest rate of just under 11 percent. Given the fact that the prime rate (the rate that banks charge their best customers) is now 3.25 percent, that augurs poorly for Endeavor's future.

Speaking to the *New York Times* about UFC's determination to promote fights during the COVID-19 pandemic, Endeavor president Mark Shapiro said, "We are not putting fights on to satisfy any contracts or because of any particular financial situation at Endeavor." But the income from UFC events is crucial to Endeavor's balance sheet.

ESPN has faced financial challenges of its own in recent months and has a vested interest in the success of the UFC telecasts. That said, its website —and particularly Mark Raimondi—has done a solid job of reporting on coronavirus issues as they relate to UFC.

UFC had hoped to move forward with a May 23 fight card at its APEX facility in Las Vegas. But the Nevada State Athletic Commission refused to approve it. White is now hoping to stage events in Las Vegas on May 30 and June 6 with Arizona as a backup site. A source who has spoken directly with NSAC executive director Bob Bennett says, "UFC was given free rein to do things its way in Florida. That won't happen in Nevada."

Meanwhile, Top Rank is working with the NSAC in the hope of ironing out plans for fights that would be contested in June and viewed on ESPN and ESPN+.

In truth, no one knows what will happen next. UFC has pushed the needle in one direction. As Dana White told *Sports Illustrated*, "While everybody was fucking lying out by the pool, hanging out and doing whatever the fuck they're doing in quarantine, we were in here fucking grinding, man. Fighting crazy wars every day to put on this first event. We pulled it off. Somebody has to be first, right? Eventually. You just can't hide forever. Who gets to determine how long we go without sports? It's a really weird situation in a weird time."

But White, who owned 9 percent of UFC when it was sold in 2016 and reportedly netted more than $300 million from the transaction, lives in a Las Vegas mansion with his wife and children. His home has a basketball court, personal gym, arcade room, and outdoor pool. His life contrasts markedly with those of the nurses, hospital orderlies, grocery store clerks, and others who are on the front lines in the battle against COVID-19.

UFC boasted that it performed more than one thousand COVID-19 tests in conjunction with UFC 249. That's enough kits to test the entire police force and fire department of a small city. A widely disseminated video showed Tony Ferguson in a hospital room "in high spirits despite a facial fracture" after his loss to Justin Gaethje. In this day and age, do we really want to encourage nonessential activities that are likely to lead to demands of this nature on already overtaxed medical resources?

It's a given that states have to begin reopening the economy. We know this will cost lives. The issue is: What is an acceptable risk-reward ratio? Driving a car entails risks. We try to make driving safer. There are speed limits and seatbelt laws. A lot of thought goes into incorporating safety features into automobiles. And because driving is essential to our way of life, we tolerate a system in which 40,000 Americans die in automobile accidents each year.

At some point, the powers that be will have to take risks to keep the economy from collapsing completely. But there should be a sensible risk-reward formula with regard to reopening. Scientifically backed medical protocols should be in place. And the reopening should be based on priorities that benefit society as a whole—hardware stores before tattoo parlors—not loopholes, lobbying, and who grabs for the brass ring first.

Too many people still don't understand how dangerous the coronavirus is. They don't have a relative or friend or even know someone who died from it. That will change. The United States has 5 percent of the world's population and 33 percent of all reported cases of COVID-19. Underreporting is a problem everywhere; probably more of a problem in Third World countries than in the United States. But even if these numbers are adjusted, it's clear that we're not doing enough to halt the spread of the virus.

People are starting to behave very irresponsibly now. They're refusing to wear masks and ignoring the rules of social distancing. There are instances where establishments have posted signs that proclaim "NO MASKS ALLOWED." We cannot accept the mindset that thousands of deaths from COVID-19 each day will be the new norm.

On the first day of summer 2020, I speculated about the future.

Will Boxing Fans Come Back to the Arenas?

The initial impact of COVID-19 was most visible on a national scale in the world of sports. The National Basketball Association, Major League Baseball, and other time-honored institutions shut down. Boxing followed suit.

Now sports are in the early stages of return. Initially, most competitions will take place without spectators on site. The powers that be will rely on television license fees to make ends meet. But inevitably, spectators will be invited back into the fold.

Will boxing fans return to arenas? At the moment, the question is academic. But there will be significant practical implications before long.

It's one thing to get fans to turn on their televisions sets or other devices to watch a fight. It will be a more formidable task to get them back to ringside.

Even before the coronavirus shutdown, boxing was struggling at the gate throughout the United States. In an interview with Fight Hub, Bob Arum asked rhetorically, "What is the real problem in boxing?" and answered, "The real problem in boxing is that people are not buying tickets to the fights."

Arum knows of what he speaks. When Tyson Fury fought Otto Wallin at T-Mobile Arena in Las Vegas last year, there were more comps (3,898) than tickets sold (3,577). Recent fights at Madison Square Garden and Barclays Center saw steep price discounts and ticket giveaways. Canelo Álvarez (boxing's biggest draw) fought his last two fights in Las Vegas with empty seats in the arena.

Boxing at its best is the greatest sport of all. But there are times when buying tickets for a fight feels like a bad habit.

No sport disrespects its onsite fans as badly as boxing. Ticket prices are high. There are long periods of inactivity between undercard fights, which are usually mediocre. Bad decisions frustrate fans, who want to see fair fights as well as good ones. Now COVID-19 has further complicated the issue.

Donald Trump would like to see fans return to sports events across the board. "We want to get it back to where it was," the president said in an interview that aired during a May 17 golf telecast on NBC. "We want big, big stadiums loaded with people. We want to get back to normal where you have the big crowds and they're practically standing on top of each other and enjoying themselves, not where they're worried. Things can happen very quickly. We're getting it back and it's going to be fast."

But it won't be that easy.

Relatively few people have gone through the past three months thinking that, once the pandemic has passed, their lives will be better than before COVID-19 hit. In a time of mass unemployment and failing businesses, discretionary income goes down. Some states might consider professional sports to be an "essential business" that should be reopened to spectators as soon as possible. But boxing fans might not consider it essential to go to fights.

Unlike team sports, boxing doesn't have the narrative of a season culminating in championship playoffs to attract attention. There are no season ticket packages to lure fans in. And lengthy travel is often required to get to a fight.

This leads to perhaps the biggest obstacle that all sports including boxing will face in bringing fans back to arenas—the health issues involved.

John Oliver recently noted, "One of the things that sports does best is bring people together in a time of crisis. Unfortunately, bringing people together is the exact thing we should not be doing now."

Some sports fans will discount health issues, just as some people discount the need for safe sex. It depends on how, and how badly, someone wants something. But realistically speaking, many sports fans won't return to arenas until there's an effective vaccine to combat COVID-19.

Promoters favor the notion that fighters must accept smaller purses. They're less enthusiastic about pay cuts where their own bank accounts are concerned. Fans might decide that their own safety is more important to them than the checking accounts of promoters, managers, and fighters.

And let's not forget; after COVID-19, there could be COVID-20.

A few major promoters might finance a few big fights with large site fees from the Middle East, Macau, or some other foreign entity. That seems to be the formula in bigtime boxing these days: solicit funds from a network or other source outside of the sport with the fights that follow failing to generate enough revenue to cover the investment.

ESPN, FOX, and DAZN have invested hundreds of millions of dollars in boxing over the past two years. Has it worked? Right now, the possibility of fifty-four-year-old Mike Tyson (who lost three of his last four fights and hasn't fought in fifteen years) facing off in an exhibition against fifty-seven-year-old Evander Holyfield (who hasn't fought since 2011) is generating more interest than anything currently on the boxing calendar.

Boxing has to reset. It hasn't satisfied its fans for a long time. That's a long-term project. But a journey of a thousand miles begins with a single step.

Sports are addictive for their fan base. It's hard to shake an addiction, but it can be done. The more time goes by, the more fans will adapt to life without sports and say, "I can live without attending a fight." In that regard, some thoughts that I received recently from a reader are instructive.

"Since the pandemic hit the sports world," the email read, "I have noticed the obsessive value that is put on sports in this county. How if people could not watch live sports, well, they were going to talk about sports. And if there were no sports to talk about, then they were going to reminisce about the old days. That thirst for sports is still there, right? Well, not so fast. There is a natural progression to some things in life. Sorta like losing a girlfriend. At first, it is painful. It hurts just not to hear the phone ring. But after a while, you find out some things. You find out that there were parts of that girl's persona you do not miss. Was she really all that much? And before you know it, bam! You see a nice swinging skirt pass by and you are over her. The promoters do not want you to find out you can possibly live without sports. And the truth is that sports in their current form can be done without."

Some Notes on the Coronavirus

In the midst of the coronavirus pandemic that's ravaging America, my thoughts turned recently to Harold Lederman.

Long before he became America's unofficial ringside scorer, Harold was a pharmacist. For much of his career, he worked for Duane Reade. Harold's assignments for HBO took him out of town for up to five days at a time. So to make up the lost hours, he often worked at Duane Reade for thirteen-hour shifts.

Pharmacies are at the center of our national life these days. In many instances, supply can't meet demand. Facemasks, hand sanitizers, disinfecting wipes—even toilet paper—are hard to find. That brings me back to Harold.

In the aftermath of 9/11, there was an anthrax scare when letters containing anthrax spores were mailed to several news organizations and two United States senators. Five people died as a result. It was common knowledge that someone who was believed to have breathed in anthrax spores should take a prescription medicine called ciprofloxacin. Patients in need were given a ten-day supply to start.

Most doctors, appropriately, wouldn't write a prescription for ciprofloxacin unless a patient was at risk. But even then, supplies grew short. People began asking themselves, "If I need ciprofloxacin, will I be able to get it?"

As a pharmacist, Harold had opportunities that the rest of us don't have. And he was generous. One fighter known for the longevity of his ring career acknowledged to me that he got performance-enhancing drugs free of charge from Harold. His PED was Viagra.

Several days after the anthrax scare began, I got a small package in the mail with a note from Harold that read, "I thought you might want this just in case."

The note came with a ten-day supply of ciprofloxacin.

★ ★ ★

The coronavirus that has wreaked havoc upon the boxing calendar also dealt a painful body blow to Jody Heaps.

Prior to retiring last year, Heaps spent three decades as a senior creative director and executive producer for boxing-related projects at Showtime Sports. In a memoir entitled *Blood in My Coffee*, former Showtime Boxing commentator Ferdie Pacheco referenced him as "a former beatnik who had washed up on the shores of Showtime as a writer" but added that Jody was "funny and lively and had wonderful insights into things."

Heaps wrote his first play two decades ago and has produced a half dozen of his works on his own dime. Several more productions were mounted by outsiders. Each of the productions was an Equity showcase with a limited-engagement run in a small theater.

"An Equity showcase costs between twelve and fifteen thousand dollars to mount," Jody explains. "If I'm lucky, I get back three or four thousand of that. I do it because I love it. I love theater. I love the collaborative process. In boxing, everyone fights with everyone. In theater, people work together. In television, everyone picks apart what the writer writes. In theater, the play belongs to the writer."

That brings us to *Punchline*, Heaps's most recent creative endeavor.

The play begins with Jake Levenstein (a struggling writer-actor) doing a stand-up comedy gig in which the fictional Levenstein plays the role of Nathan Rossenkowski (a deceased fighter).

"So, I hear the ref counting 'four, five, six.' And I think to myself, 'What happened to one, two, three?'"

The one-liners continue.

"Anyways, after that fight, I realized it was a whole lot safer dying on stage than in the ring. So I hang up my gloves and go into standup comedy."

Punchline then takes an intriguing turn when Rossenkowski's daughter appears in the audience. More unexpected turns follow. It's an entertaining journey.

The play was scheduled to run for ten days at the 13th Street Repertory Theater in New York, starting on March 19. Heaps was funding the production, which was to be directed by Mary Linehan with a cast that included

Drew Valins, Moti Margolin, Victoria Meade, and Nicholas Delany. Then the coronavirus intervened.

"The theater seats sixty people," Heaps says. "Crowds wouldn't have been a problem. But the virus shut down theater in New York. It was as simple as that. We were at the second-to-last rehearsal when the cancellation hit. That meant we were at a point where I'd paid for almost everything and couldn't get any of the money back. I lost about ten thousand dollars."

Heaps has seen fighters' dreams destroyed by an unexpected punch. This time, it happened to him. But like a fighter who rebounds from a knockout defeat, he hopes to mount a production of *Punchline* in the future.

★ ★ ★

A boxing analogy, if I may.

COVID-19 is a puncher. And it's relentless. You can't let your guard down. That means wearing a mask, social distancing, washing your hands. You know the moves. Your trainer taught them to you. If you're careless or too stubborn to follow the advice, you'll get whacked. And like a fighter in the ring, even if you do what you're supposed to do, you might get hit. Hard.

Maybe you'll shake it off without much damage. Maybe you'll be hurt but recover. Or maybe—like Jimmy Glenn and some others we loved—you'll be out for the count.

They say that boxing is a metaphor for life. So true.

The boxing scene, it's often said, is like a dysfunctional family drama. That said, in 2020, I missed it.

I Miss the Boxing Scene

Boxing shut down in March of this year due to COVID-19. In recent months, there has been a resumption of activity. But most of it has taken place in "bubbles" and under circumstances far different from the way things were before.

I've been one of the lucky ones. I live in New York, which was the early epicenter of the coronavirus in the United States. But so far—knock on wood—I've stayed healthy. I wear a mask when I go out. I practice social distancing. I live in a nice apartment and don't have to worry about where the money will come from to pay my bills.

That said, like many people, I miss things I used to do. Activities that were part of my daily routine are now off limits. Social interaction that was second nature to me has been curtailed. One of the things I miss most about my life the way it was is the boxing scene.

I have a life apart from boxing. I've written about Charles Dickens and Beethoven, not just Canelo Álvarez and Muhammad Ali. I've authored books on subjects ranging from race relations to United States foreign policy, not just the sweet science. Many of my friends aren't involved with boxing. They don't even watch fights on television. But over the years, the sport has been central to my work as a writer and intertwined with my social life.

I understand what Larry Merchant was saying when he told me recently, "I started as a newspaper guy. Then I was with HBO. I was around the fight game for a long time, but I didn't realize how much I'd miss the social aspect of it until it was gone. You meet new people. The relationships can be casual or they can evolve into meaningful friendships. I've made some good friends through boxing."

The boxing scene is a circus. Going to the circus can be fun. Over the years, being in the media has afforded me access to a sometimes magical world and placed me midway between fans on the outside looking in and active participants in the drama.

I've often said that some of the best people I've met in my life are in boxing and many of the worst people I've met in my life are in boxing. But it's never boring.

Boxing is unique. It has its own culture. There's nothing quite like the boxing scene. So many of its denizens are like characters in a novel.

"I love being around boxing people," Harold Lederman once said. "There's something special about them. Even the bad ones are fun to be around."

There's a sense of belonging and being part of a community for those of us who are involved with boxing. Rituals become an enjoyable part of life's routine. Whenever Michael Buffer and I are in the same city for the same fight card, we have lunch on fight day. When Bruce Trampler is in New York for a Top Rank event, we go to the Tick Tock Diner two blocks from Madison Square Garden before or after the weigh-in. Gerry Cooney and I sit together during the fights at Barclays Center. In theory, I'm "working" on these occasions. But as the centuries-old proverb counsels, "Find a job you love and you'll never have to work a day in your life."

The boxing scene is about so much more than the fights.

Formal press conferences can be boring. Too often, the promoter speaks for forty-five minutes and the main event fighters talk for two minutes each. That's entertaining if the promoter is Don King. Unfortunately, DK hasn't hosted many press conferences lately.

But the kickoff press conference is when I start thinking about how I'll frame an article that I might not write for weeks. I'm gathering pieces for a puzzle that I'll put together later on. Being at the press conference adds texture to my writing. It enables me to look a fighter in the eye. Also, some of the best material I get at press conferences comes from time spent in conversation with people before the formal press conference begins.

Weigh-ins can be tedious. I remember a conversation I had with David Tua years ago as he sat waiting for an hour to weigh in. "This is the hardest part," Tua groused. "Things that should take fifteen minutes drag on and on and on." But for a writer, the waiting offers ample opportunity to talk, listen, and learn.

Then there are the fights.

Mingling at some fight cards is more entertaining than the fights themselves because—let's be honest—too many of the fights that fans see these days are mediocre. But regardless of what's going on inside the ring, club fights have an ambience of their own. The feeling, the mood, the excitement when the action heats up; that's special. I miss moving around in the early hours of the evening, sitting next to Russell Peltz, Don Elbaum, Ron Katz, or some other "boxing guy" and talking boxing.

Big fight weeks are a world of their own. It's electrifying when a big event catches fire.

I don't travel often for fights. When I do, it's usually to Las Vegas. I don't miss standing on line to go through airport security and the long flight to Sin City and back. I do miss the theatrics of the final days before a big fight. When Manny Pacquiao was at his peak, Pacquiao events had the feel of a world convocation.

I miss hanging out in the media center at the MGM Grand in Las Vegas and shmoozing with Al Bernstein, Norm Frauenheim, and Bill Caplan. There's always someone to talk with. Sometimes that someone is a legend like Ray Leonard or Roberto Duran. I miss going through the buffet line at the final pre-fight press conference and eating what I want.

I don't miss standing on line to pick up my fight-night credential. But I do miss the rush I feel each time I'm handed my credential. I arrive at the arena early for a big fight and let my mind wander.

I miss the crowd filing into Madison Square Garden to root for Félix Trinidad and Miguel Cotto. I miss sitting at ringside and watching the brutal artistry of Lennox Lewis and Bernard Hopkins.

I've been privileged over the years in that dozens of fighters have allowed me to spend the hours before and after a fight in the dressing room with them. Nothing in sports is as serious as two men getting in a boxing ring. Pre-fight promotion is the propaganda before the war. Now the soldiers have to do battle. I miss sitting close enough to a man to touch him as he readies to leave his sanctuary, knowing that, win or lose, his life will be very different when he returns to the dressing room in a little more than an hour.

I miss the opportunity the boxing scene has given me to get to know people like Don Turner, Freddie Roach, and Russ Anber. I miss spending time with people who are no longer with us like Eddie Futch, Emanuel Steward, Angelo Dundee, Naazim Richardson, Jimmy Glenn, Don Chargin, George Kimball, and Artie Curry.

It's human nature to get a bit jaded. Sometimes we take things for granted more than we should. Then we miss them when they're gone.

The next big fight in Las Vegas when things are up and running again will be like a reunion. But boxing will be slow to come back. The return won't happen all at once. For the foreseeable future, big press conferences, a crowded media center, and onsite crowds will be a thing of the past.

In the words of the Persian Sufi poets, "This too shall pass." The question is when.

Muhammad Ali and the Coronavirus

Someone asked me recently what I thought Muhammad Ali would make of the burgeoning coronavirus crisis.

Let's start by noting what Ali was not. He was a not a doctor. He was not a scientist. He was not a socioeconomic planner. He was not always a practical rational thinker. But the world could use his voice today.

Ali in the 1960s was a divisive figure. But he inspired people in need of inspiration and gave people hope.

He projected as being fearless. He wasn't. Sonny Liston scared him. The assassination of Malcolm X weighed heavily upon him. But he was willing to take risks and journey into the unknown.

In later years, he became a symbol of people coming together and a unifying force.

Now, as was the case in the 1960s, there's a sense that the world is falling apart. What would Ali do today?

He didn't always take advice from the government. That's for sure. And some common-sense directives would be hard for him to follow. Muhammad loved crowds, the bigger the better. He loved being surrounded by people. Social distancing would have been contrary to his nature. His first reaction to the current coronavirus crisis would probably be to urge people to trust in God. But Ali understood that faith alone can take a person just so far; that not all prayers are answered; that prayer should be supplemented by practical acts (such as training hard for a fight—or taking proper medical precautions).

On a more whimsical note, one can imagine the poet in Ali proclaiming:

"There will be an end to the crisis
When I beat the coronavirus"

I mentioned that to Jim Lampley earlier this week, and he supplemented my offering with the lines:

"It might take our jobs and fire us
But we will whup the coronavirus"

In search of yet another opinion, I turned to George Foreman.

There was a time when Foreman modeled himself after Sonny Liston. But he has evolved since then and is now a warm, almost spiritual presence. George is as qualified as anyone to speak for Ali.

"Ali would have a public service message today," George told me. "He'd be telling everyone, 'Get your soap out, wash your hands, and sing along with me.'"

And how would that song go?

It would be called "The Hand-Washing Song," George suggested. And it would go something like:

"When I was floating like a butterfly and stinging like a bee,
        Sonny Liston, Joe Frazier, George Foreman,
They all tried but couldn't put a hand on me,
        so their hands were clean
In twenty seconds, your hands can be clean too."

There are times when I think that George is a genius. Advertising agencies are paid millions of dollars to create lines like that.

We know what Ali wouldn't do today. He wouldn't blame the current crisis on the Chinese people. He wouldn't be more troubled by the stock market going down than by people dying. He would be one of many voices urging compassion.

He would be an inspiration. But he would be quick to remind us that, in this time of crisis, we should look to the front lines for inspiration. To hospital workers and their counterparts in other essential professions who are risking their lives every day to safeguard us. And he would be wise enough to tell us that we should look to health care professionals like Dr. Anthony Fauci for guidance.

I've written many times that Muhammad Ali in the 1960s stood as a beacon of hope for oppressed people all over the world. Every time he looked in the mirror and uttered the phrase, "I'm so pretty," he was saying "Black is beautiful" before it became fashionable. When he refused induction into the United States Army, he stood up to armies everywhere in support of the proposition that, unless you have a very good reason for killing people, war is wrong. But in his later years, there was an even more important component of Ali's legacy. He shortened the distance between people. He became the embodiment of love.

Now more than ever, the world needs Ali's message. It's an uplifting counterpoint to the ugliness and fear that pollute our surroundings today. In his absence, let's all reach down for the goodness within ourselves, be kind to each other, and be a bit more like the best of Ali.

More than most years, 2020 was a time for reflection.

Some Notes to End On

When Black Lives Matter was formed in 2013 after the acquittal of George Zimmerman in the aftermath of the shooting death of Trayvon Martin, my reaction was similar to that of many well-intentioned Americans: Shouldn't we say that "All Lives Matter?"

But Black Lives Matter has now acquired a meaning that goes far beyond a literal interpretation of the phrase. It symbolizes opposition to systemic racism and injustice.

In recent weeks, many of our elected leaders and their enablers have made a point of refusing to speak these three simple words in sequence: "Black . . Lives . . Matter."

What does that have to do with boxing?

Refusing to say the words "Black Lives Matter" reminds me of the bigots who refused to call Muhammad Ali by his chosen name.

★ ★ ★

Twenty years ago, I had a long conversation with George Foreman about religion. George became a born-again Christian in 1977 and an ordained minister in 1978.

"Good is good, whether or not one believes in Jesus," George told me. "To be good is to be saved."

On another occasion, George recounted telephone conversations he'd had with Muhammad Ali as the two men matured. "We agreed," George remembered, "that good is good and bad is bad. And most people, whatever their religion is or even if they don't follow a particular religion, know the difference."

These are ugly times in America. We're very much in need of healing voices. This past week, I reached out to George and asked what else he remembered about his telephone conversations with Muhammad.

"Ali and I really went at it at times," George recalled. "But he never wanted to hurt me and he always wanted another chat. He was determined never to leave me on a bad note. And when I'd hear his voice on the phone, it would always bring me happiness again. It seemed with us there was something greater than religion—a longing to love and belonging to each other, a thankfulness we had each other. First time I am able to put this into words. Brought a tear."

★ ★ ★

John Lewis, a titan in the Civil Rights Movement and member of Congress for thirty-three years, died on Friday (July 17, 2020) at age eighty after a struggle with pancreatic cancer.

I had the honor of interviewing Lewis in 1991. It was a wide-ranging conversation and the last question I asked was, "Are there other societies that you think have dealt with the issues of race more successfully than we have?"

"No, not at all," Lewis answered. "See, I think we're so different. I think we have to travel down this road by ourselves, really. We are involved in an experiment in America. We have to make it work. I believe that we can make it work. And it must work. There may be some setbacks. There may be some interruptions, disappointments here and there. But you know, we're on that long march. We're on that road. We're traveling down that road toward a society based on equality and equal opportunity. We're on our way toward the building of a loving community, that open society, that interracial democracy. We may slow down and walk and sort of march in place, but I think we're on our way. There are going to be different forces rising up from time to time, trying to slow down that effort or interfere with that effort. But as a nation and as a people, there won't be any turning back."

Some things are more important than boxing.